GLOBAL ECOLOGICAL POLITICS

ADVANCES IN ECOPOLITICS   VOLUME 5

GLOBAL ECOLOGICAL POLITICS

EDITED BY

LIAM LEONARD

*School of Business and Humanities, Institute of Technology,
Sligo, Republic of Ireland*

JOHN BARRY

*School of Politics, International Studies and Philosophy,
Queens University Belfast, UK*

United Kingdom – North America – Japan
India – Malaysia – China

Emerald Group Publishing Limited
Howard House, Wagon Lane, Bingley BD16 1WA, UK

First edition 2010

British Library Cataloguing in Publication Data
A catalogue record for this book is available from the British Library

ISBN: 978-1-84950-748-6
ISSN: 2041-806X (Series)

Awarded in recognition of
Emerald's production
department's adherence to
quality systems and processes
when preparing scholarly
journals for print

INVESTOR IN PEOPLE

CONTENTS

LIST OF CONTRIBUTORS

Jon Anderson	School of City & Regional Planning, Cardiff University, UK
John Barry	School of Politics and International Studies and Philosophy, Queen's University, Belfast, Northern Ireland
G. Honor Fagan	National University of Ireland, Maynooth, Ireland
James Hanrahan	IT Sligo, Ireland
Liam Leonard	IT Sligo, Ireland
Darren McCauley	Queen's University, Belfast, Northern Ireland
Peter North	Liverpool University, UK
Victor Ojakorotu	Monash University, Australia
Michael O'Kane	Monash University, Australia
Ann Pettifor	New Economics Foundation, London

LIST OF REVIEWERS

Peter Doran
Law, Queens University,
Belfast, UK

G. Honor Fagan
Sociology, NUI Maynooth,
Ireland

Alejandra Maria Gonzalez-Perez
Business, Eafit University, Colombia

Niamh Hourigan
Sociology, University College, Cork,
Ireland

John Karamichas
Sociology, Queens University,
Belfast, UK

Miriam Kennet
Green Economics Institute, UK

Paula Kenny
Humanities, Institute of Technology,
Sligo, Ireland

Carmen Kuhling
Sociology, University of Limerick,
Ireland

Michael O'Kane
Monash University, Melbourne,
Australia

Ariel Salleh
University of Western Sydney,
Australia

PREFACE

This edition of the *Advances in Ecopolitics* Series with Emerald Publishing examines the range of environmental campaigns that are in occurring across the planet. As world leaders attempt to tackle climate change, this edition presents a collection of case studies on global grassroots initiatives and activism in diverse areas such as green economic alternatives in Anne Pettifor's study on 'The Green New Deal: Restoring Balance and Stability to the Global Financial and Ecosystem' or John Barry's chapter 'Towards a Model of Green Political Economy: From Economic Growth and Ecological Modernisation to Economic Security' or regional activism in defense of communities as presented in Victor Ojakorotu's study on 'the Dilemma of Justice: Foreign Oil Multinationals and Human Rights Violation in the Niger Delta of Nigeria'.

Advances in Ecopolitics 5 goes on to explore alternative or utopian communities in Peter North's 'Alternative Currencies as Localised Utopian Practice' and Jon Anderson's 'Elusive Escapes: Everyday Life and Ecotopias'. Michael O'Kane's study 'Green Politics and Anthropology' examines the theoretical understandings of green politics from the perspective of his discipline, whereas James Hanrahan's chapter investigates the current understandings and potential outcomes of 'Ecotourism and Sustainability in the Tourism Sector'. Honor Fagan's chapter ends this exploration of Global Ecopolitics with an analysis of The 'Politics of Waste, Consumption and Sustainability in the Republic of Ireland'.

This extensive array of ecological participation demonstrates that viable green alternatives are available in this current era of legitimation crisis across the formal political and economic sectors. *Advances in Ecopolitics 5: Global Ecological Politics* presents an important collection of articles for researchers, lecturers and academics in the socio-economic and political sector. As editor of this series, I acknowledge the team at Emerald Publishing, including Claire Ferres, Chris Hart and Emma Smith for their support for this project.

I also thank those involved with the international Editorial Board of the Ecopolitics Series, including my co-editor John Barry, in addition to Board members Peter Doran, Maruis De Geus, Honor Fagan, Carmen Kuhling,

Hilary Tovey, Maria-Alejandra Gonzalez-Perez, Ariel Salleh and Paula Kenny amongst many for their contributions to date. I look forward to further editions of the *Advances in Ecopolitics* Series and will endeavour to continue to bring further significant works on the crucial topics surrounding ecological politics in the future.

Liam Leonard
Series Editor

CHAPTER 1

INTRODUCTION: THE BACKGROUND TO GLOBAL ECOPOLITICS

Liam Leonard

INTRODUCTION

To better understand the key issues surrounding Global Ecopolitics, it may be beneficial to examine the background to the environmental movement over time. The environmental movement is perhaps the most significant contemporary global movement to have emerged in recent decades. The relationship between humankind and nature has been the subject of much debate and enquiry over time. The environmental movement had its cultural origins in literary accounts of humanity's relationship with nature, beginning from the romantic poets such as William Blake, John Keats, Percy Bysshe Shelley, and Lord Byron, whose works were concerned with the reconciliation of man and nature. This aesthetic could also be found in subsequent transcendentalist American literature, such as Henry David Thoreau's *Walden*, published in 1854 (Shabecoff, 2003, pp. 37–71). The transcendentalists were interested in the spiritual connections that connected humankind and nature with God and could be seen as the forefathers of deep green ecologists. Charles Darwin's *Origin of the Species* was published in 1859, creating further interest in the understanding of nature. George Perkins Marsh wrote of the destructive impact of agriculture in his book

Global Ecological Politics
Advances in Ecopolitics, Volume 5, 1–18
Copyright © 2010 by Emerald Group Publishing Limited
ISSN: 2041-806X/doi:10.1108/S2041-806X(2010)0000005005

Man and Nature in 1864. President Teddy Roosevelt would develop the National Parks with Gifford Pinchot of the Forestry Service in the early 1900s. In the aftermath of the Industrial Revolution, concerns about protecting wildlife led to the emergence of a progressive conservation movement, alongside federal regulation of natural habitats and the establishment of national parks. Influential conservation groups included the National Audubon Society, founded in 1886, and the Sierra Club, founded by John Muir in 1892. Muir and Pinchot would become adversaries in the campaign to prevent the building of a dam in Yosemite National Park in the early decade of the nineteenth century (*ibid.*).

The preservationist and conservationist movements were prominent in the United States during the final decades of the 1800s and the early decades of the past century. Muir had been successful in having the Yosemite National Park created during the 1890s. He was also a central figure in the foundation of the Sierra Club in 1892, which focused on the preservation of the wilderness. The Audubon Society was concerned with the protection of birds, and both groups contributed to the founding of the National Park services in 1916. Franklin D. Roosevelt would also consider the importance of conservationalism as part of his "New Deal" during the Depression years of the 1930s. Americans had become concerned about the "Dust Bowl" phenomenon that characterized that era, and the Civilian Conservation Corps was founded to address both the ecological and the economical problems of the day. Aldo Leopold came to prominence as an advocate of forests and wilderness regions in the 1920s. In the post–World War II era, conservationists were active in highlighting the degradation caused by the urbanization of US society, as well as other concerns such as nuclear warfare. Scientists concerned by the threats posed by industrialization began joined with conservationists to present an environmental critique of modernity. The 1950s witnessed a major controversy about the building of the Echo Park Dam in Colorado in the United States. This campaign led to the signing of the Wilderness Act of 1964 that protected millions of acres of wilderness and forests throughout the United States (Shabecoff, 2003, pp. 103–121).

Rachel Carson's (1962) book *A Silent Spring* highlighted concerns about the impact of science on nature. Beat poets such as Gary Snyder were also influential on the early environmental movement. During the 1960s, a widespread social movement emerged around environmental issues; the environmental movement emerged alongside the mobilization of student, feminist, and anti-war movements. The growing threats of a "population explosion" were expressed in Paul R. Ehrlich's (1968) book *The Population*

Bomb. Ehrlich predicted the onset of famine from overpopulation and a growing scarcity of resources. Concerns about toxicity and pollution inspired an urban-based environmental movement, as an educated population began to question the environmental costs of continued industrialization and urban sprawl. Other influential environmental publications include Garrett Hardin's (1968) *The Tragedy of the Commons*, which highlighted humankind's propensity to overconsume commonly held resources, and Donella Meadows' (1972) *The Limits to Growth*, which measured the impact of such overconsumption on the earth's finite resources, as many came to realize the fragility of planet earth in the wider universe in the aftermath of the Moon landings in 1969 (Garner, 2000, pp. 2–33).

THE MODERN ENVIRONMENTAL MOVEMENT

A series of environmental organizations emerged from the counterculture; Friends of the Earth (FOE) was founded in 1969, the Natural Resources Defense Council (NRDC) in 1970, and Greenpeace in 1971. These organizations would provide the platform for a bourgeoning interest in environmental issues following the first Earth Day in 1970. The establishment of the US Environmental Protection Agency (EPA) (also in 1970) was a response to this wider interest in environmental issues, leading to an increase in environmental regulation. The Brundtland Report (titled *Our Common Future*) from the World Commission on Environment and Development (WCED) of 1987 set out an understanding of sustainable development on a global level. This was followed by further initiatives such as the 1992 Earth Summit (which introduced Agenda 21), the Rio Declaration, and the Commission on Sustainable Development. Many environmental groups advocated for the Kyoto Protocol on Climate Change in 1997, and environmental nongovernmental organizations (NGOs) continue to lead on issues such as climate change (*ibid.*).

The increased incidents of environmental catastrophes such as Three Mile Island, Bhopal (India), and Chernobyl led to increased concerns about environmental degradation globally. In 1992, the Earth Summit led to a further growth in green consciousness; environmentalism became a fashionable cause, with celebrity endorsements and an increased focus on environmental issues from a newly globalized media. Major concerns such as the depletion of the ozone layer, acid rain, global warming, and climate change led to a surge in interest in environmental issues and broadened the scope of environmental movement activism. In recent years, the environmental movement has continued to campaign on a range of issues including sustainable development based on increased ecological and global equity, green consumerism, and green politics with a focus on dignity for all species. Green political parties have not met with varied degrees of political success, remaining marginalized in the United States and United Kingdom. However, green parties have participated in coalition governments in Germany, Finland, France, Belgium, the Czech Republic, Mexico, and the Republic of Ireland. China's environmental movement is expanding, and as China's economic growth continues, the Chinese environmental movement may be one of the most significant of the coming century.

PRINCIPLES OF THE ENVIRONMENTAL MOVEMENT

The environmental movement includes a diverse set of philosophies and principles, which ranges from conservation of species and ecosystems, preservation of habitats and natural areas of special interest, promotion of ecological issues, embracing of "deep green" notions about the primacy of nature over human development, promotion of sustainable development, biocentrism, and green politics. The late Arne Naess wrote of a deep green life based on his concept of "ecosophy" in 1972. James Lovelock's (1979) book *Gaia: A New Look at Life on Earth* argues that the planet is a single living, self-regulating entity. The concept of "social ecology" was put forward by Murray Bookchin in the 1960s. Bookchin argued that because environmental problems were based on human injustice, environmental issues must be linked with issues of social justice. For Bookchin, the impulse to dominate nature or other humans was at heart of all environmental and social problems. Social ecology's questioning of the impulse toward growth and development has become one of the environmental movement's most significant critiques of overconsumption. The environmental movement incorporates a range of ideologies across a spectrum that includes what Australian writer Timothy O'Riordan terms "deep green ecologists," who value nature over economic growth, through to "light green technocentrics" who favor growth (Leonard, 2008).

This division between "ecocentric" ecologism and "anthropocentric" human-based concerns has characterized the divisions that are inherent in the environmental movement. The environmental movement recognizes that humanity has a role to play in the planet, but that that this creates certain obligations in relation to maintaining a sustainable present so as not to jeopardize the planet's future. The environmental movement's principles are based on the promotion of a balanced approach to ecological and human rights. However, the environmental movement has been criticized for being too focused on Europe and North America, while the emergence of corporate "greenwash" in response to environmental concerns has reduced the environmental movement to the role of a special interest lobby group, lacking a wider appeal in spite of increased interest in environmental issues among the wider public.

EXAMPLES OF ENVIRONMENTAL MOVEMENT ACTIVISM

The environmental movement includes many groups with participatory activist roots, such as Earth First!, while others have embarked on a more professionally negotiated platform, such as the World Wildlife Fund (WWF). However, it was the sinking of the Greenpeace ship The Rainbow Warrior in Auckland Harbor in 1985 that gave rise to the environmental movement's global activist appeal. The Rainbow Warrior was en route to protests against nuclear testing in Moruroa, in the French Polynesian Islands of the South Pacific. New Zealand became a nuclear free zone as a result of the outcry of the sinking and loss of life. The Greenham Common Women's camp protestors campaigned against nuclear weapons at the Greenham American Air Force base in the United Kingdom between 1981 and 2000. The Women's camp participants were protesting about both the human and the environmental costs of nuclear war, and the last Trident missiles were removed from the base in 1991. The Sea Shepherd Society led by Paul Watson has led direct activist campaigns against the whaling industry, sinking two Icelandic whaling vessels in 1986.

The anti-nuclear movement was central to the development of the wider environmental movement. In the aftermath of the atomic bombs at Hiroshima and Nagasaki in Japan at the end of World War II, public concerns about nuclear power spread to nuclear energy production and transportation. The proliferation of nuclear weapons during the Cold War between the United States and Soviet Union highlighted the need to oppose nuclear production for many in the environmental movement. The first major anti-nuclear protests in the United States were at Seabrook nuclear power plant in New Hampshire in 1977 and 1978. In 1978, 500 people were arrested at a protest against the Diablo Canyon nuclear power plant in California. In 1979, 70,000 people attended a "No Nukes" rally against nuclear power in Washington D.C. and 38,000 people attended a protest rally at Diablo Canyon. The cultural impact of the anti-nuclear movement was captured in the 1979 album and 1980 documentary titled "No Nukes," and featuring contemporary artists such as Bruce Springsteen and Jackson Browne. The year 1979 was also the year of the meltdown at the Three Mile Island nuclear power station in Pennsylvania, USA (Szasz, 1994). The accident occurred in the same week that the "China Syndrome" movie was released. The movie, starring Jane Fonda, documents a nuclear accident. In 1986, a meltdown at the Chernobyl nuclear plant in the Ukraine was the largest of its kind globally. These events increased public opposition to nuclear power. In 2004, the environmental writer James Lovelock argued that nuclear power was an alternative to fossil fuels and needed to be considered as a clean energy for the future, alongside solar, wind, and wave technologies.

The Environmental Justice Movement emerged during the 1960s when farm workers led by Cesar Chavez challenged the use of pesticides such as DDT in California, USA. African American communities mobilized against regional toxic plants in Houston and Harlem during the 1960s. In 1978, families were evacuated from the Love Canal township near Niagara Falls, New York, in the United States, in response to concerns about high rates of cancer and birth defects. Toxic waste had been buried in the region in previous decades. The community-based Environmental Justice Movement developed further in the 1980s in response to the siting of hazardous plants or dumps, often in economically disadvantaged non-white neighborhoods. As a result, the Environmental Justice Movement became associated with the civil rights movement. Attempts to dump toxic waste in the primarily African American community of Afton, Warren County, North Carolina, USA, in 1982 led to protests and arrests. In 1987, the Commission for Racial Justice (CRJ) published the Toxic Wastes and Race in the United States report that confirmed the extent of dumping in minority communities throughout the United States. In 1990, the First National People of Color Environmental Leadership Summit met in Washington D.C. Robert Bullard (1990) published a further study on the issue, titled *Dumping in Dixie: Race, Class, and Environmental Quality*. Further support for the Environmental Justice Movement was provided by the Clinton administration (Clifford, 1998).

The growth in consumption in western society has led to a waste management crisis in many countries. The emergence of incineration in response to this crisis has led to a global mobilization against incineration by communities concerned about the health and environmental risks posed by emissions. In the United States, campaigns against incineration and dumps became an important part of the environmental movement. In addition, moves to promote recycling and waste reduction have been a central part of environmentalists' alternatives to incineration. The "waste hierarchy" that favors reduction and recycling over dumping and incineration has been adopted as best practice by many municipal authorities. Love Canal residents had founded the Citizens Clearinghouse for Hazardous Wastes (CCHW) in 1981. The CCHW would prove to be an important resource for the anti-incineration campaign. This combination of concerns about hazardous waste, incineration, dumps, and environmental justice led to the development of a wider anti-toxics movement that extended links globally, allowing community campaigns to present themselves as more than merely NIMBY-based or "not in my backyard" groups. In 1994, Andrew Szasz published a study on community campaigns titled *Ecopopulism: Toxic Waste and the Movement for Environmental Justice*, which charts the development of local community groups who move "beyond NIMBY" and become part of the wider environmental movement (Szasz, 1994).

Dave Forman's Earth First! has been at the center of direct action activism since 1979. Earth First! was influenced by Edward Abbey's (1975) book *The Monkey Wrench Gang*, and the group became synonymous with the anti-logging campaign in the North western states of the United States in the 1980s. Earth First! activism has been described as "ecotage"; their environmentally minded campaigns of sabotage have included tree sitting, tree spiking, road blockages, and tunneling to protect forests. A more radical offshoot of Earth First! called the Earth Liberation Front (ELF) was seen as "eco-terrorists" by some critics of direct action tactics. The Animal Liberation Front (ALF) was another group whose tactics in defense of animal rights were criticized. The anti-fur campaign of People for the Ethical Treatment of Animals (PETA) also attracted considerable support, but was also criticized for its "shock tactics." PETA's targeting of corporate groups who violated animal rights brought the group widespread media coverage and celebrity support during the 1990s.

Greenpeace are perhaps the most recognizable of all environmental groups. From their origins in Vancouver, Canada, in 1971, Greenpeace have been at the center of environmental movement activism globally. Their protests against nuclear testing in the South Pacific brought the group into conflict with the French authorities and led to the sinking of the flagship

Rainbow Warrior in 1985. In 1995, Greenpeace was involved in one of its most significant campaigns. The group prevented Shell Oil from dumping the decommissioned oil platform Brent Spar in the North Sea. Greenpeace occupied the Brent Spar. With the support of public protests and boycotts across Europe, Shell relented and recycled the oil rig. Greenpeace's Brent Spar protest led to an international moratorium on the dumping of oil rigs. Rex Weyler published a book about Greenpeace titled *Greenpeace: How a Group of Ecologists, Journalists, and Visionaries Changed the World* in 2004. Today, Greenpeace is an international organization that highlights global environmental campaigns on many diverse issues such as providing information about climate change and working toward the preservation of the rainforests. Based in Amsterdam, the Netherlands, Greenpeace has 2.8 million supporters worldwide and maintains offices in 41 countries (Weyler, 2004).

The WWF was founded in 1961 in Switzerland. The WWF is known as the World Wide Fund for Nature outside of North America. With 5 million members, it is the largest environmental group in the world. The WWF is committed to "halting and reversing the destruction of our environment." The group's focus is on biodiversity, pollution, climate change, and the conservation of forests and oceans. The WWF engage with many multinational corporations to promote education about environmental issues and to prevent further environmental destruction. The WWF's Panda logo is one of the most recognizable icons in the modern environmental movement. FOE was founded by David Brower following his departure from the Sierra Club in 1969. This represented a new departure for the previously conservationist environmental movement, as FOE would go on to oppose nuclear power plants and embrace social as well as environmental justice issues in the subsequent decades. FOE has confederations in 69 separate countries, with each national group retaining a degree of autonomy. These national groups are supported by FOE International, based in the Netherlands. FOE groups campaign on issues such as climate change, desertification, corporate accountability for pollution, nuclear power, and biodiversity issues (Mertig, 2007, pp. 239–262).

The NRDC was founded in 1970. The NRDC developed with a focus on a reform agenda and now has offices in Washington DC, San Francisco, Los Angeles, Chicago, and Beijing. The group has over 1.2 million members worldwide. The NRDC has had success as a lobby group and has good influence among legislators in Washington D.C. where they argue for a balanced approach to conservation and sustainable development. The NRDC has remained relevant during recent crisis, implementing a study on the health impacts of the 9/11 attacks in New York and working with communities in the aftermath of Hurricane Katrina in New Orleans. The NRDC has also reached out to a younger demographic and has developed a platform with the band Green Day to raise social and political conscious-ness among audiences worldwide. The NRDC has also worked with political leaders such as Robert Kennedy, Jr. to maintain challenges to protect coastlines in Alaska, and the group continues to advocate for sustainable development and political justice issues and has focused on clean air and protection of the oceans (*ibid.*).

The environmental movement influenced anti-globalization protests on development from the 1999 protests in Seattle, USA, against the World Trade Organization or in Davos, Switzerland, against the World Economic Forum through to the 2002 Johannesburg, South Africa World Summit on Sustainable Development and the G8 protests at Edinburgh, Scotland, and Hamburg, Germany. In the United Kingdom, protestors used direct action to prevent the disposal of the Brent Spar oil rig platform in the North Sea in 1995. The image of "ecowarriors" tunneling into the earth or chaining themselves to trees as part of their campaigns to protect nature has become a part of contemporary iconography. Earth First's anti-roads movements in the United States, United Kingdom, and Germany in the 1990s have been followed in the 2000s by Climate Action's "Plane Stupid" protests against airport extensions in the United Kingdom as part of a wider campaign about reducing carbon emissions. The environmental movement has also included mainstream media events such as former US Vice President Al Gore's (2006) *An Inconvenient Truth* book and documentary. The Live Earth concerts of 2007 also served to increase awareness and participation in environmental issues. Scientific evidence of the anthropogenic basis for climate change was presented by the Intergovernmental Panel on Climate Change (IPCC) in 2007, providing a new impetus for the environmental movement of the future. With the election of President Barack Obama in 2008, green issues will remain at the forefront of the political agenda in the coming era, as the challenge of climate change becomes one of the priorities of the age.

THE ANTI-TOXICS MOVEMENT

Background

The anti-toxics movement's origins can be traced back to Rachel Carson's (1962) *A Silent Spring*. The book highlighted the impact of pesticides such as

DDT on plant and wildlife in America in the years following the introduction of scientized methods of agriculture in the United States. In the aftermath of a wider public concern and scientific debate about Carson's work, President John F. Kennedy called on the Science Advisory Committee to investigate issues surrounding the use of pesticides. This inquiry confirmed Carson's position and led to the regulation of the use of chemical pesticides in the United States. Carson has been subject to a number of subsequent criticisms from scientists working for the chemical industry.

The Environmental Justice Movement developed further during the 1960s when migrant agricultural workers led by Cesar Chavez also challenged the use of pesticides in California, USA. African American communities mobilized under a racial justice and anti-toxics agenda as part of a number of regional campaigns against toxic plants in Houston, Texas, and Harlem, in New York City during the 1960s. In 1978, communities campaigned against the dumping of toxics near their homes in the Love Canal Township near Niagara Falls, New York, in the United States. The campaign emerged in response to concerns about high rates of cancer and birth defects in the area. The toxic waste had been buried in the region by the Hooker Chemical Company in the 1920s and had begun to seep into the local water supplies (Szasz, 1994).

THE LOVE CANAL CONTROVERSY

The land surrounding Love Canal was developed for a school and housing despite the warnings of the Hooker Company in the 1950s. Over 50 drums of chemical waste were found at the site during excavations, and the school was built away from the area. In 1957, low income housing was built on the site. With the construction of a superhighway in the 1970s, floods began to occur in the area, often containing toxic residue. In 1978, Lois Gibbs of the "Love Canal Homeowners Association" led residents in protests about the number of serious illnesses occurring with children in the Love Canal community. The activities of the Homeowners Association led to the discovery of the toxic materials underneath the homes in the area. This information had been withheld from the community when the homes were first built. The Homeowners Association found that over 50% of their residents suffered in some way from the effects of the toxic waste underneath their housing.

US President Jimmy Carter allocated funds to assist with the Love Canal controversy, which had begun to make national headlines and found coverage in television new broadcasts. An investigation by the EPA in 1979 found that the Love canal area suffered from an abnormally high number of serious illnesses and miscarriages. Pregnant women were evacuated from the Love Canal area as a precaution. The EPA Report also found that up to a third of residents had detectable damage to their chromosomes due to exposure to the chemicals at the site. Love Canal was declared a National Emergency site in 1980. Over 700 families were evacuated and re-housed, and the Comprehensive Environmental Response, Compensation, and Liability Act (CERCLA) or "Superfund" Act was signed into law, and in 1995, the EPA won nearly 300 million dollars in compensation for the incident. Legislation against toxic industries continued to be introduced in the aftermath of increased agitation from the public. Many industries would relocate to nations that lacked similar legislation but would find that local opposition would occur as communities discovered the effects of toxics in emissions over time (*ibid.*).

The community-based Environmental Justice Movement developed further in the 1980s in response to the siting of hazardous plants or dumps, often in economically disadvantaged non-white neighborhoods. This section of the anti-toxics movement developed in conjunction with the civil rights movement and was organized in response to repeated incidents of siting toxic plants or dumps in minority neighborhoods. Suspicions about toxic industries were heightened by the industrial accidents at Three Mile Island, Chernobyl, and Bhopal in India. Campaigns against incinerators emerged in the 1980s. The emissions from the incineration of waste released dioxins and furans into the atmosphere, and communities near incineration plants began to oppose the incineration industry as a result. While the concept of "Waste to Energy" (WTE) was attractive to many municipalities due to the dualistic outcomes of waste incineration and energy creation from the same process, concerns raised about emissions by the anti-toxics movement were gradually extended to incineration plants.

CAMPAIGNS AGAINST INCINERATION

The first major campaigns against incineration in the United States occurred at the same time as a "garbage crisis" was being highlighted in the media. This crisis emerged as a result of regional landfills reaching capacity, and in some cases closing down. In addition, scientists such as Barry Commoner and Paul Connet were highlighting the carcinogenic risks posed by incinerator emissions. Another contributory factor was the discovery of a document prepared for the incineration industry in California, which suggested ways of overcoming "Political Difficulties Facing Waste to Energy Conversion Plant Siting." The document, sometimes known as the "Cerrell Report" after the company that had commissioned it, was a handbook in overcoming community resistance to incinerators. It fell into anti-incineration activist's possession and would later be used to demonstrate the technocratic approach taken by the industry when dealing with local communities (Walsh, Warland, & Smith, 1997).

Lois Gibbs of the Love Canal campaign had formed the "CCHW" in the early 1980s. The CCHW would prove to be a major resource for the anti-toxics and anti-incineration movements. The CCHW provided advice for communities opposing municipal and private plants or sites, which came to be known as "LULU" or Locally Undesirable Land Use cases. The campaigners came to be known as "NIMBY" mobilizations. However, the CCHW and scientific experts such as chemistry professor Paul Connet went beyond the local for the scientific evidence that was provided to local communities; information was utilized from Europe, Japan, and Australia to provide the data for opponents to toxic plants throughout North America. One significant fact that emerged from this approach was the dramatic increase in dioxin ingestion from the food chain surrounding incinerators. This figure was believed to be as high as 500 times greater than airborne emissions (ibid.).

The result of the campaigns of the anti-incinerator and anti-toxics campaigns has been increased legislation on emissions and a decline in the construction of incinerators in the United States. The incineration industry has improved its filtering system to reduce emissions to address community concerns. However, the anti-incineration movement also contributed a positive initiative to the toxics debate, through its promotion of recycling. The internationally accepted waste hierarchy that locates reuse, reduction, and recycling at the top of its pyramid also places incineration and landfilling at the bottom. Paul Connett would also become a lead spokesperson of the "Zero-Waste" movement that advocated for the reuse of all materials in production processes (ibid.).

Campaigns against incineration continue in the United Kingdom, the Republic of Ireland, and throughout Europe. In the United Kingdom, a number of campaigns against incineration have occurred in areas such as Guilford and Brent's Cross and Bristol. Anti-incineration campaigns have also emerged in Russia. Campaigners have the benefit of national and international support networks that evolved from the work of the CCHW and Professor Connett. Anti-toxics campaigners have also been able to link their concerns with the wider issue of climate change by highlighting the negative impact of toxic emissions on the ozone layer. The internet became a valuable resource for local anti-toxics campaigns that might once have been isolated (Leonard, 2005; Rootes & Leonard, 2009).

CULTURAL ACCOUNTS OF THE ANTI-TOXICS MOVEMENT

In 1994, sociologist Andrew Szasz wrote of the methods in which the anti-incineration movement was able to move beyond its NIMBY inceptions in his book *Ecopopulism*. The anti-incineration movement in the Northeast of the United States was the subject of a study by Edward Walsh Rex Warland and D. Clayton Smith titled *Don't Burn it Here*. The real-life anti-toxics activism of a local mother and legal activist was the subject of a movie titled "Erin Brockovic" starring Julia Roberts in 2000. A movie of the week about the Love Canal campaign titled "Lois Gibbs and the Love Canal" was made in 1982. The issue of communities opposing toxics plants has become a part of contemporary culture and is regularly featured in television news, documentaries, movies, books, and even comics. Like the nuclear industry, the wider toxics and incineration industries have developed a considerable amount of public opposition to their products, and the introduction of innovations or changes is met with a degree of skepticism from concerned communities (Szasz, 1994).

GREEN PARTIES

The US Green Party

The first Green Party was established in Tasmania, Australia, in 1972 emanating from a clean water conservation campaign. Green parties were founded in New Zealand (the Values Party) in 1972 and in the United Kingdom (the Ecology Party) in 1973. The German Greens or Die Grünen was also established in 1979 and ran candidates in the 1980 national election. By the mid-1980s, a Green Party had been established in the United States in the aftermath of wider campaigns by environmental movement participants around issues such as conservation and preservation, opposition to nuclear power, and campaigns against toxic industries. The first

Green group in the United States was known as the "Green Committees of Correspondence" (CoC), and it organized in local confederations until 1991. This group organized under the principle of decentralization and maintained local structures. An interesting facet of the Green Committees is its organizational structure that was based on bioregional rather than political considerations. The group was focused on local politics and was initially opposed to involvement with national politics (Rensenbrink, 1999).

The CoC was renamed as "The Greens/Green Party" in 1991. This group continued to organize at the sub-state level; national politics was seen as outside of the local ethos of green politics. The Association of Autonomous State Green Parties emerged with an agenda to participate in national elections in the 1990s. The Association of State Green Parties (ASGP) put forward consumer activist Ralph Nader as a candidate in the 1996 presidential campaign. These moves led to a nationally based party called the "Green Party of the United States" (GPUS) being formed in 2001. The GPUS became the third party in US politics at this point and organized on a political platform similar to the established Green parties operating in Europe at that time. GPUS set out "10 key values" as guiding principles for their activists:

1. Grassroots democracy
2. Social justice and equal opportunity
3. Ecological wisdom
4. Non-violence
5. Decentralization
6. Community-based economics and economic justice
7. Feminism and gender equity
8. Respect for diversity
9. Personal and global responsibility
10. Future focus and sustainability (www.gp.org)

A further group known as the ASGP worked to develop the electoral capacity of local green organizations, often in tandem with GPUS. In the 2000 presidential election, the Green Party again nominated Ralph Nader and Native American activist Winona LaDuke for president and vice president. The Green Party was on the ballot in 44 of the 50 US states and received 2.7% of the vote. The candidacy of Nader was criticized in the aftermath of George W. Bush's marginal success over green-minded Democratic candidate Al Gore. The Green's response was that they represented a platform for change from the policies of both mainstream parties. The ASGP took on the name "Green Party of the United States" in

2001 and successfully applied for recognition from the Federal Electoral Commission.

In 2002, John Eder became the first Green Party candidate to win a seat on a state legislature, winning in Maine House of Representatives, a seat that Eder would go on to successfully defend in 2004. The 2004 presidential campaign was marked by Ralph Nader seeking an endorsement rather than a nomination from the Green Party, although prominent party member Peter Camejo would run as Nader's vice presidential candidate. The Green's nominated candidate was David Cobb. The controversy between supporters of the endorsement and the nomination approach again divided the Greens. The year 2006 witnessed electoral successes for Green Party candidates at local level, although the removal of candidate Carl Romanelli from the Pennsylvania ballot created further problems for the party, including the loss of their third party status in that state. The Green's presidential candidate in 2008 was former congresswoman Cynthia McKinney alongside Rosa Clemente for vice president. They received 0.5% of the national vote. Ralph Nader declined the Green Party endorsement as part of his independent campaign (*ibid.*).

European Green Parties

The first Green Party in Europe was the "Ecology Party" in the United Kingdom in 1972. The party has prominent spokespersons such as their chair, Jonathon Porritt, author of the environmental books such as *Seeing Green: The Politics of Ecology Explained* (1984) and *Capitalism: As if the World Matters* (2007). The Ecology Party received 40,000 votes in the 1979 general election and 54,000 votes in the 1983 general election, increasing its profile and membership considerably in the process. Under the title of Green Party, nearly 90,000 were won in the 1987 general election. However, the UK Green's most successful campaign came in 1989 when the party won 2 million votes, representing 15% of the overall vote in the European elections. This result pushed the Liberal Democrats into fourth place, but the Greens were unable to gain any seats due to the UK's majoritarian electoral system. The UK Green Party was divided into the Green Party of England and Wales in 1990, after the Green Parties of Scotland and Northern Ireland organized independently. The groups still co-operate, although the Northern Ireland Greens merged with their counterparts in the Republic of Ireland in 2007 (O'Neill, 1997). The Green Party in the

Republic of Ireland has been a participant in the coalition government of that state since 2007.

The Australian Green Party emerged from its origins in Tasmania to form from a coalition of conservationists and anti-nuclear protestors. Regional green groups organized under a national banner in 1984, after encouragement from German green activist Petra Kelly. The Australian greens are organized through federal structures and has a consensus-based National Council (Doyle, 2000). The Australian Green Party was formed from that alliance in 1992. The Australian Green's charter contains the following principles:

- Social justice
- Sustainability
- Grassroots democracy
- Peace and non-violence

The Australian Greens won an increase in support for their campaign of support for asylum seekers in 2001. The party won 7.2% of the vote in the federal elections of 2004. This percentage increased to 9% of the federal vote in 2007, representing 1.38% of the overall national vote. The party continues to poll well in regional elections across Australia. The Green Party of Aotearoa New Zealand is committed to environmental principles and preservation of the indigenous Maori culture. The New Zealand Greens emerged from "the Values Party," the first nationally organized Green Party in the world in 1972. The Greens became associated with the left-wing alliance during the 1990s but set out on an independent path to raise their profile from 1997. The party achieved 5.16% of the vote in the 1999 general elections, rising to 5.30 in the 2005 elections and 6.72 in the general election of 2008.

In Europe, the German Greens or Die Grünen was founded in 1979. Leading figures such as Petra Kelly united the party around political issues such as opposing nuclear power and weapons as well as highlighting concerns about increased industrialization. The party split in 1982 with a faction forming the "Ecological Democratic Party." The remaining members of Die Grünen organized the party around campaigns of political protest. After the re-unification of Germany in 1990, Die Grünen achieved 7.3% of the national vote, gaining 49 seats (O'Neill, 1997). In 1998, the party went into coalition with the Social Democrats for the first time, and the Greens had some policy successes, including the phasing out of nuclear weapons. By 2002, Die Grünen was up to 8.6% of the vote and continues to gain support in opposition. Green parties have also participated in coalition governments in Finland, France, Belgium, the Czech Republic, and Mexico. In France, Les Verts formed in 1982. In 1989, the party received 10.6% of the vote in elections to the European Parliament. Green parties in the European parliament formed the European Green Party in 2004, the first political grouping to do so.

The European Green grouping has been Eurosceptic in the past, as the European Union (EU) was seen to be the opposite of the decentralization ethic favored by most greens. The European Greens also oppose increased links between the EU and the North Atlantic Treaty Organization (NATO). The Greens have since become more pro-active on EU affairs, and were supportive of wider European integration. In Africa, the "Federation of Green Parties of Africa" links the Green parties of the continent, whereas in the Americas, "the Federation of the Green Parties of the Americas" united Greens from both North and South America. "The Asia-Pacific Green Network" unites Green parties from Asia and the Pacific Ocean. In the contemporary era, Green parties continue to work for environmental politics and justice under their slogan of "think globally-act locally."

REFERENCES

Abbey, E. (1975). *The monkey wrench gang*. Philadelphia: Lippincott Williams & Wilkin.
Bullard, R. (1990). *Dumping in Dixie: Race, class, and environmental quality*. Boulder, CO: Westview Press.
Carson, R. (1962). *A silent spring*. London: Houghton Mifflin.
Clifford, M. (1998). *Environmental crime*. Gaithersburg, MD: Aspen.
Doyle, T. (2000). *Green power: The environment movement in Australia*. Sydney: UNSW Press.
Ehrlich, P. (1968). *The population bomb*. New York: Ballantine.
Garner, R. (2000). *Environmental politics: Britain, Europe and the global environment* (2nd ed.). London: Macmillan.
Gore, A. (2006). *An inconvenient truth*. London: Rodale Books.
Hardin, G. (1968). The tragedy of the commons. *Science, 162*, 1243–1248.
Leonard, L. (2005). *Politics inflamed: GSE and the campaign against incineration in Ireland greenhouse press ecopolitics series 1*. Drogheda: Choice.
Leonard, L. (2008). *The environmental movement in Ireland*. Dordrecht: Springer.
Lovelock, J. (1979). *Gaia: A new look at life on earth*. Oxford: Oxford University Press.
Meadows, D. (1972). *The limits to growth*. New York: Universe Books.
Mertig, A. G. (2007). The 'nature' of environmentalism: Nature protection in the USA. In: C. S. A. Van Koppen & W. T. Markham (Eds), *Protecting nature: Organizations and networks in Europe and the USA*. London: Edward Elgar.
O'Neill, M. (1997). *Green parties and political change in contemporary Europe*. Aldershot: Ashgate.

Rensenbrink, J. (1999). *Against all odds: The green transformation of American politics.* New York: Leopold Press.

Rootes, C., & Leonard, L. (2009). *Environmental movements and waste infrastructure.* London: Routledge.

Shabecoff, P. (2003). *A fierce green fire: The American environmental movement.* Washington, DC: Island Press.

Szasz, A. (1994). *Ecopopulism: Toxic waste and the movement for environmental justice University of Minnesota.* Minnesota: University of Minnesota Press.

Walsh, E., Warland, R., & Smith, D. (1997). *Don't burn it here: Grassroots challenges to trash incinerators.* Pennsylvania: Pennsylvania University Press.

Weyler, R. (2004). *Greenpeace: How a group of ecologists, journalists, and visionaries changed the world.* London: Rodale Books.

CHAPTER 2

THE GREEN NEW DEAL: RESTORING BALANCE AND STABILITY TO THE GLOBAL FINANCIAL AND ECOSYSTEM

Ann Pettifor

INTRODUCTION

We are today in the middle of the greatest economic catastrophe – the greatest catastrophe due almost entirely to economic causes – of the modern world ... I see no reason to be in the slightest degree doubtful about the initiating causes of the slump... .

The leading characteristic was an extraordinary willingness to borrow money for the purposes of new real investment at very high rates of interest – rates of interest which were extravagantly high on pre-war standards, rates of interest which have never in the history of the world been earned, I should say, over a period of years over the average of enterprise as a whole. This was a phenomenon which was apparent not, indeed, over the whole world but over a very large part of it.

– John Maynard Keynes (First of the Harris Foundation Lectures, 1931)

We are once again in the middle of the greatest economic catastrophe of our time, and as in the 1930s, high rates of lending at high real rates of interest are the cause. Only this time the threat posed by economic failure is compounded by the much greater threat of climate change and the threat of peak oil. It was this 'triple crunch' that led to a small group of experts, of which I was one, convening over several months in the Spring of 2008 to

Global Ecological Politics
Advances in Ecopolitics, Volume 5, 19–42
Copyright © 2010 by Emerald Group Publishing Limited
All rights of reproduction in any form reserved
ISSN: 2041-806X/doi:10.1108/S2041-806X(2010)0000005006

prepare the way for a major new policy initiative published in July by the New Economics Foundation : the 'Green New Deal' (Green New Deal Group, 2008).

In drafting the Green New Deal, we recognised that the triple crunch was inter-linked. That globalisation's easy but costly money manifested as the global credit bubble of the past three decades had fuelled 'easy consumption'. In other words the Anglo-American economies had used their derivatives trading, securitised lending, mortgages, credit cards and over-drafts to max out on shopping – whether for mergers and acquisitions, goods, or services.

This led to, among other things, a rise in consumption which, through a parallel expansion of manufacturing and carbon use, fuelled toxic greenhouse gas emissions. So for Green New Dealers de-regulated finance, consumption and emissions are inextricably linked. If we are to deal with the threat of climate change, our report concluded, we must deal with the role of the finance sector in inflating a global credit bubble, which in turn inflated consumption, and a global climate 'bubble'.

Our analysis, however, is not widely shared. Although there is widespread public anger at the role of the finance sector in causing and exacerbating the current financial crisis, no major Anglo-American political party is willing to admit that the world's financial centres are responsible, or to make the links between the financial crisis and the rise in emissions. Very few politicians are willing to analyse the cause of the crisis as the collapse of a global credit bubble, inflated by the liberalisation and de-regulation policies of Anglo-American economies. Nor are they willing to concede that it was the credit bubble that fuelled in turn a range of asset bubbles – including, among others, the property bubble, the stock market bubble and the commodity bubble.

Instead, much blame for global economic failure is laid at the door of poor sub-prime borrowers in the United States. Alastair Darling, the UK Chancellor, made this blame explicit in his remarks to the UK parliament during the debate on the Pre-Budget Report of 24 November, 2008, 'a crisis which began, as America itself has said, in the US housing market has seen...benign conditions undermined...The problems in the sub-prime housing market rapidly spread to the entire global financial system, causing a disastrous tightening in credit and undermining confidence' (http://www.hm-treasury.gov.uk/prebud_pbr08_speech.htm).

Why are western politicians unwilling to lay the blame for this great depression on the finance sector – and in Darling's case the finance sector in his own backyard – the city of London? The fact is politicians may be too compromised. After all, it was they, supported by those 'guardians of the nation's finances' – central bankers – that de-regulated the finance sector back in the 1970s and 1980s and cheered on 'light-touch regulation' over the city.

For political links to the finance sector, one need just think back to events on an oligarch's yacht in Corfu in the summer of 2008 in which both of Britain's major political parties were implicated. Or to the recruitment of a man until recently Labour's Prime Minister by J. P. Morgan in 2008 – at just £2 million a year. Or to Chancellor Gordon Brown's recommendation in 2002 that an honorary knighthood be bestowed on the man that carries a great responsibility for this crisis – Alan Greenspan.

The latter was an extraordinary act of deference in the light of Greenspan's views about the role of government. As recently as the 4 August 2008, writing in the *Financial Times*, he celebrated the role that 'Adam Smith's invisible hand' had played in 'quietly displacing government control of economic affairs. Since early this decade' he wrote 'central banks have had to cede control of long-term interest rates to global market forces'. Greenspan went on to warn of '*the danger* that some governments...will endeavour to reassert their grip on economic affairs' (my italics).

Just three months after this was written, governments on both sides of the Atlantic had broken with long-held taboos. Both the Prime Minister Gordon Brown and the President George Bush used taxpayer resources to avert danger and effectively nationalise a range of financial institutions, including two of the biggest banks in the world – Citigroup and the Royal Bank of Scotland (RBS) – to protect them from the punishing discipline of global market forces.

And still politicians would not concede that the cause of the crisis lay with these institutions. Until they do, politicians and policy-makers will not be able to analyse correctly and then deal with the devastation of what will come be known as the bankers' depression, or indeed with the imminent threat of climate change and peak oil. To tackle all three of these 'crunches', the interests of the finance sector will have to be subordinated to society's and the ecosystem's interests.

Second, Anglo-American politicians will have to abandon the certainties of orthodox monetary theory. Namely that money is a commodity and that its 'price' – the rate of interest – is set, and should be set, by the forces of supply and demand, just as the price and distribution of oil is set by the forces of supply and demand.

This orthodoxy is a nonsense. Money is not a commodity. It is not dug out of the ground, nor does it grow on trees. Credit, and in particular the concept of bank money, is man-made and based on confidence and trust. Furthermore, the creation of credit – and with it bank deposits – does not arise from the volume of savings deposited in the banks. Interest rates are a social construct – they are decided by a committee of men, taking into account the interests of finance and the economy. And as such, unlike oil or copper or diamonds, money and credit is a free good, and therefore, 'there are no intrinsic reasons for the scarcity of capital' as Keynes argued in the General Theory.

Because the creation of credit is effectively costless (if not risk-free) and because credit is therefore a free good, there is no reason for it to be scarce, and absolutely no reason for the 'price' of capital – interest rates – to be high. Indeed the sustainability of the ecosystem requires that interest rates should at best be at 0% – or 'the natural rate' – so that we never try to extract from the ecosystem more than it provides. (From this point of view, Islamic banking – which is a form of stakeholder banking in which interest is abhorred – would be far more appropriate to an ecologically sound economic system.)

To develop appropriate policies for financing and sustaining investment in the Green New Deal, our group concluded that society and governments must first manage and regulate the creation of credit, the movement of capital and the setting of interest rates. Until we, as a society, acknowledge the need to do that, there will be little hope of financing a Green New Deal in a way that is sustainable (i.e. easily repayable) in the long-term and of ensuring that investments in the Green New Deal do not require additional economic growth to generate the funds needed to repay debts and interest. In other words, to limit economic growth, to ensure the sustainability of the Green New Deal and to maintain a 'steady state economy' requires, in the first instance, firm regulation and control of the finance sector and very low, if not zero rates of interest.

THE HISTORICAL BACKGROUND

Our international financial system was, until relatively recently, reasonably stable, equitable and fair, at least for the 'developed world'. Lending and borrowing was under control, low rates of interest led to high investment and affordable government expenditure; these led to relatively high incomes and high rates of saving in OECD countries. Income inequality was at its lowest. The crisis of the 1920s and 1930s had taught western societies grave lessons about the folly of allowing 'the money-lenders to take over the temple' – the main theme of President Franklin D. Roosevelt's inaugural speech, in 1933 (http://www.bartelby.com/124/pres49.html) – at the height of the international financial crisis.

> A host of unemployed citizens face the grim problem of existence, and an equally great number toil with little return. Only a foolish optimist can deny the dark realities of the moment.

> Yet our distress comes from no failure of substance. We are stricken by no plague of locusts...Nature still offers her bounty and human efforts have multiplied it. Plenty is at our doorstep, but a generous use of it languishes in the very sight of the supply. Primarily this is because the rulers of the exchange of mankind's goods have failed, through their own stubbornness and their own incompetence, have admitted their failure, and abdicated. Practices of the unscrupulous money changers stand indicted in the court of public opinion, rejected by the hearts and minds of men.

> Faced by failure of credit they have proposed only the lending of more money. Stripped of the lure of profit by which to induce our people to follow their false leadership, they have resorted to exhortations, pleading tearfully for restored confidence. They know only the rules of a generation of self-seekers. They have no vision, and when there is no vision the people perish.

> The money changers have fled from their high seats in the temple of our civilization. We may now restore that temple to the ancient truths. The measure of the restoration lies in the extent to which we apply social values more noble than mere monetary profit.
> – Roosevelt (1933)

In 1944, before the end of World War II, world leaders and a group of economists, including John Maynard Keynes, gathered at Bretton Woods and vowed, effectively, never to allow bankers to rule the international economy again. Instead, they created a new and more stable international financial architecture – the Bretton Woods System. Under this improved, but imperfect system, governments co-ordinated and co-operated to construct an international financial architecture:

- that imposed controls over the movement of capital – capital controls and exchange controls;
- this control over capital flows gave governments the power to set the rate of interest over loans of different terms and risk, at levels most appropriate to domestic conditions;
- and thereby restored to governments one of the most vital levers over the economy.
- at the same time, the Bretton Woods conference created the key-currency standard whereby, through international co-operation, the dollar helped anchor and co-ordinate the value of world currencies, by linking its value

to gold, so each dollar was worth 1/35 of an ounce of gold, or $35 an ounce.

- introduced a system of international co-operation and co-ordination to ensure that currencies did not drift too far apart in value;
- fixed but adjustable rates gave governments effective control over exchange rates, another vital lever for the economy;
- [confusion here – in my view the point is that concerns about exchange should not have greatly impinged on domestic policy setting, and fixed but adjustable rates provided a good degree of stability.]
- thereby regaining the initiative for governments, giving them room for manoeuvre, or policy autonomy; and finally
- encouraged governments to ration, or cut back on foreign imports and balance these with exports.

The International Monetary Fund (IMF) was created to supervise these arrangements and to act only as a firefighter lending to countries with temporary exchange of difficulties and negotiating any necessary changes to the fixed exchange rates. (The IMF's board later gave the institution greater powers, in particular to begin lending for 'development' on the basis of conditions, to low-income countries.)

John Maynard Keynes favoured an International Clearing Union – not the key-currency standard that was finally adopted, but was overruled. He also wanted the IMF to have a matching power to draw funds from countries with surpluses – to give it the even-handed capacity to maintain international equilibrium between countries. The United States, at the time the only surplus country, vetoed this proposal.

To discipline and restrain the international money-lenders who had wreaked such havoc on the global economy in the 1920s and 1930s and to restore *policy autonomy* to governments, the Bretton Woods architects had, above all, recommended capital controls.

Keynes and his fellow Bretton Woods architects argued that democratic states should regain from financial markets the right to control over key levers of the economy, namely the flow of capital, and its corollary, the management of interest rates. In his view, 'the whole management of the domestic economy depends upon being free to have the appropriate rate of interest without reference to the rates prevailing elsewhere in the world. Capital control is a corollary to this' (Keynes, Collected Writings, Volume XXV, p. 149). The aim of domestic monetary policy was to be the cheap money that he saw as necessary to prosperity.

The Bretton Woods Agreement ensured that people should be free to exchange any national currency for any other for purposes of trade or travel. But for the first 14 years after 1945 most governments kept control of their citizens' access to foreign exchange. Some restricted foreign investment and ownership within their territory. Broadly speaking, they did their best to restrict imports to what could be paid for (Milward, 1977). Under the Bretton Woods system, while the dollar was key, the US government was nevertheless subject to stiff constraints and was obliged to ration imports in balance with earnings from exports. All governments were obliged to balance their books – their trade and capital accounts – with the rest of the world, and co-operated and co-ordinated internationally to ensure that there was no build-up of large deficits or large surpluses.

The Bretton Woods system, though not perfect and though not the full realisation of Keynes's ideas, remained in place for almost 30 years, until the 1970s. During that period the world, including continents such as Africa and Latin America, enjoyed unprecedented economic stability, rising growth in income, and expanded trade. There were no financial crises of any magnitude. Barry Eichengreen and Peter Lindert, distinguished economic historians, have noted that, 'In retrospect, the three decades following World War II seem to have been a golden era of tranquillity in international capital markets, a fulfilment of the benediction "May you live in dull times"...Sovereign defaults and liquidity crises were relatively rare' (Eichengreen & Lindert, 1991).

The evidence for these benign conditions can be seen in the charts later in text, which track debt, house prices, inflation and the consumer price index in the United States and the United Kingdom over the period from about 1950 to 2008. (If there are gaps, it is because of gaps in data, and in particular in the consistency of data over this period.) They reveal the direct correlation between de-regulation and the rise in debt, inflation and property prices. All were low and stable during the Keynesian period of 1945 until the end of the 1960s. After President Nixon's unilateral default on the US's obligations to repay its debts in gold, which lead to the collapse of the Bretton Woods system in 1971; and after the gradual de-regulation of the finance sector in the 1970s and 1980s, the break with the post-war 'golden age' is very distinct.

Thus ended the Bretton Woods era and was launched the era of unfettered capital flows and easy, if costly credit: the era of globalisation. This era came to an abrupt end on 9 August 2007 with the global freezing of lending between banks.

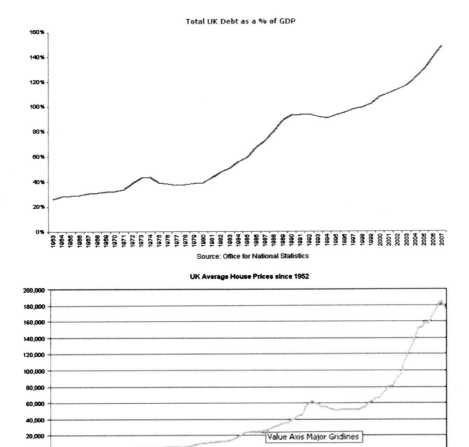

MANAGING MONEY AND DEBT-CREATION

It is well enough that people of the nation do not understand our banking and monetary system, for if they did, I believe there would be a revolution before tomorrow morning.
– Henry Ford, American industrialist and pioneer of assembly-line production method

Money and its link to debt-creation are not well understood. However, the link is firmly established. By creating money at virtually no cost, charging high real rates of interest on loaned money and then adding additional 'charges', banks and creditors:

- extract assets from the productive sector in a manner that can fairly be described as parasitic;
- extract assets from the ecosystem at rates that are unsustainable;
- transfer assets from those without to those with assets;
- make a claim on the future;
- build up exponentially rising levels of debt – both financial and ecological – which are unlikely to be repaid in full.

The debt becomes ultimately unpayable because the rate of interest, or the rate of return on this privately created credit, exceeds the rate at which society (broadly industry and labour, to use Polanyi's terms) and the ecosystem can be renewed, can generate additional resources and can repay.

This would be bad enough, but costly credit is a crime against society and against nature for another reason: it demands exponential rates of return on an asset, money, which is costless to create. Whereas those who grow for example tomatoes have to engage on the one hand with land in the broadest sense and with labour, and because land (including the climate) and labour can affect the profit and loss rate of growing tomatoes, this way of making money carries risks. Those on the other hand that grow money or credit do not have to either engage with land or with labour to create credit. It is effectively effortless activity, which requires minimal staff for basic banking services. The creation of credit, unlike the growing of tomatoes or Nike shoes or McDonald's hamburgers, does not involve land or labour. In other words, it is what economists call 'a free good' – like the air we breathe or the wireless radio waves we may encounter in a public library. And as a free good, its price should be free – or else very low, to cover the diminishing fixed costs of creating credit.

Money's great benefit is that it facilitates exchanges. Furthermore, as Keynes noted, it can do that without 'ever coming into the picture as a substantive object' (Keynes, Collected Writings, Volume XIV). In other words, we can get paid our wages/salaries or can pay taxes without notes or coins – substantive monetary objects – ever being required.

Today money enjoys much greater sophistication than it did in the past. Even then, it was a significant innovation and evolution over a system of exchanges based on *barter*. Today we benefit from another form of money: *bank money*. Over time money has evolved. The original token money (including the bank note) was, at the first stage of its evolution, based on a commodity – a bead, or shell or metal, and then a precious metal, silver or gold. During the second stage of money's evolution commodity money was changed into *bank money*, based not on a tangible object but on something more ephemeral: trust and confidence.

In today's economy, most transactions no longer involve *cash* (i.e. notes and coins) but entries in a ledger or account – that is, *bank money*. Our taxes are, on the whole, not paid in tokens, coins or notes; instead employers pay salaries and make PAYE transfers with bank money. Goods are purchased by direct debit or credit card or by bank transfer. Everyday *consumption* (clothes, food, magazines, entertainment) can be paid both through *bank money* (using credit, debit cards and cheques) and *cash*.

Bank money, unlike commodity money, is *intangible* – you never see or hold it. The amounts held by economic actors at any point in time are simply figures entered into a ledger or a computer, printed occasionally on a bank statement. Of course you could choose to withdraw the amount on the ledger of your bank account and hold it as notes and coins, in which case bank money is turned into 'real' money but generally people do not do this – they keep their money in the bank and spend a large part of it in transactions that do not involve cash. As Geoff Tilly notes:

> There is no tangible quantity corresponding to the aggregate of bank money in an economy at any point in time. Such a tangible quantity/quality is not a necessary characteristic of money. The acceptability and hence validity of bank money is due to its being able to facilitate...transactions.
>
> – Tilly (2005)

In understanding bank money, we need to understand that money held in banks does not necessarily correspond to what we understand as income. Nor does it correspond to savings or depend on the volume of savings. *It does not necessarily correspond to any economic activity.* The one-to-one link that existed between metal tokens and economic activity back in the middle ages – the exchange of a silver token for a pig, for example – does not exist in today's banking system. As John Law, the Scottish economist who was one of the first to understand and advocate bank money, is credited by Schumpeter as saying:

> Money is not the Value for which Goods are exchanged, but the Value by which they are exchanged. (Schumpeter, 1954, p. 322).

A second, vital point to understand about bank money is this: bank money does not exist as a *result* of economic activity. Instead, bank money *creates* economic activity.

As long as 50 years ago, the economist Joseph Schumpeter noted that:

> it proved extraordinarily difficult for economists to recognise that bank loans and bank investments do create deposits. And even in 1930, when the large majority had been converted and accepted the doctrine as a matter of course, Keynes rightly felt it necessary to re-expound and to defend the doctrine at some length...and some of the most important aspects cannot be said to be fully understood even now.
> – Schumpeter (1954, p. 324)

Things have not changed much since 1954. The quotation below, from a recent Question and Answer session with Ministers in the United Kingdom's House of Lords (about a report by James Roberts of the new economics foundation on creating new money) demonstrates that it is still extraordinarily difficult for economists, officials and ministers to recognise that bank lending does not depend on the receipt of deposits; that loans create deposits.

> Contrary to the report of the New Economics Foundation, banks are not provided with a hidden subsidy. Funds loaned out to customers must either be obtained from depositors or the sterling money markets, both of which usually require the payment of interest.
> – Lord McIntosh of Haringey (UK Government minister), 2001, in Boyle (2002, p. 84)

Like Lord McIntosh, many of us still assume that bank loans represent a gift from someone (either locally or internationally) who, unlike ourselves, has taken the trouble to deny themselves a portion of their income and to deposit this in a piggy-bank or savings account – or to lend it out on the international capital markets. Most mainstream economists still believe that banks have 'savings' – either theirs or those of others – and extend these savings to others as credit – charging interest. This is not the case. *The money for a bank loan does not exist until we, the customers, apply for credit.*

Nor do banks have to hold 'reserves' to lend. All they need to hold is the collateral (e.g. a guarantee against a property) on a loan. In other words, far from the bank starting with a deposit or reserves, and then lending out money, the bank starts with our application for a loan, the asset against which we guarantee or secure repayment, such as our house, and the promise we make to repay with interest. A clerk then enters the number into a ledger. Having agreed the loan, the commercial bank then applies to the central bank (e.g. the Bank of England) for the cash element of the loan. This cash element (notes and coins) is the small proportion of the loan that will be tangible to the borrower. The rest is bank money, which is intangible. The central bank provides – on demand – the necessary cash element.

Once the commercial bank has obtained the cash from the central bank we the borrowers, then obligingly re-deposit both the bank money (the undrawn part of the loan) and the cash, which together make up the sum of the loan, in either our own, or in other banks – creating deposits. Even if we spend the cash, the recipient of our cash will deposit it. By this means do new loans create deposits in banks. Because printing and minting the cash costs the central bank a fair sum, the central bank charges a rate of interest to the commercial bank when it issues notes and coins to that bank. The commercial bank pays this in due course and passes on the cost both of the central bank's fee (interest rate), and its own, to the borrower.

Although an increasing number of transactions can be carried out without cash, there are many that still depend on cash, like coins for parking meters so we, the bank's customers, want to hold a portion, albeit (in the United Kingdom) only a small proportion, of our money as cash. A bank is therefore obliged to offer cash to its customers according to demand, depending on their credit standing or overdraft limit. As a consequence banks have to hold a ratio of deposits in the bank, as cash. This is known as the cash ratio or 'reserve requirement'. This tends to be a small fraction of total deposits. In any case, as noted earlier, any cash issued and spent (mostly in retail transactions) very quickly returns to the banking system as deposits. If a shopper were to go to a hole-in-wall and draw out £100 in cash to spend at her local coffee shop, newsagent or cinema, this money would quickly be re-deposited in banks.

This being the case, a popular illusion nevertheless persists: that banks can only lend on the basis of reserve requirements. In other words, to lend £1,000, banks need a reserve requirement of £100 in their vaults. The reality is exactly the opposite. *Reserves are created to support lending.* The Bank of England (for example) provides cash to British commercial banks, *based on public demand for that cash.* Cash is created by the central bank only once borrowers apply for loans.

It is important to note that central banks place no limit on the cash made available to banks. Because the central bank provides cash on demand, there is therefore no limit to the cash, bank money or credit that can be created by commercial banks. The only restraint on the bank money or credit that can be created is the ability of the loan to be matched, or 'secured' by collateral – for example a property. In the Anglo-American economies that so eagerly de-regulated credit creation after the 1970s, the upward spiralling prices of assets provided as 'security' (e.g. property, stocks and shares, works of art, race-horses, veteran cars) enabled private banks to follow and even accelerate for example the property spiral by pushing lending upwards too, to create a vast global credit – or more precisely debt-bubble. This bubble is unprecedented, historically, in scale.

In the United Kingdom in 1982, the ratio of coins and notes to bank deposits was 1:14. At the end of 2005 the ratio had more than doubled to 1:34. Put differently, in 1982 there was about £10.5 billion in circulation as notes and coins. Retail and wholesale deposits amounted to almost 14 times as much £144 billion. By 2005 there was only £38 billion circulating in notes and coins, and almost 34 times as much – £1,289 billion – held in banks as retail and wholesale deposits (Office for National Statistics, May 2006). So for every £1 circulating in cash in 2005, £34 took the intangible form of bank deposits.

These historic numbers demonstrate that the ratio of cash to bank money is not a constant: cash declines over time as confidence in bank money grows, and we make ever-greater use of, for example, credit cards, bank transfers, Oyster cards and Internet banking.

Today in the United Kingdom and the United States (but not in many countries in Africa, for example) a larger and ever increasing proportion of transactions will be carried out as simple account transfers that do not involve coins and notes. The increased use of credit cards and the increased use of Internet banking are two of the most visible examples of this non-cash bank money.

INTEREST AS A SOCIAL CONSTRUCT; MONEY AS A FREE GOOD

The rate of interest is effectively, the price of bank money, set by commercial banks, and largely (but not always) linked to the official or base rate, set by the central bank (e.g. the Bank of England, the ECB or the Federal Reserve.) The initial basis for this 'price' of bank money is set by the central bank when it sets the base or official rate. Since 1994, the private banking sector, led by the British Bankers Association (BBA) has set a parallel rate – the London Inter Bank Offer Rate (LIBOR). This rate – which covers loans in a range of countries and for a range of risk and terms – has always closely tracked the official or bank rate. However, during the current financial crisis, LIBOR has diverged dramatically from the base rate. In other words, central banks have lost control over rates of interest set by the private banking system.

So how are interest rates set? Remember, the central bank enjoys the sole power to issue notes and coins. No other private bank can issue notes or coins, while every private bank can create credit. In the past publicly controlled central banks would have had the power to create or regulate the creation of bank money, and therefore credit. Today that power has been privatised, with commercial banks granted power to create unlimited volumes of credit – through the creation of intangible, costless, bank money. However, it is the sole power to issue notes and coins that provides central banks like the Bank of England with the mechanism for setting the official, base rate of interest. The central bank does this by providing cash on demand that is without limit to a commercial bank, in exchange for collateral owned by the commercial bank (collateral can take the form of assets, e.g. Treasury bills or bonds).

To give a practical example, if Citibank UK intended to make a loan of say £6,600 to Josephine Bloggs, the bank could demand £300 of that loan from the Bank of England in cash (the amount that Josephine is likely to draw in cash). Remember that the cash to bank money ratio in the United Kingdom in 2004 was 1:22. In return Citibank would offer an asset of £300 to the Bank of England. The central bank holds this 'collateral' or asset for a period – say two weeks, and then returns it to Citibank at a *discount* of its value, retaining say 5% of the asset, or £15. The difference between the original value of the asset and the new value – that is 5% – is *the rate of interest* (an arrangement known as a repurchase agreement or 'repo') on a specified date. In other words, the central bank takes it cut and returns the commercial bank's asset to the bank, less 5%. The rate at which these assets are discounted is the rate set by (in the case of the Bank of England) the Monetary Policy Committee (MPC) and is known to us as the bank rate of interest.

It is important to note at this point that the rate of interest is a social construct. The Bank of England arrives at its decision as a result of consultation between members of the MPC and the Governor of the MPC – all of whose members are there by *political appointment* of the United Kingdom's finance minister, the chancellor of the exchequer. The rate of interest is fixed bearing in mind the various interests within the economy, broadly represented by finance, labour and industry. *The official rate of interest is not set according to the demand for money.* The less cash there is in the economy, the more free money the banks create.

So how much can banks lend given that they do not need to find money/deposits in the first place? The answer is that there are no limits to the creation of bank money and therefore of credit, and like other free goods, the price (or interest) should therefore be very low. The cost to a bank or finance company of entering numbers into a ledger is ludicrously low or non-existent. Note too, that the cost of obtaining cash from the central bank is passed on to the borrower. If pushed, bankers would explain that their costs involve an infinitesimally small share of the cost of the ledger, of the pen or computer; of the wage of the member of staff that enters the number; and of the rental costs of the building. With the development of technology, and with the growth of credit, these fixed costs disappear. Josiah Charles Stamp (1880–1941), President of the Bank of England in the 1920s said that:

> The modern banking system manufactures money out of nothing. The process is perhaps the most astounding piece of sleight-of-hand that was ever invented. Banking was conceived in inequity and born in sin...But if you want to continue to be slaves of the bankers and pay the cost of your own slavery, then let the bankers continue to create money and control credit. (cited in British Association for Monetary Reform, 2007)

Given these very low costs, and given that there is no limit to the volume of credit/debt that can be created, then credit is essentially a free good. Prices in free markets are supposed to rise for scarce resources. There is (as yet) for example no price for the air we breathe, because there is no (apparent) limit to it; and it is not scarce. In the same way, there is no scarcity of credit, no limit to its creation.

To understand how the cost of an almost free good can be multiplied, it might be useful to compare the interest charged by commercial banks on 'free' bank money, to the rates paid for the use of wi-fi, or wireless networks in hotels, airports, restaurants etc. Like bank money, the cost of generating wireless has an initial fixed cost and is subsequently very low for the provider, so in the US public authorities like libraries offer free access to the radio frequencies needed to transmit data. But by capturing and controlling access to this essentially free good, private sector providers are able to charge a rent on units of time-use of radio frequencies, and to make extraordinary capital gains from this rent.

Keynes understood that money was essentially a free good. In his *Treatise on Money*, he wrote, 'Why then...if banks can create credit, should they refuse any reasonable request for it? And why should they charge a fee for what costs them little or nothing?' (Keynes, 1930). The answer of course is that if the bank is a publicly owned bank, a bank answerable to the citizens of a nation, then there is no reason why it should charge a fee, or interest, for what costs little or nothing. There is no reason why it should not create debt-free (i.e. non-interest bearing) money for public works. If publicly owned banks, or the government, exercised the power to create credit, citizens would be saved a great deal in taxation.

During the Second World War, and in the years afterwards, Keynes helped both the Bank of England and the Federal Reserve understand the monetary system and to devise money operations that enabled the central bank to offer low, very low rates of interest on a range of loans – short and long, safe and risky. As we in Britain have just realised, in 1950 interest rates were as low as 2% and have not been as low since then. With the de-regulation of capital flows, and with the privatisation of interest rate-setting, central bank governors and elected politicians gave away these vital powers to keep interest rates low – to international capital markets the private finance sector, embodied by the BBA.

GLOBALISATION AND THE DISMANTLING OF BRETTON WOODS

The contrast between economic conditions today and the low rates of interest, the high levels of investment, employment and wages of the Bretton Woods era could not be greater. Low rates of interest are anathema to money-lenders but are vital to all those who engage in productive work, those who undertake vital research, and develop new medicines and other products. They will be vital to the financing of the massive expansion of home insulation and clean technology central to the Green New Deal. If we are to mobilise a carbon army of green-collar workers, then raising the finance to pay these workers without bankrupting the economy, and without making unsustainable claims on taxpayers, the ecosystem and the future, will be vital.

One of globalisation's most destructive legacies is high real rates of interest. Indeed it was high rates of interest that eventually burst the global credit bubble in August 2007. Real interest rates long-term loans (as opposed to the official rate set by the central banks for short-term loans) were, and remain high in most economies, deterring investment in research and development – and in new green investments.

Giant oligopolies now control our market places, and the governmental response to the credit crunch is strengthening their hands. Nowhere is this clearer than in the 'consolidation' or monopolisation of the banking sector. Oligopolies, encouraged by loose government regulation, eliminate competition. Ignoring the cheerful, blind ideology of free marketers, they force up prices for vital goods like drugs and capture disproportionately high profits. As the *Financial Times* noted:

> in a production system marked by extreme outsourcing, oligopoly does not result in the end of competition so much as the redirection of competition downwards, as lead companies capture more power to set supplier against supplier, community against community and worker against worker.
>
> – *Financial Times* (Leader, 14 February 2006).

How was Bretton Woods dismantled? The truth is that it was done stealthily, behind the closed doors of a small group of the world's political and financial elites, with little public and academic debate. To this date the events of 1971 are little known, little understood and seldom studied. Bretton Woods was replaced by a system still in force today. This system of financial liberalisation is different from the old gold standard, in that it is not anchored in gold or any other commodity for that matter. Instead it is anchored on a system of debt, US debt.

The story, summarised briefly, began thus. By the late 1960s, the United States had become the world's biggest creditor and had used its position to displace the United Kingdom as a super-power. However, it had begun to build up a deficit, as a direct result of military spending on the Vietnam War. The United States refused to sell its gold reserves and international investment to reduce this deficit. Instead on 13 August 1971 at Camp David, President Nixon made an extraordinary policy reversal and announced unilaterally that the United States would no longer conform to the Bretton Woods system. Nixon made clear that the dollar would no longer be linked to gold, nor would payments be made in gold. Nor would the United States sell its gold or international investments to raise funds to pay for imports or to pay off debts. (van der Wee, 1987). In other words, the United States declared that it would unilaterally default on its foreign obligations to repay debts in the form it had contracted to do so. This represented, at the time, the biggest-ever default by a sovereign government.

As Herman van der Wee has written, 'such a fundamental decision as the abolition of the gold-dollar standard, taken unilaterally by the United States and without any prior consultation with the rest of the world, was regarded as an arrogant expression of the American policy of domination' (Van der Wee, 1987). Instead of paying its debts by selling exports and earning gold, with which to repay its creditors, the United States offered something much less tangible: bank money in the form of US debt – US Treasury Bills. In other words it was suggested to creditors that they might want to hold new loans to the United States as a form of collateral for the debts they were owed!

THE DESIGN OF A GLOBAL, DEBT-BASED FINANCIAL ARCHITECTURE

At the same time, US policy-makers invited the IMF to design a new international financial system. An effort was made; some insist that the effort was serious but that it came to nothing. Instead, and by default, the dollar became the global reserve currency; and US debt – low-cost loans to the United States – formed the basis of all international reserves. Central banks would no longer hold gold, as evidence of their reserves and to pay for foreign purchases, as evidence of the general health of their economy. Instead they would hold US debt – IOUs of the US Federal Reserve Bank printed on paper.

It is important to note that this new financial system was not the result of considered, planned and co-ordinated action by the international community of world leaders. That although the Bretton Woods system worked well overall, there were clearly strains, and it had become necessary to make changes and improvements, in particular to the exchange rate system. But these changes were not then made as a result of careful deliberation by wise scholars, responsible leaders and their expert advisers. Instead they were made in reaction to the unilateral default on its foreign obligations by the US government in 1971.

The effect of these new arrangements was to dramatically transform the international financial system. First, by dismantling a cornerstone of the Bretton Woods system, the link of the reserve currency to gold, the removal of controls over the movement of capital, in particular US capital, began. The United States could expect to borrow money in the currency it printed. By re-valuing or de-valuing that currency, the United States could, therefore, increase or lower the value of its foreign debts. Furthermore, because there was no longer any benchmark (i.e. gold) against which its currency would be measured, or indeed any constraints against which its balances (imports/exports) would be assessed, the United States need never again be obliged to structurally adjust its economy to restore it to balance (a requirement regularly made, since the 1980s, of poor, debtor nations). This meant that the United States, just by issuing billions of dollars of IOUs to willing buyers, could now borrow limitless amounts of money on the international capital markets without restraint and use these resources to pursue apparently endless consumption.

That is not to say that constraints to international borrowing were all removed instantaneously. Potential creditor countries still maintained capital controls, which made it difficult for money to be transferred to the

United States in the form of a loan. The United States, supported by the finance sector and the United Kingdom government, then began a sustained campaign to discredit and lift international capital or exchange controls – a campaign that succeeded with the elections of Margaret Thatcher as British Prime Minister and Ronald Reagan as the US President in 1979.

Today, instead of holding gold reserves, all countries mainly hold low-cost loans (IOUs or Treasury Bills) issued by the United States – as reserves. These huge holdings of reserves represent staggeringly large loans to the United States, at very low real interest rates. (Poor countries that need to borrow on international capital markets pay much higher rates of interest). Rich and poor countries alike hold these Treasury Bills in their Central Banks, as evidence of their creditworthiness, and of the health of their economies. Larry Summers, until recently the US Treasury Secretary or finance minister, has noted that 'The largest international flow of fixed-income debt today takes the form of borrowing by the world's richest nations at (probably) negative real interest rates from countries with very large numbers of poor' (*Business Times*, 9 March 2004).

The silent, revolutionary changes to the international financial system began the process that was to remove the stabilisers which had ensured that international trade remained balanced, without countries accumulating deficits or surpluses.

The result, after more than 25 years is the build-up of substantial imbalances. The United States today imports half as much again as it exports. Not only does it have the biggest deficit run by a G7 economy in the past 30 years, at approximately 7% of national output, but it needs to raise from abroad an approximate $1 trillion a year, about $3 billion a day. As a share of America's economy, this external deficit had more than doubled by 2005 (IMF, *World Economic Outlook*, April 2005). Recently it has fallen to about 18% of GDP.[1]

The United States is not the only country to build up trade deficits: Britain's trade deficit has recently hit record levels.

Somewhat alarmingly for the central banks and private lenders that have lent money to the United States, American policy makers have indicated that America's Federal Reserve could use its the power to cancel its own debts, by printing more dollars and lowering the value of the reserve currency. A speech in 2002 by the new governor of the Federal Reserve, Mr. Bernard Bernanke, caused considerable controversy, but is illuminating:

Like gold, U.S. dollars have value only to the extent that they are strictly limited in supply. But the U.S. government has a technology, called a printing press (or, today, its electronic equivalent) that allows it to produce as many U.S. dollars as it wishes at essentially no cost. By increasing the number of U.S. dollars in circulation, or even by credibly threatening to do so, the U.S. government can also reduce the value of a dollar in terms of goods and services, which is equivalent to raising the prices in dollars of those goods and services.

– Bernanke (2002 [speech]).
http://www.federalreserve.gov/boardDocs/speeches/2002/20021121/default.htm

Mr. Bernanke has helped ensure that the reproduction of bank money, by means of a mechanical or digital printing press, will remain at the centre of the debate about international finance. Above all he has demonstrated that the United States has extraordinary powers to manipulate the global economy.

Today's financial system resembles the earlier periods of globalisation in almost every respect. It prioritises the interests of the finance sector and in particular the creators of credit. It provides for the unregulated growth of trade – regardless of imbalances between nations, environmental or other impacts, and certainly with little regard for those I will loosely define as 'Industry' and 'Labour' within nations.

The United States' ability to use its financial assets to obtain, cheaply, additional resources; its ability to leverage its political hegemony to hoover up assets from poor countries; the absence of any form of international framework to discipline the US (and other sovereign) countries building up imbalances: all these issues raise profound ethical questions about the unjust edifice that is today's international financial architecture. Above all, President Nixon's unilateral actions in 1971 granted the United States powers and rights to embark on a path of sustained and unchecked consumption. As a result, the United States has massively increased consumption in a way that appeared to have no limit until checked by the Bankers Depression that began on 9 August 2007 when inter-bank lending froze.

Today the United States has plunged into a deep recession and moved from being the world's biggest creditor to the world's biggest debtor and consumer. As the World Bank has noted, this means that today, in contradiction of orthodox neo-liberal economic theory, money often flows from where it is scarce (low income countries like India and China with large numbers of poor) to where it is plentiful (high income countries like the United States and the United Kingdom). In other words, money flows from the poor to the rich. This is the very reverse of what orthodox economists teach in all our universities when they write of wealth trickling down from rich to poor. Neo-liberal economists imply that the trickle down effect is as natural a law of economics as gravity is a law of physics. Today's international financial system proves that it is not.

GREEN NEW DEAL: THE FINANCIAL PROPOSALS

The Green New Deal involves a dual approach: first, proposals for the renewal of the domestic and international financial system, including a changed regime of taxation, and second, proposals for state intervention to allow higher public and private expenditure – targeted at environmental projects that will dramatically cut fossil fuel use and hence help tackle climate change and peak oil. Central to the transformation of national economies and the global economy will be the re-regulation and restriction of the international finance sector. Finance will have to return to its role as servant, not master, of the global economy: to return to its given role of dealing prudently with people's savings and providing regular capital for productive and sustainable investment. The initial proposals of the Green New Deal group for financial renewal involve:

- Holding the Bank of England's interest rate at a low level indefinitely.
- Very much tighter controls on lending and on the generation of credit.
- The forced demerger of large banking and finance groups. We want to see retail banking split from both corporate finance (merchant banking) and from securities dealing. This would echo the Glass-Steagall legislation of inter-war America, which separated retail and investment banking but was repealed in the 1990s by President Clinton, advised by Larry Summers and Robert Rubin.
- Breaking these demerged financial entities up into smaller banks, on the principle that mega banks make mega mistakes that affect us all. Instead of institutions that are 'too big to fail', we should aim for institutions that are small enough to fail without creating problems for depositors and the wider public.
- Subjecting all derivative products and other exotic instruments to official inspection. Only those approved would be permitted to be traded. Anyone trying to circumvent the rules by going offshore or on to the internet would face the 'negative enforcement' – their contracts would be unenforceable in law.
- Offering the same protection for our remaining top-class industrial companies as is routine in France or the United States – and perhaps go further.

Ultimately, our aim is an orderly downsizing of the financial sector. Our Green New Deal relies for funding on a mixture of public and private spending financed by borrowing. Such borrowing is essential during a depression, when the government must intervene as the corporate sector shrinks. This government intervention generates employment, income and saving, and associated tax revenues repay the exchequer. This is the multiplier process, attributed to Richard Kahn, Keynes's closest follower. Any public spending should be targeted so that domestic companies benefit, and then the wages generated create further spending on consumer goods and services. So combined heat-and-power initiatives generate income for construction and technological companies, and then workers' salaries are spent on food, clothes, home entertainment, theatre and so on, creating demand for those industries.

The mathematics of the process are such that the public investment should create an exactly increased amount of new saving, rather than being a draw on existing saving. Equally the higher level of saving as a result of public works will create demand for new savings instruments. This can be met with innovative government instruments such as green savings bonds. The same argument demonstrates that there is nothing wrong with reliance on public expenditure for a good part of national economic activity. The extent of that activity should be a matter for political and democratic choice, for it merely directs real resources into certain uses, whereas private impetus may direct resources elsewhere. The issue is surely complementarity of purpose and full utilisation of resource.

A Green New Deal will to some extent replicate the three major planks of the original 1930s New Deal, designed to deal with the aftermath of the credit crunch of the late 1920s. These were:

1. Franklin Roosevelt's strict regulation of the cause of the problem – a greedy and feckless financial sector. This had been the major culprit in causing the Great Depression, made worse by governments thinking they had to let the market rule.
2. The provision of funding for infrastructure, part of which was paid for by an increase in taxes on big business and the rich – a measure which also had the positive effect of dramatically decreasing inequality.
3. The investment of billions of dollars in a wide range of infrastructural projects such as highways, dams and bridges, as well as in training and better working condition. Its purpose was to get people back to work and generate business opportunities. The Green New Deal will, however, differ from its 1930s predecessor in that there will be a much bigger role for investments from private savings, pensions, banks and insurance. Today's economic and business downturns, and consequent rises in unemployment, are not yet on the scale of the Great Depression. But we believe they will inevitably increase as debt-fuelled demand is curbed in

response to the present credit crunch. To fill this deflationary gap the Green New Deal will encourage investments that are labour intensive, generate huge business possibilities and help solve the triple crunch all at once.

CONCLUSION

Climate change is a global phenomenon and requires a global response. However, if governments are to be able to co-ordinate and co-operate to forge agreements on methods for abatement and adaptation, then it will be vital that they first co-ordinate and co-operate to stabilise the global financial system. For, as the Green New Deal report argues, imbalances in national and international financial systems are inextricably tied to imbalances in consumption and fuel emissions. To stabilise emissions, it is also vital to stabilise financial systems and to subordinate the finance sector to the interests of humanity and the ecosystem.

NOTE

1. Federal Reserve Bank of Cleveland 'The Net International Investment Position' Owen F. Humpage and Michael Shenk, June 2008 (http://www.clevelandfed. org/research/trends/2008/0808/01intmar.cfm). The US net international investment – the broadest measure of US external debt – is currently estimated at year end 2007 at –\$2,4 trillion (US Bureau of Economic Analysis, June 27 2008, http://www.bea.gov/ newsreleases/international/intinv/intinvnewsrelease.htm).

REFERENCES

Boyle, D. (Ed.) (2002). *The money changers.* London: Earthscan.
British Association for Monetary Reform. (2007). Available at http://www.monetaryreform. org/moneytextbook/New_Money_Text_Book004.htm
Business Times. (2004). Siow Li Sen, Editorial. *Business Times*, March 9, p.14. Singapore: Singapore Press Holdings.
Eichengreen, B., & Lindert, P. H. (1991). *The international debt crisis in historical perspective.* Cambridge, MA and London: MIT Press.
Financial Times, Leader. (2006). Martin Wolf, Editorial. *Financial Times*, February 14, p. 12. London: Financial Times/Pearson Newspapers.
Green New Deal Group. (2008). *A green new deal: Joined-up policies to solve the triple crunch of the credit crisis, climate change and high oil prices.* London: New Economics Foundation.

Keynes, J. M. (1930). *Treatise on money and the general theory of employment, interest and money*. New York: Harcourt Brace and Co.

Milward, A. S. (1977). *War, economy, and society, 1939–1945*. London: Allen Lane.

Office for National Statistics. (2006, May). *Report of the UK Statistics Authority*. The Office for National Statistics (ONS), Newport.

Schumpeter, J. (1954). *History of economic analysis*. London: Allen and Unwin.

Tilly, C. (2005). *Contention and democracy in Europe, 1650–2000*. Cambridge: Cambridge University Press.

van der Wee, H. (1987). *Prosperity and upheaval: The world economy 1945–1980*. pelikan books. First published by Deutscher Taschenbuch Verlag GmbH & Co. KG in 1983. Translation published in Britain by Viking, 1986.

CHAPTER 3

THE DILEMMA OF JUSTICE: FOREIGN OIL MULTINATIONALS AND HUMAN RIGHTS VIOLATION IN THE NIGER DELTA OF NIGERIA

Victor Ojakorotu

ABSTRACT

The crisis in the Niger Delta predates discovery of oil in large quantities at Oloibiri in 1956. Before independence in 1960, conflict in the region took the form of agitation for political representation and protection against marginalization by the dominant ethnic groups. However, this crisis took a new dimension in the early 1990s as oil became a major source of foreign exchange and the derivation formula was changed in favour of the federal government with negative consequences on the local people (the need to maintain constant flow of oil have resulted to gross violation of the local people's rights by the state and the oil multi-nationals) especially under the military regimes. The entrenchment of democracy in the late 1990s further escalated the tripartite conflict between the state, oil multinationals and host communities as the complex crisis drew global attention. The formation of Movement for the Survival of Ogoni People (MOSOP) and Ijaw Youth Council (IYC) in the 1990s

Global Ecological Politics
Advances in Ecopolitics, Volume 5, 43–72
Copyright © 2010 by Emerald Group Publishing Limited
ISSN: 2041-806X/doi:10.1108/S2041-806X(2010)0000005007

to challenge the abuse of human rights over four decades was overwhelmed applauded by the local people of the region. More importantly, MOSOP was the first social movement in the region to have internationalized the plight of the local people while IYC took over from the period when MOSOP had some internal crises that undermined its struggle.

Equally the achievements of MOSOP and IYC have instigated the formation of other social movements in the Niger Delta as a whole. The pressure from these social movements might have accounted for sudden change of policies by the state and the major oil multinationals in the mid-1990s. However, the fundamental question is to what extent the social movements (MOSOP/IYC) and International civil society have been successful with the issue of human rights abuse in the region.

INTRODUCTION

The Niger Delta and Colonial State of Nigeria

The Niger Delta was the Oil Rivers that served European economic interests, for which rival economic competition among European business groups promoted as source for various needed raw materials in western industrialization process. The Ijaws who are the major ethnic group making up the Niger Delta resisted the penetration of Europeans severally in many areas of the coastal zone. For there were many cases of violent confrontation against European penetration. The colonial state was created eventually in Nigeria. Following the 1914 amalgamation of the Lagos colony, southern and northern protectorates became a defining moment in respect of how the colonial state was to respond to the fears of the Niger Delta people in the months preceding independence.

Preparation for independence created fears of marginalization. The forced *marriage* of northern and southern Nigeria through the amalgamation of 1914 was considered unhealthy and insensitive of the needs of the minorities of the Niger Delta. In any case, the departing colonial state set up the Willink's Commission in 1958 to look into the fears of the people and recommend solutions. The outcome included prescription for constitutional mechanisms for allaying the fears of domination and marginalization of the Niger Delta by majority ethnic groups in Nigeria. It led to the establishment of special development agencies such as the Niger Delta Basin Authority.

The Niger Delta and Post-Colonial State of Nigeria

Perception of threat to the economic, political, environmental and social security of the oil-bearing communities of the Niger Delta began to sharpen from the time oil was discovered in commercial quantity. By the 1960s, the first violent confrontation against the Federal Government by armed revolutionary group led by Jasper Adaka Boro under the platform of the Niger Delta Volunteer Force (NDVF) had been recorded.

The Federal Government crushed the revolution by the use of force, arrested Boro and his colleagues, tried them for treason and eventually jailed them. In any case, with the Biafra rebellion and events leading to the civil war, Boro was freed along with his colleagues. His decision to join the war on the side of the Federal Government was in compensation for the creation of states in Nigeria but more in determination to fight against the eastern regional government headed by Odumegu Ojukwu whose calculation and intention for leading the rebellion and declaration of sovereign state of Biafra included the control of the oil resources of the Niger Delta.

In 1967, the Federal Government created 12 states out of the existing regional structure of the federation of Nigeria. Rivers, Bendel and Cross Rivers states were created and became the core states of the Niger Delta where Nigeria's oil deposits are found and mined. This action brought respite to the people of the region in terms of addressing their sense of marginalization and representation. Yet for the Federal Government, it was much more to destroy support for Biafra from the then eastern minority communities of the Niger Delta. It is important to note that the war was partly funded with revenue generated from oil exploration and production. With the increasing importance of oil for national development, the Federal Government began to shift the revenue sharing formula in its favour as against the structure that favoured the regional and state governments in the years earlier. This chapter highlights the causes of the perennial violence in the Niger Delta, the reasons that inform sudden upsurge of social movements in the region in the 1990s; the assessment of the Movement for the Survival of Ogoni People (MOSOP) and Ijaw Youth Council (IYC) activities in challenging the state and foreign oil multinationals on issues of human rights abuse in the region

THEORETICAL FRAMEWORK[1]

Several theories were propounded by scholars to explain the occurrences of conflict over the year's most especially resource-driven violence that have caused havoc, destroyed and ruined millions of life in Africa. Some of these theories, especially dependency, could vividly capture the bases for conflicts in the Niger Delta, as this theory did not have explanation for the complex relations among the principal actors involved in the struggle – the state, oil multinationals and local people of the region.

To properly understand the Niger Delta conflict and the gross violation of the local's rights, this chapter situates itself within the framework of frustration-aggression theory. It argues that frustration increases the likelihood of aggression, like what the people of the region have exhibited over four decades against the state and the major oil multinationals operating in the region. All aggression has its origin/root causes in the frustration of one or more of an actor's goal achievement. Therefore, conflict is as a result of unfulfilment of individual or group objectives and the frustration that this breeds. Generally, human needs have always exceeded supply, and the failure to meet all these demands informs series of conflicts in the international system (Barker, Dembo, & Lewin, 1941).

This theory vividly illustrated why the ethnic militias in the Niger Delta resorted into violence as a last option. At different times, it has been argued by the Niger delta militants, activists and scholars that it was accumulated frustration arising from the policies of the state and international oil multinationals that accounted for violence activities in the area. The youths were totally discontented with the deliberate policy of marginalization, alienation, environmental degradation foisted on the locals of the region from the extractive acts of the oil multinationals.

OIL PRODUCTION IN THE NIGER DELTA

The extraction of oil has two basic characteristics: profit maximization and its negative impact on the environment (Falola, 1987; Olatunbosun, 1975). As noted earlier, mineral extraction in the developing world is associated with exploitation, environmental degradation and pollution. The Niger Delta is not an exception in this regard. It was in this direction that Godwin Ojo contends that 'mineral resource extraction across the world, particularly, developing economies, shows that the history of resource extraction is the history of resource appropriation, reckless exploitation with serious threat to the people, environment and livelihoods'.[2] The Niger Delta has witnessed a heavy disregard for environment by the oil multinationals for over four decades. This has translated to severe oil pollution, which has affected the atmosphere, soil fertility, waterway sand mangroves, wildlife, plant life and human health in general. The consequences of this on human were in forms of diseases (resulting from gas flaring), water diseases and the spread of HIV/AIDS. Oil pollution also impacts on the physiology of plants. Worthy of note is its effect on transpiration and photosynthetic activities of these plants.[3]

The unfulfilled expectations that prompted widespread indignation and unprecedented restiveness over the environmental/social effects of oil extraction in the Niger Delta attracted the attention of the international community in the early 1990s. The heightened tension in the region and subsequent violence that followed have compelled the state and oil multinationals to revisit their policies towards the local people especially in the areas of corporate social responsibility and human rights. Notwithstanding the changes that occurred in the late 1990s, the local people have directed their protest against the foreign oil companies operating in the Niger Delta region.

Nigeria is the largest oil producer in Africa and the fifth largest in the Organization of Petroleum Exporting Countries (OPEC) (Manby, 1999). The huge oil wealth the state derives from the sale of petroleum has not turned it into one of the most developed and prosperous on the African continent. This commodity has benefited only a few while the people of the region where oil is extracted have become increasingly impoverished. The country is also ranked among the poorest nations of the world due to mismanagement of petrodollars by those in power.[4]

There is no gainsaying the fact that oil-related activities have done much damage to the fragile Niger Delta environment as well as the health of its people. This stems from the continued unbridled exploitation of crude oil and natural gas, which has led to numerous oil spills and gas flaring.[5] Massive oil spills have not only polluted the sources of drinking water available to the people but have also denied them access to safe water for domestic use. Other deprivations the people suffer are in the form of displacements and strangulation of the means of livelihood in a predominantly fishing and agrarian population. The consideration of a few instances for the purpose of illuminating our analysis here will suffice.

Exxon Mobil, the dominant transnational oil company operating in Eket, Akwa Ibom State in the Niger Delta, has often been accused of flagrant disregard for the environment in the course of its operations. Apart from Mobil, Addax and Elf are also located in the area. Regrettably, the activities of these transnational companies have resulted in pollution, environmental degradation and terminal diseases such as cancer and birth defects. Their operations have had negative impact on forests, marine life as well as the lives of people of the Niger Delta, including even the future generations.

However, in terms of causing ecological horrors to the Niger Delta environment, Mobil is not the worst offender. Shell has equally been criticized for its activities in the area. For instance, 'Shell has callously left uncapped wells in which three young children have so far drowned. Elf, with its deep offshore platform and Floating, Production, Storage and Off-loading Vessels (FPSOs), continue to treat the Akwa Ibom government and people with ignominy'.[6]

The manner in which oil multinationals respond to reported cases of oil spillage seem to confirm this 'ignominy'. For instance, in July 2000, a major oil spill occurred at the Batan flow station, an oil facility owned by Shell. The spill reportedly caused extensive ecological damage in the community and led to loss of the means of livelihood of the local people. Since then, a line of enmity (exacerbated by mutual suspicion) seems to have been drawn between the community and the Shell. With the outcry over the Batan flow station crisis yet to abate, another major spill occurred at the oil company's Batan delivery line on 20 October, 2002. The actual cause of the spill going by divers' claims was a 'slack' in two bolts and nuts used in the 8-inch tie-in manifold locked under water at the delivery line. The communities have not only lamented the economic hardship they have been plunged into by the spill, but they have also alleged recession in their fishing business, lack of 'good' drinking water in the affected areas and the refusal of the oil company to provide relief materials to cushion the effect of the spill.[7]

Despite this ugly incidence, Shell was not eager to accept responsibility for the spill. The Western Division of the oil giants claimed that the Ijaw community subjected its staff to 'gruesome ordeal, duress and manhandling' Shell also alleged that the oil spill was an act of third party interference. This in the language of the oil company means an act of sabotage. According to the oil multinational, 'the inspection report of the diver who inspected the leak point leaves no reasonable person in doubt that the leakage occurred due to unauthorized tempering by unknown persons with two bolts and nuts on the flange of the manifold'.[8] On the contrary, the people insist that the oil company owes the Batan community an obligation of providing relief materials and replacement of ageing oil facilities in the community and stopping the alleged use of military personnel to harass the local people. Mr. Alex Ebi, a community leader, alleged that Shell was using armed security operatives to repress them, insisting that the community was not responsible for the spillage. Although the cause of the major spill in the area has been in dispute, what however appears clear is the fact that there has been an extensive ecological damage in the community.[9]

This development has generated a barraged of criticism against these oil multinationals nonchalant or lethargic response to such environmental crisis in its operational procedure in Nigeria. For example, a university lecturer, Dr. Uwem Ite, recently blamed the environmental hazards in the Niger Delta on the years of oil exploration by oil multinationals in the region. He described the period when the company first set foot in the Niger Delta region as a rip-off. He maintained that these companies' business approach has led to a high 'dependent culture', resulting in confrontation between oil-producing communities and the multinationals, stating that this 'dependent culture' was adversely affecting its operations. He further argued that when the oil multinationals realized that it was responsible for community restiveness due to failed promises, it opted for *community development*, launched in February 2004 in Warri, Delta State, as opposed to *community assistance* that it had consistently practiced.[10]

What is most worrisome is the failure of government to muster the needed political will to ensure that oil companies honor their commitments towards the host communities whenever environmental crises and ecological disasters occur. Environmental degradation continues in spite of Nigeria's accession to many international environmental agreements. Some of these international legal instruments (to which Nigeria is signatory) include the Vienna Convention for the Protection of the Ozone Layer, the Montreal Protocol and the London Amendment, Convention on Biological Diversity and the International Convention on Oil Pollution Preparedness, Response and Coordination.[11]

Today Nigeria is grappling with the recurrence of violent protests by the youth of the Niger Delta as result of the negative impact of oil production on the people of the region. The grievances of the local people over oil production in their region will be categorized into environmental damage, economic deprivation, political exclusion and social factors.

STATE AND FOREIGN OIL COMPANIES VERSUS HOST COMMUNITIES

A poignant issue in the administration of oil activity is lack of local participation in the administration of the transnational oil corporations. This is also referred to as the lack of equity participation in the oil industry – a development that has been interpreted as a strategic means of keeping the people and Niger Delta states out of the dividends of the resource, which belongs to them and which they agitate to control.[12] The Nigerian state and oil companies of course frown at any agitation to alter the status quo. Therefore, the resistance by the Ogoni against oil production has always been considered a direct threat by the Nigerian state and oil companies, which are answerable to their headquarters in Europe and North America. It is therefore necessary to consider some of the major resistance in the region that attracted the counter resistance by the state/multinational companies (MNCs) to ensure uninterrupted oil activities.

For the sustenance of oil flows in the region, the Nigerian state (in collaboration with oil companies) put in place regular security arrangements and special task forces. This informed the establishment of the notorious and brutal task force known as the Rivers State Internal Security Force, a paramilitary force created on the eve of MOSOP's protest against oil production in Ogoni. Similarly, the core states of the Niger Delta also formed their own special security forces with different names, for example, 'Operation Salvage' (created by Bayelsa State to protect oil installations) and 'Operation Flush' (established by Rivers State).

The state and oil companies have always emphasized their commitment to the forceful protection of oil companies' activities and installations. This underscored the states leaders' pronouncements of warning against the disruption of oil production because oil is the lifeblood of the country. Indeed, the former Petroleum Minister during the Abacha regime, Dan Etete, at various times spoke against violent protest from the local people, insisting that 'the present [Abacha's] administration will not tolerate a situation where every political grievance is taken out on oil installations and operations of oil companies' and that community leaders should restrain their youths from such acts.[13]

Similarly, he stated in 1998 that the destruction of oil companies' property would meet the full wrath of the law because the state was (and still is) in a joint partnership with the foreign oil companies.

Accordingly, the repression of the people of the Niger Delta has been conducted by the state and major oil companies (that are acting in concert with the government). However, the oil companies at various times have resisted the claim that they have always collaborated with the state in perpetuating gross human rights violations in the Niger Delta. It has been proven however that oil companies have, at different times, assisted the state to suppress protests in the region. For example, they collaborated with the Rivers State Government Security Force (made up of the Mobile Police Force) in 1990 to attack protesters in Umuechem where more than 80 persons were killed and 495 houses reduced to ashes. Moreover, the Judicial Commission of Inquiry that was set up to look into the incident discovered that there was no evidence of threat from the villagers and submitted that the mobile police force had displayed a reckless disregard for lives and property (Pegg, 1999).

The Umuechem incident became a special case study in the analysis of brutalization in the Niger Delta. First, it marked the first time in which serious human rights violations were carried out. Secondly, it was the first time that arms were directed at protesters. A monarch and two of his sons died with 493 people declared missing. Whereas this community produced about 76,981,735 barrels of oil between 1982 and 1985 and produced about 1,568,378,000 of natural gas[14] in the same period, yet there were no good roads, hospitals, electricity and good drinking water when the researcher visited the community in 2003. The most devastating incident occurred in 1990, when the youths of the community demanded for social amenities and compensation for oil pollution of their farmlands and rivers (Nwauzi, 2000). Incidentally, the security agents of the state and oil company misunderstood the demands of the local people and turned the episode into festival that led to the death of about 500 people and the destruction of houses all in the name of protecting oil production in the region.

All the measures adopted by the state to contain the spate of violence in Ogoniland have severed and insulated the local people the more. On several occasions, prominent Ogoni leaders were arrested by security agents and detained. For instance, in January 1993, MOSOP leaders – Leton, Kobani and Saro-Wiwa – were arrested in Lagos for questioning. A similar arrest of MOSOP leaders took place on 23 June, 1993, and criminal charges were brought against them on July 1993 (Ibeanu, 1999a, 1999b).

Given the strategies employed by the state to create divisions among the Niger Delta communities, several communal conflicts have erupted since 1993. Among the prominent cases of conflicts in Ogoniland were those involving Andoni (July 1993), Okrika (December 1993) and Ndoki (April 1994). Apart from these, other incidents of violence between communities in the region have led to loss of thousands of lives and the destruction of property especially in Warri, that is, the conflicts between Ijaw, Itsekiri and Urhobo, and between the Urhobo and the Isoko communities in Delta state. In addition, the state had used extra-judicial killings to eliminate prominent activists who are perceived as threats to oil production in the region. To substantiate these actions, series of decrees were rolled out by the state in the 1990s not only to silence opposition from the community and the activists but were also invoked by the military regime to sentence and execute the Ogoni 9 in 1995.

The situation in Ogoni deteriorated in 1993, when some oil workers were beaten by aggrieved youths in the community. The response of the state and oil company was so dramatic that it marked the extension of (continual) military harassment and eventual use of military force against protest in the Niger Delta region especially in Ogoniland.

Similarly, on 30 April, 1993, when about 10,000 Ogoni people protested in Nonwa against pipeline construction by Wilbros (an American oil servicing firm working for another oil company), the response of the military was so severe on the people. In this particular incident, about 15 people were wounded and the owner of the farmland where the firm (Wilbros) was working lost her arm. This particular episode resulted in the death of one Mr. Agbarator who was shot by Nigerian soldiers on 4 May, 1993.

Another important incident that aggravated the state's harassment of Ogoni leaders was the decision taken by MOSOP to boycott the 12 June, 1993, presidential election. In fact, this incident marked a watershed in the annals of MOSOP. The election divided the leadership of the organization such that the militant group wanted an outright boycott while the conservatives favoured participation in the election. On the basis of this, name-calling ensued. It was assumed that those who opted for participation had been bought over by the government. The situation got to a head on May 21, 1994, when four of Ogoni leaders – Albert Badey, Edward Kobani, Samuel Orage and Theophilus Orage – were murdered in Gokana. Those killed represented the conservatives within MOSOP. Almost immediately government swung into action arresting the militants including the entire MOSOP leadership and subsequently charged them under military law. This single event resulted in the death of about 1,000 persons (Boele, 1995; Crow, 1995; Ibeanu, 1997; Robinson, 1997).

Another facet of the state's response to the Niger Delta issue merits consideration. The state evolved a strategy that would create a disharmony among the ethnic groups in the Niger Delta as could be seen in the war between the Andoni and the Ogoni which led to loss of lives and the destruction of property worth millions of naira.

This unwieldy situation made it possible for the state to sustain its determination to silence opposition in the region. Professor Claude Ake (1996) (who was appointed to look into the remote and immediate causes of the inter ethnic conflict), noted,

> I don't think it was purely an ethnic clash, in fact there is really no reason why it should be an ethnic clash and as far as we could determine, there was nothing in dispute in the sense of territory, fishing rights, access rights, discriminatory treatment which are the normal causes of these communal clashes.[15]

The change of government in November 1993, which brought General Abacha to power, exacerbated the state violence against the local people. A series of measures were taken by the government to permanently incapacitate the opposition by minorities in the region. It is interesting to note that some of the oil companies are also in collaboration with the Abacha government in this act of repression. To this charge, the MNCs provided a rebuttal. But evidences abound that some of them are indeed culpable.[16] The government has continued to pay oil company back by providing armed security and other logistics at its installations[17] to avert the shutting down of flow stations and disruption to oil activities. This is to prevent loss of revenue which should accrue to government. For instance, major oil companies in the region estimated that they lost about 200 million dollars in 1993 due to incessant protests and unfavourable conditions in the Niger Delta. They have consistently called for urgent measures from the state to forestall such occurrence in the future. Such measures almost always include the use of force to suppress dissent and legitimate demands by the people.

Supposedly heeding the above admonition by the oil companies, the state collaborated with these MNCs to deal with aggressive communities. A report in a leaked memo from the Rivers State Commissioner of Police urged 'the Nigerian Army, the Nigerian Air force, the Nigerian Navy and the Nigerian Police' to 'restore and maintain law and order in Ogoniland ... The purpose of this operation order is to ensure that ordinary law abiding citizens of the area, non-indigenous resident of carrying out business ventures or schooling within Ogoniland are not molested'.[18]

While in another memo of May 12, 1994, it was stated that because one of the oil companies could not continue with its oil production, Ogoni leaders should be wasted. The memo was reportedly signed by Lt. Col. Paul Okuntimo of the Rivers State Internal Security Task Force.[19]

This same task force was linked with many dastardly acts against the oil minorities in the 1990s. The head of the task force stated in one of his unguarded utterances that

> I will just take some detachments of soldiers; they will stay at four corners of the town. They have automatic rifles that sound as death ... We shall surround the town at night ... The machine gun with 500 rounds will open up and then we are throwing grenades and they are making *eekpuwaa* ... and they know I am around.[20]

He went further, 'what do you think the people are going to do? We have already put roadblocks on the main road; we do not want anybody to start running ... so the option we have made was that we should drive all these people into the bush with nothing except the pants and the wrapper they are using that night'.[21]

Despite all these repressive measures, the Ogoni responded to state violence by increasing their mobilization and campaign against the state and oil companies. This approach was considered as the most viable way to portray the oil company's battered image abroad. In addition, MOSOP adopted a measure to raise money through *'one Naira per Ogoni Person'* in 1993 with a view to sustaining the cause of the Ogoni within Nigerian federation and at international fore. Most importantly, MOSOP was able to sensitize other communities in the Niger Delta to embrace the struggle by the Ogoni. This accounted for the dramatic increase in protests by other communities in the region. It also gave impetus to the adoption of a series of bill of rights that was presented to the state and oil companies in the region. For the Ijaws, they took up the struggle in a violent way consequent upon their adoption of the *Kaiama Declaration* in 1998. The Oron, the Urhobo, Isoko, Ikwerre and other ethnic communities followed suit.

One fundamental factor that weakened the Ogoni struggle in the 1990s was the implosion of MOSOP, which culminated in the killing of other prominent Ogoni citizens on 21 May, 1994. The rancor among the Ogoni leaders which resulted in the death of four of their leaders gave the state the 'opportunity' to nail the organization that had been a thorn in the flesh of the state/oil companies.

Generally, see below the response of the state, oil companies and local communities to the activities of oil multinationals.

Human rights violation	The response of the oil companies	The response of the state	The reaction of the local communities
Pollution of water	Initiation of community development projects	Militarization of the communities	Making representation to government
Destruction of farm land	Supply of arms to the state as a measure of protecting facilities	Divide and rule tactics among the communities	Embracing dialogue
Destruction of aquatic lives	Very lukewarm, at times, nonchalant and discouraging	Settlement of the elites and community leaders	Peaceful demonstration
Destruction of wildlife		Establishment of some dysfunctional bodies	Hostage taking

Source: Compiled by the researcher.

Overall, the factors that culminated in the fall of the Ogoni can be summarized, as Bob (2002) argues, in terms of the shrinking of domestic and international opportunities that had engendered the formation of social movements. The developments that undermined MOSOP's struggle and ultimately led to its fall are as follows:

- The differences (between the radical and conservative wings) within the MOSOP leadership over the issues of organizational structure and strategies.
- The activities of the conservative elite who bargained for and accepted political offices offered by the Federal Government as these frustrated MOSOP in its attempt to forge a cohesive front against the multinational oil companies (MNOCs) and the government.
- The withdrawal of the conservative elements within MOSOP's ranks vis-à-vis the boycott of the Presidential elections of June 12, 1993.
- The failure of the international community to sustain its support for MOSOP in the aftermath of the internal crisis.
- Increased repression of the civil rights movement in general by the Abacha regime.

The eventual transition from military rule to civilian administration in 1999, coupled with the interest of international community, gave impetus to the Ijaws to carry out militant struggle against the state and oil companies in the Niger Delta.

THE OBASANJO REGIME AND THE NIGER DELTA

There was a general assumption that the enthronement of democracy in Nigeria in 1999 will automatically translate to demilitarization and development of the Niger Delta as it was also assumed for other regions as well. This position arose from the opportunity that would be provided by entrenchment of rule of law and other institutions associated with democratic regimes. While it is true that the Obasanjo administration improved on its predecessors' policies in the Niger Delta, the initial action of the government especially the 'Odi Massacre' dented the regime's policy towards the region. Notwithstanding the Odi episode, in other areas like the Warri crisis, the legal battle between the littoral states and the central government, and the onshore/ offshore debacle, the Nigerian state policy towards the local people improved considerably. The action of the president in his first month in office established his sympathy for the region through a draft Bill that established the Niger Delta Development Commission (NDDC). The president thus demonstrated the need to urgently address the plight of the region; this effort invariably paid off with the takeoff of the commission as an intervention agency to facilitate development in the region.

The agency was plagued with series of difficulties, especially the inability of the commission to effectively discharge its statutory duties due to lack of fund. The National assembly noted that the foreign oil multinationals were reluctant to contribute the required 3% of their annual budget to the body; on the side of the central and state governments, there are backlogs of its financial commitment to the commission. Therefore, it is likely that the ideas behind the establishment of the body are far from being fulfilled.

The composition of the governing council of NDDC witnessed a huge protest in 1999 from the youths because there is an unsettling conviction that the NDDC would fail like the defunct Oil Minerals Producing Areas Development Commission (OMPADEC) that enriched few individuals to the detriment of the populace. Their protest stemmed from the involvement of the governors and other bureaucratic bottlenecks in the operation of the body. Given this uncertainty, the deputy director of Environmental Rights Action (ERA) insisted that the organization would be politicized and drift from the part of addressing the fundamental issues of resources control, self-determination and environmental protection.[22] Similar to these problems is the government under-contribution to the commission as it was confirmed that the state had a backlog of almost N70 billion between January 2001 and December 2003.

Despite these shortcomings, the commission prides itself as having achieved considerable success in the Niger Delta. As at 2003, the organization had executed some notable projects in the region as could be seen in the table below.

Projects	Units Executed
Roads	40
Water	90
Electricity	129
Shore protection/Jetty	47

Source: www.nddconline.org

Similarly, the body also undertook some major projects in the area of erection of school buildings, educational equipment supplies, agriculture and fisheries and hospital. As part of its impact on health infrastructure in the region, it donated an ambulance and X-ray facilities worth millions of naira to the General Hospital, Calabar. NDDC built a number of health centres, doctors' and nurses' quarters and donated ambulances to specialist hospitals in other parts of the region. According to the body (NDDC) as at 2003, a total of 127,148 patients were given free quality medicare, 478 received eye surgeries, 2,683 had general and gynecological surgeries, 19,490 received free eyeglasses and 4,497 had dental surgeries.[23]

Before the formation of the NDDC, majority of the people of the oil-bearing communities in the Niger Delta had to rely almost exclusively on traditional medical treatment save for the existence of a few primary health centres managed by the local or state governments. The MNCs also operated a few, barely equipped hospitals scattered across the Niger Delta. Little wonder that the initiatives by the NDDC in reversing the trends of the past have been commended by a number of people.[24] However, it may be argued that the community projects embarked upon by the NDDC need not draw any special applause from the people given that the Commission was just doing what the state should have been doing all along. The arguments and counterarguments notwithstanding, some observers have commended the NDDC for its efforts at addressing the problems in the Niger Delta.

It was in recognition of NDDC's efforts at developing the Niger Delta that the organization was awarded an International Award by European Marketing Research Centre (EMRC), Brussels, Belgium, on 15 December, 2003. At the presentation ceremony, the Director of EMRC, Professor Mathijsen, praised the efforts of NDDC for its 'spirit of initiative in developing a region that is key to Nigeria's economic fortunes' and that if the organization is properly encouraged and financed it will truly make a difference in the lives of the poverty-ridden region.[25] President Olusegun Obasanjo also established a new federal ministry that would address one of the major problems facing the people of the Niger Delta (Ministry of Environment). His regime established the Environmental Monitoring Committee under the Ministry of Environment and appointed 'a youth director' for the directorate of Youths Development in the NDDC. The president later signed into law a bill abrogating the dichotomy between onshore and offshore that sparked up a heated debate in Nigeria. A series of administrative panels were raised at the local and the national levels to proffer solutions into the crisis in the Niger Delta. Some of the multinationals have at different time argued and placed the responsibility of development and human rights violation in the region on the Federal Government.[26]

But when the companies came under intense pressure to intervene on Saro-Wiwa's behalf, it was forced to issue a statement that called for quiet diplomacy. While on environmental issues, critics have asserted that oil multinationals are operating double standards, '[One of the foreign oil companies] admitted that it tailors the implementation of its environmental policy to meet local circumstances' (Carr, 2001). In response to a series of these allegations, one of the companies initiated a long-term survey known as Niger Delta Environmental Survey in 1995 to provide baseline ecological and socioeconomic data. It was an independent steering committee of all the stakeholders in oil industry but was saddled with the responsibility of providing terms of reference and appointed the consultants and the initial funding was provided by one of the oil firms. A case of putting the cart before the horse! After years of human and environmental hazards unleashed on the region, the oil firm felt obliged to undertake baseline studies that should have determined its operations in the region. Similarly, one of the multinationals confirmed in 1996 that their expenditure on environment-related projects exceeded the US$150 million it spent in 1995 and its budget for community projects of providing schools, hospitals, water, roads and other facilities was in excess of US$20 million a year in the Niger Delta. It was asserted that 'we have never denied that there are environmental problems in the Delta. While many of these are not attributable to the oil industry, we accept that oil operations in general, …, do have an impact'.[27]

Aside all these general changes in oil multinational operations in Niger Delta, they took a decisive step in 1996 to address some demands of the Ogoni. The company offered a plan of action in Ogoniland on 8 May, 1996, that if an agreement was reached between the company and the Ogoni communities, it will clean up all oil spills since 1993 when the company withdrew from the area, whether or not they were due to sabotage.

One of the oil companies agreed that as a matter of urgency rehabilitate and take over its past community projects and provide further development projects in the areas that needed such. All these were aimed at reconciling the oil company and Ogoni communities.[28]

Over the years, gas flaring has been regarded as one of the most serious environmental impacts of oil production. With series of allegation levelled against these oil giants, they have since reduced gas flaring to about 20% and it approved $400 million in 1998 for gas gathering projects. These companies, with NNPC, Elf and Agip, in a joint venture signed a contract worth $65 million with Italian oil company – Nuovo Pignome in 1998 to harness gas from its flares in the Niger Delta.

This project called Odidi Project was launched in 1996 due to an approval by an Environmental Impact Assessment (EIA) undertaken by the industry's environmental regulatory authority and the Department of

Petroleum Resources.[29] By 2003, oil company's aspirations to meet the gas flares, out target of 2008, brought about two sets of pipelines in the Offshore Gas Gathering System (OGGS) and have been completed: the 32-inch 2,565-km trunk line and 24-inch 90-km Forcados spur line. The offshore section of the trunk line has been successfully hydro tested while a similar integrity test with water is planned for the onshore stretch.[30] The company has made some progress in recent years in its efforts to address the impacts of its operation on the health of the local people in the Niger Delta. It was to this effect that two of the oil companies signed a partnership agreement to establish a $4.5 million health care program in Nigeria in 2003. The focus of this partnership is to reduce child and maternal mortality from malaria and to compliment government efforts in her Roll Back Malaria program. The company has also been involved in the building of clinics and hospitals in various parts of their areas of operations in the Niger Delta. It is also instructive to note that the oil firms have been of assistance to the NDDC in the discharge of the Commission's duties. In 2003, one of these oil giant contributed some $54.5 million to NDDC.[31]

This is in addition to its direct *community development* interventions that supplanted the company's *community assistance* programs in 1998. For instance, in one of the oil giants' annual report of 2003, it highlighted the projects and activities of the company vis-à-vis its social responsibility component:

- Some 2,500 secondary and 840 university scholarships were awarded to deserving students.
- Provision of leadership skills training for approximately 70 school prefects from some 15 schools.
- Building and renovation of classroom blocks at around 20 schools.
- Completion of the computer and telecommunications centre at the University of Port Harcourt in Rivers State.
- Completion of nine agro-processing micro-projects in various communities under the Agricultural Extension Services Scheme.
- Completion of the Women's Development Centre at Egbemo-Angalabiri as part of Shell's Women-in-Development Program.
- Provision of support for the incorporation of 29 community-based enterprises.
- Establishment of 14 micro-credit schemes.
- Provision of seven hand-pump equipped boreholes and deep-water reticulated systems in 13 communities.
- Completion of Otuabagi concrete bridge.[32]

These palliatives have had little impact on the region; the long period of neglect has made it imperative that any intervention would necessarily take some time to make any positive change in the environment. That the state and multinational oil companies have started something is welcome, but these must be carried to conclusive ends and new ones also injected.

Beyond the foregoing, this chapter evaluates the success or failure of social movement activity vis-à-vis their quest to alter the attitude of both the government and the MNOCs towards the social dislocations including human rights violations in the Niger Delta. In other words, the fundamental question is whether the social movements have been successful with regard to realizing the advantages they have been seeking. The answer to this question finds its relevance in a similar study of social movement efforts at mobilizing for action. Gamson, in his study of 53 active social movements between 1800 and 1945, advances a typology that stresses the criteria of acceptance by the social movement's audience and advantage (Gamson, 1975).

Pegg modifies Gamson's typology in evaluating the outcomes of social mobilization by groups. According to Pegg, a social movement can be considered successful if it gains acceptance and if it secures advantage with reference to its stated objective(s). A social mobilization actor is deemed to be partially successful if it gains either acceptance or secures advantage while it is rated unsuccessful if it gains neither (Pegg, 2003).

An extrapolation of the evaluative criteria of this typology to suit the discourse of MOSOP and IYC as social movements in the Niger Delta is instructive in reaching definitive conclusions. It can be safely concluded that the social movements in focus were successful in that they were recognized as the linchpins of the minorities' struggle against marginalization, environmental degradation and inequitable revenue allocation among others. Their recognition as such not only by the ethnic groups they represent but also by the government and the oil multinationals is noteworthy. Such recognition served as a necessary prelude to acceptance by the main actors. The foregoing finds expression in these movements' *locus standi* as negotiating partners and stakeholders in the recent processes aimed at addressing the problems of the Niger Delta. For instance, one or some of the oil firms have been compelled to recognize MOSOP as the valid representative of the Ogoni. The same recognition has been accorded the group by the government especially during failed peace processes in the past. The people at the grassroots have also reposed their confidence in social mobilization groups. That the government and the multinationals have been forced to negotiate with these movements on occasions especially whenever developmental issues (as they affect the Niger Delta) are on the agenda substantiates the conclusion premised on the first evaluative criterion, that is, the acceptance of the social movement by the audience as a valid spokesperson.

The second criterion that determines the success or failure of social movements, that is, securing advantage, also lends itself to the evaluation of MOSOP and IYC's efforts in the Niger Delta. The findings of this research suggest that the social movements in the Niger Delta succeeded albeit partially with regard to securing advantage vis-à-vis the cardinal objectives they have been seeking. That the success of the social movements in the Niger Delta is relative is premised on the fact that not all of the objectives of these groups have been realized. For instance, goals such as the restructuring of the Nigerian state to engender true federalism, equitable political participation and resource control have not been attained. Be that as it may, the social movements have succeeded in taking the Niger Delta issue to the front burner of international environmental politics. They have also succeeded in changing the attitude of both the government and the oil multinationals towards the Niger Delta through the series of methods and approaches discussed in this study. More than ever before, the state and the MNOCS have been compelled and are being compelled to take more action aimed at ameliorating the situation in the Niger Delta. The establishment of the NDDC was informed by the resonance of the agitation by the people under the aegis of the social mobilization groups.

At another level, increased social responsibility on the part of the oil multinationals is indicative of the success of community agitation over the years. As noted earlier, oil company's adoption of *community development*, as opposed to *community assistance*, represents a shift in company policy in the Niger Delta. The author gathered from both the leaders of the oil-bearing communities and oil firms that these companies have increased their financial contributions to the communities. The change of company policy and increased financial commitment lend credence to the conclusion that the social mobilization groups succeeded albeit partially with reference to the second evaluative criteria as extrapolated from Gamson's typology.

THE WAY FORWARD

The increasing spate of armed violence in the current Niger Delta crisis is a combination of related fundamental issues that generated the crisis in the first place. Therefore, it follows that any attempt aimed at addressing this dangerous trend should be premised on finding solutions to the fundamental issues that form the bedrock of the crisis in the oil-bearing region. The resolution of the issues at the core of the Niger Delta problem goes beyond the palliatives that the government and the multinationals have handed out to the communities and the people of the region. This is imperative given that the problems of the Niger Delta impinge on the very nature of the Nigerian state. Expressed differently, the knotty issues that have precipitated crisis in the region cannot be addressed satisfactorily without the encumbrances of the Nigerian state as presently constituted. It has been put beyond doubt that past attempts at solving the problems of the Niger Delta without due cognizance of the overall problematic character of the Nigerian state have failed. A crucial step towards building peace in the Niger Delta is the convocation of a conference of ethnic nationalities where all stakeholders in the polity could come together and discuss the future of Nigeria. A conference of this nature would allow both the majority and the minority to put their heads together and fashion out workable machinery for restructuring the country in such a way that each section of the country would have its own fair share of available opportunities. In addition, there would be equal representation in the real decision-making mechanism of the state.

Some observes of the Nigerian political scene reject the idea of the national conference in that it would create more problems than it was meant to solve. Their argument is that it is difficult for even a handful of Nigerians to come to an agreement on any issue let alone the more fundamental ones that border on the continuity of the state. This writer strongly believes that a national conference would not necessarily unleash other problems on the polity if the managers of the process and other stakeholders steer the process so as to build national consensus around the key issues of Nigerian federalism. This conviction is further reinforced by the understanding that majority of Nigerians still subscribe to the oneness and indivisibility of the Nigerian state. National conferences have worked elsewhere[33] and Nigeria stands a chance of making the best of such inclusive dialogue. The government, through National Political Reform Conference (NPRC) under Olusegun Obasanjo, attempted to deal with the issues (Niger Delta).

However, the forum ended abruptly and without success as the delegates from the South-South (representing the [oil] minorities) boycotted proceedings on account of the refusal of delegates from other parts of the country to accede to increased revenues for the oil-producing states. Besides, the conference was not truly representative of the people for the governments at the federal and the state levels nominated delegates without any input whatsoever from the people. Therefore, it is difficult to attribute the recommendations of the conference to the people, which of course poses challenges to the legitimacy of any structures, arrangements and policies resulting there from. The failure of the NPRC therefore makes the convocation of a sovereign national conference or a people's conference imperative. It is instructive to note that the people of the Niger Delta have rejected the NPRC and overwhelmingly lent their support to the rival conference to be organized by the Pro-National Conference Organizations (PRONACO) later in 2005. It is apt to include a caveat though: the convocation of a sovereign national conference is not necessarily an antidote to the myriad of problems facing the Nigerian state. Perhaps, it should be added as an aside that Nigerians seldom agree about any issue. In fact, the convocation of a sovereign national conference may even throw up new issues that might complicate Nigeria's problems.

As a logical corollary of the preceding, the fundamental questions of Nigerian federalism should be resolved, and this could be done in a national conference as suggested above. At present, Nigerian federalism is skewed, and it does not adequately take care of minority interests. This question of federalism must be an integral part of the project to create and nurture true democracy and good governance, enhance the position of ethnic minorities and institutionalize transparent fiscal control.

The government, as a matter of urgency, should devise a workable environmental policy that would regulate oil operations in the Niger Delta. The destruction of the ecosystem of the region by the activities of oil companies has remained an important issue in the Niger Delta question over the years. Setting up of environmental agencies is not enough. Government should enact laws that would protect the environment from being degraded, polluted and damaged by activities of all sorts. In addition, effective machinery should be put in place to see to the strict enforcement of such laws. In the case of the MNOCs, they should be made to become more responsible to the local people in their operations. Government should not compromise the welfare and survival of its citizens because of its profit-motivated partnership with the oil companies. A situation where governments (or some actors in government) protect(s) the oil companies against its own citizens, and oil companies casting themselves as neutral in the conflict between government and the people, does not help matters.

Local people continue to associate oil companies with government, either good or bad. This is why it is necessary for the oil companies to review their relationship with government and become closer and accountable to the local oil-bearing communities. An essential plank on which this 'new' partnership and understanding could be forged is the formation of oil companies–communities relations committees for the purpose of constant dialogue and exchange of ideas.

An interim measure, as a prelude to realizing the long-term ends advanced in this chapter, is the payment of adequate compensation to (affected) local communities even as this is expected to continue in view of the fact that oil activities are not incident free. However, compensation in this sense does not mean putting money into the pockets of the people. Recent events in the Niger Delta have shown that the leadership of many oil communities has compromised their struggle for selfish motives or monetary gains. Some elites and leaders in these communities have turned compensation entrepreneurs, who devise different methods in claiming compensation or grants from government, oil companies and international relief agencies. At times, government and oil company officials collaborate with these greedy leaders in this compensation game. The tragedy of this development is that such monetary compensation so collected only end in private pockets to the exclusion of the ordinary local citizens thus creating feelings of mutual suspicion between the community leaders and the youths in particular. This often sets the tone for rancorous relations among the inhabitants of the same community thereby complicating the already dire situation in the region.

In view of the above, monetary compensation to individuals and middlemen should be discouraged. Instead, government and oil companies should embark on community development projects, which are agreed upon by the local residents. In addition, schools, scholarship schemes, hospitals, good transportation system, electricity, gainful employment, good tele-communications and drinkable water supply should be adequately provided in the communities. This is the only way by which the ordinary people in the Niger Delta could benefit from compensation.

Following from the above, there should be a master development plan for the Niger Delta. Interestingly, government has taken a giant stride in this direction. When General Abdulsalami Abubakar took over the reins of power in 1998, he set up a 22-member committee headed by Major-General Oladayo Popoola. This committee was to appraise various recommendations made to the government on how to tackle the festering crisis in the Niger Delta and produce practical plans for implementation. In its report, a total financial outlay of about 15 billion naira was to be devoted to the establishment of basic infrastructure such as marine transportation, telecommunications and electricity supply. At present, the Integrated Master Plan for the development of the Niger Delta has been rejected by some of the communities in the region as they insist that they were not consulted during its drafting.[34] There are fears that its implementation could be fraught with difficulties (if it would not meet with outright failure) given the lack of popular support. This necessitates local community inputs into whatever arrangement that is intended to address the problems of the Niger Delta. Put differently, whatever initiatives that would be expected to succeed must be generated by the people and owned by them, not foisted on them by all-wise politicians who are less conversant with the enormity of the environmental problems in the region. The import of this recommendation is that the people are more willing to support any initiative they conceive as theirs thus boosting the chances of its success.

It is instructive to note that the regime of President Olusegun Obasanjo made some major steps in addressing the Niger Delta question. In 2000, the NDDC was set up to replace the OMPADEC. In addition, the revenue derivation formula of the Niger Delta and other oil-producing areas outside the region has been increased to 13%. However, these measures have not gone far enough in dealing with the more fundamental demands for the control of oil resources by the oil minorities. At present, there is a raging agitation in the Niger Delta for control of local resources. The agitators have posited that Nigeria is the only country in the world which has so cruelly plundered its oil-producing districts without any policy of compensation and repatriation. In view of these recent developments in the Niger Delta, government needs to reappraise its policies, especially the revenue allocation formula, in tackling the problems in the region.

Not to be overemphasized is the need for both government and the oil communities in the Niger Delta to embrace dialogue. The present crisis in the region is partly being fuelled by the lingering militarist disposition on both sides. The Nigerian political life has been militarized for several years since independence, no thanks to years of military rule. This military phenomenon has inculcated a culture of violence in the society. The frequent deployment of military forces to the Niger Delta to quell local riots in recent years has equally further militarized local ethnic militia. Even the present democratic government is not spared, as recent invasion of communities in the Niger Delta by military forces has shown. Therefore, to stem this tide of violence and armed confrontation in the region, government should systematically deemphasize the use of maximum force and embrace the aggrieved communities in meaningful dialogue. However, this could only be achieved by tolerance from both sides.

The question of leadership in the Niger Delta struggle deserves some serious attention. As was noted earlier, some leaders in the oil-bearing communities have compromised the interests of their own people to achieve selfish ends. The crass opportunism and greed of such leaders tend to

destabilize resistance movements or weaken collective agitations. This factor
was responsible for the destabilization of the Ogoni struggle. Some Ogoni
leaders were essentially interested in personal power and money. As a matter
of fact, some Niger Delta leaders, like leaders at other levels of national life,
are greedy and compromised. They find it easier to line their pockets with
compensations from the oil companies than to fight a principled and
courageous battle for reparations that would make a real difference in the
lives of their people. It is not surprising then that youths in several
communities have come out publicly to denounce their leaders, saying that
they represent themselves, not their people.

Therefore, to appear realistic, determined and resolute in their struggle,
the people of the Niger Delta should lay their trust in the hands of leaders
of proven integrity and good track records.

The distribution of government patronage and resources among
communities and ethnic groups in the Niger Delta should also be addressed.
It is on record that part of the conflict in the Niger Delta has to do with
politics, most especially local government creation. Three main ethnic
groups in the region – Ijaw, Urhobo and Itsekiri – are at daggers drawn over
land ownership and creation of local government.

Therefore, government should ensure that separate local governments are
created to reflect the composition and origins of these warring ethnic groups
to stem the tide of politically motivated wars in these areas. Some argue that
the creation of local governments on the basis of ethnicity does have
implications for (national) unity, cohesion, democracy and governance.
Sound as this argument may be, this writer noted (during his field trip) the
deep-seated feelings of the main ethnic groups in the Warri area and their
hard-line posture concerning the idea of their coexistence. This recommendation is therefore apposite (even if in the short term) so as to defuse inter-
ethnic tensions and avert crisis with a view to finding a lasting solution
to the problem.

The overwhelming reliance on oil and revenues derived from its exploitation has done more harm than good to the Nigerian state. Therefore, the
government should diversify the economy as the neglect of other economic
sectors like agriculture and tourism has remained a bane to Nigeria's
development over the years. Records from the country have shown that
there are abundant solid minerals (mainly in commercial quantities) in
other parts of the state and exploration of these minerals will minimize
over-reliance on oil. It will also downplay the constant push and pull by the
dominant ethnic groups to maintain the flow of oil at all cost. It is
interesting to note that the country can also secure foreign exchange and

further monies for accelerated development by exploiting other vital resources across the country. The harnessing of these solid minerals will gradually reduce Nigeria's over-reliance on oil and vitiate the unnecessary competition for control of oil which can be likened to the zero-sum contest for power. Indeed, solid minerals provide a high development potential for Nigeria. It must be granted that energy is not only an item for revenue generation but a very volatile political commodity. A look at world events (in the Middle East, the United States and the Gulf Region) would confirm this. Whereas this chapter is not suggesting a neglect of crude oil as an economic commodity, it strongly holds that other commodities would reduce its volatile political nature in the local scene.

There is a paradox about the ability of the Nigerian state to manage crises since independence. Somehow, crises have been resolved without leaving too much bitter taste in the mouth, including the management of the civil war and the reconciliation, rehabilitation and reconstruction that followed. Aside the civil war that plagued the country for almost 30 months, the Nigerian state has witnessed a series of challenges that threatens the corporate existence of the country. In view of these challenges (Sharia in the north, Yoruba national separatism, Igbo marginalization, militarization of politics and the Niger Delta debacle), Nigeria can be safely classified as a state that may be drifting towards disintegration. Therefore, there is urgent need for series of reforms in terms of the practice of federalism.

Looking at the challenges posed by the Niger Delta crisis, Nigeria would risk further crisis and tension in the region if the state failed to accept dialogue and rational bargaining with the local people from the region. On the contrary, oil multinationals have a role to play to guarantee their operations in the Niger Delta. The Niger Delta problem cannot be resolved without dealing with the youths who have been at the forefront of the struggle since 1990s. As peace is a major step towards development, the state and oil companies in the region must urgently address the shortcomings of NDDC. Similarly, the international NGOs in the areas of socioeconomic development are to be encouraged to invest in the region. The incessant wave of youth restiveness in the Niger Delta will pose a serious threat to the operation of these international NGOs or scale down their involvement, but the operation of United Nations Development Program must be commended in alleviating the suffering of the local people.[35]

While the stakeholders in the oil industry have made a lot progress to minimize the impact of oil production on the people of the region, there is still some way to go to restore peace and minimize violence in the region. In addition to the suggestion made above, the oil companies and state functionaries must establish constant channels of communication with the local people as a measure to defy further occurrence of conflict in the region.

More importantly, the issues of onshore/offshore dichotomy should be properly addressed. Despite the abrogation act by government in February 2004, scholars from that region have espoused a lot of contradictions, even suggesting that it is another means of bringing dichotomy through the 'backdoor'.[36] After series of contention between the president and the member of senate over the use of terms like 'Contiguous Zone' and 'Continental Shelf', these terms were eventually replaced by 200-meter isobaths. Given the basic Law of the Sea, it means that the derivation principle applies to those areas within 200 meters to the Nigerian coast while the Nigerian Continental Shelf is outside the principle. Therefore, the proceeds of resources from outside 200 meters into the sea will go to the federation account. The Federal Government has obviously not considered that what is called 'Continental Shelf' would not belong to Nigeria if these states that border the waters were not part of the Nigerian state.

Therefore, the implication of this development is that it will further heighten tension in the region in the nearest future as onshore/offshore was not abolished but reduced and each state of the Niger Delta will have different breadth of sea for derivation purpose.[37]

Professor Sagay argues that there would be significant difference in the states of Niger Delta length in the sea. He went further to give some rough estimates of the states derivation zones into the coast.

States	Length into the Coast
Lagos	15.5 miles (28 km)
Ogun	15.5 miles (28 km)
Ondo	27.7 miles (50 km)
Delta	33 miles (60 km)
Bayelsa	38.8 miles (70 km)
Rivers	38.8 miles (70 km)
Akwa Ibom	44.4 miles (80 km)
Cross River	44.4 miles (80 km)

The implication of this variation is that the government has sown another seed of violence that would eventually lead to another prolonged crisis in the region. This analysis has shown that Akwa Ibom and Cross River states have 200-meter isobaths derivation zone three times more than some states. It also means that the proceeds from some gigantic oil and gas fields in the deep sea bed is out of the Niger Delta states derivatives rights. These fields include Bonga, Bosi, Abo, Agbami, Erha, Akpo and Bonga-SW.[38] Apart from these, it was confirmed that at the end of 2003, 110 wells had been drilled in the deep offshore. With increasing focus on the deep shore oil and gradual exhaustion of shallow offshore (200 meters), the deep sea oil fields will be the bone of contention in the future, which the state must address now. This became necessary because the state governments failed to recognize that the negotiation and arrangement that brought all the regions together as a single entity approved for the purpose of derivation, the continental shelves of regions were deemed to be part of that region or state as the situation is in the present 36-state structure. This particular provision was entrenched in section 140(6) of the 1960 independence and 1963 republican constitutions.[39] In the light of all these, the state and oil companies and local people under the umbrella of the social movements must seriously address the explosive issue of Niger Delta crisis to guarantee unrestricted oil production and development of the region.

It would be safe to conclude that in the face of continued agitation in the Niger Delta, all actors must become proactive in resolving lingering and future flashpoints as highlighted in the preceding sections. There is no doubt that international NGOs have helped to place the local palaver effectively in international discourse, and this has helped in a very significant way to sharpen the focus of local agitators. State and MNOC oppression did not have the impact of cowing the agitators but have produced a culture of violent resistance not only in the Niger Delta but also in other areas in the polity. The bottom line remains that where equity and fair play are compromised, peace and development are certain to become impossible. The Nigerian state must therefore come to terms with the problem of the Niger Delta that brought out the international dimensions of a local crisis.

NOTES

1. For comprehensive details on this, see Ojakorotu and Whetho (2008).
2. See http://www.petroleumworld.com/
3. The *African Guardian*, October 1993; Sule (1986).
4. *Ibid.* This position was strongly expressed through interview with the local people of Yenagoa and Ogoni communities and Afiesere/Oleh when the author visited Rivers, Bayelsa and Delta states between 20 and 28, May 2003, for fieldwork.
5. See *Vanguard* (Lagos), 7 September, 2004, p. 38.
6. See *Vanguard* (Lagos), 7 September, 2004, p. 38.
7. See *Daily Independent* (Lagos), 27 August, 2004, p. A7.

8. See *Daily Independent* (Lagos), 27 August, 2004, p. A7.

9. See *Daily Independent* (Lagos), 27 August, 2004, p. A7.

10. See *Daily Independent* (Lagos), 27 August, 2004, p. A9.

11. See *Vanguard* (Lagos), 7 September, 2004, p. 38.

12. *Ibid.*

13. The Human Rights Watch.

14. *The Weekend Concord* (Lagos), 21 March, 1993.

15. http://www.ratical.com/corporations/*OgoniFacts*.html

16. Author's empirical findings.

17. See Ake (1996), Kretzman (1995), Ghazi and Dudu (1996), and Rowell (1996).

18. http://www.ratical.com/corporations/*OgoniFacts*.html

19. *Ibid.*

20. http://www.ratical.com/corporations/*OgoniFacts*.html. Inhabitants of some communities visited in Ogoniland strongly confirmed this position, but this could not be confirmed from the leaders of the communities, as they were reluctant to comment on the issue. The aggressiveness and wickedness of the task force was widely reported by the Nigerian media and human rights organization in Nigeria and abroad.

21. *Ibid.*

22. *The Guardian*, Lagos, 11 July, 1999.

23. See http://www.guardiannewsngr.com/news/article31, 1 April, 2004.

24. NDDC in the eyes of the people, *Tell Magazine*, 7 April, 2003. For instance, HRH King J. C. Egba stated that, 'my council of chiefs and I, as well as the entire people of my kingdom want to say big thank you to the NDDC fore making us enjoy the benefits of oil exploration in our community for the first time'. In a similar vein, the Chairman, Toun Titigha Ogbo of Izonland, wrote on behalf of the entire member of his community to express their sincere appreciation to NDDC for award of major road projects in their community. More importantly, a commendable comment on behalf of Ken Saro-Wiwa Estate and Family.

25. NDDC Press release: NDDC wins International Award. Press Release No. 1 of 5 January, 2004.

26. SHELL, The Environment, Nigeria Brief, Lagos, Nigeria, 1995, and The Ogoni Issue, Nigeria Brief, Lagos, Nigeria.

27. See http://www.Shellnigeria.com/ (Shell responds to environmental allegations, 13 May, 1996).

28. Shell Nigeria offers Plan for Ogoni. See http://www.Shell.com/nigeria

29. http://www.Shellnigeria.com. Shell signs $65 million contract to harness gas from flares, 15 April, 1998.

30. This is based on information obtained from Shell headquarters in Lagos and Port Harcourt, Nigeria.

31. See Shell's Annual Report for 2003 entitled 'People and the Environment', p. 18.

32. *Ibid.*, pp. 18–21.

33. National conferences have been held in a number of Francophone countries in Africa, for example, Republic of Benin, Niger and Chad. The experience in Benin is a case in point. The national conference became absolutely necessary to stem the tide of political instability, authoritarianism, dictatorship, bankruptcy of the State, economic and social crises and to put the country on the path to sustainable democracy and harmonious coexistence.

34. Author's extensive discussions with inhabitants of a number of communities in the Niger Delta during his fieldwork. These communities are Afiesere, Uzere, Arogbo Ijaw, Odi, Sagbama, Ekakpamre, Patani, Yenagoa, Bonny, Uvwie, Evwerni, Eket and in Ogoniland.

35. When the author visited Bayelsa in April 2003, the landmark of UNDP projects was felt by the people as the interview with the local people made us to understand.

36. Majority of the Governors of states in the North and a few of their counterparts in the South oppose the abrogation of the onshore/offshore dichotomy.

37. Professor I. E. Sagay's view on the Onshore/Offshore Dichotomy Abolition Act in *The Guardian* (Lagos), April 2004.

38. I. E Sagay, *op. cit.*

39. *Ibid.*

REFERENCES

Ake, C. (1996). Shelling Nigeria ablaze. *Tell* (Lagos), 29 January.

Barker, R., Dembo, T., & Lewin, K. (1941). Frustration and aggression: An experiment with young children. *University of Iowa Studies in Child Welfare, 18*(1), 1–314.

Bob, C. (2002). Political process theory and transnational movements: Dialectics of protest among Nigeria's Ogoni minority. *Social Problems, 49*(3), 395–415.

Boele, R. (1995). *Ogoni: Report of the UNPO mission to investigate the situation of the Ogoni of Nigeria*. The Hague: Unrepresented Nations and Peoples Organisation.

Carr, S., Douglas, O., & Onyeagucha, U. (2001). The Ogoni people's campaign over oil exploitation in the Niger Delta. In: A. Thomas, S. Carr & D. Humphery (Eds), *Environmental policies and NGO influence* (pp. 159–162). London: Routledge.

Crow, M. (1995). *The Ogoni crisis: A case study of military repression in South Eastern Nigeria* (Vol. 7, Iss. 5). New York: Human rights watch/Africa.

Falola, T. (1987). *Britain and Nigeria: Exploitation or development*. London: Zed books Ltd.

Gamson, W. (1975). *The strategy of social protest*. Belmont: Wadsworth Publishing Company.

Ghazi, P., & Dudu, C. (1996). How shell tried to buy Barretas for Nigerians. *The Observer*, 11 February.

Ibeanu, O. (1997). Oil, conflict and security in Nigeria: Issues in the Ogoni crisis. *AAPS Occasional Paper Series, 1*(2).

Ibeanu, O. (1999a). Insurgent civil society and democracy in Nigeria: Ogoni encounters with the state, 1990–1998. A research report for ICSAG programme of the centre for research and documentation (CRD), Kano.

Ibeanu, O. (1999b). Ogoni-oil, resource flow and conflict. In: T. Granfelt (Ed.), *Managing the globalised environment*. London: Intermediate Technology Publications.

Kretzman, S. (1995). Nigeria's drilling fields: Shells role in repressions. *Multinational Monitor, 26*(1&2), 8.

Manby, B. (1999). The role and responsibility of oil multinationals in Nigeria. *Journal of International Affairs, 53*(1), 283–301.

Nwauzi, L. (2000). *Etche and oil exploration in the Niger delta in boiling point: A CDHR Publication on*. The Crises in the Oil Producing Communities in Nigeria, pp. 133–143.

Ojakorotu, V., & Whetho, A. (2008). Multinational corporations and human rights abuses: A case study of the Movement for the Survival of Ogoni People and Ijaw Youth council of Nigeria. *Resistance Studies*.

Olatunbosun, O. (1975). *Nigeria's neglected rural majority*. Ibadan: Oxford University Press.

Pegg, S. (1999). The cost of doing business: Transnational corporations and violence in Nigeria. *Security Dialogue, 30*(4), 473–484.

Pegg, T. J. (2003). Re-establishing the link: Social mobilization actors in the Niger Delta. Paper presented at the Workshop in Political Theory and Policy Analysis, Institutional Analysis and Development Mini-Conference, Indiana University, Bloomington, Indiana, USA, May 3 and 5.

Robinson, D. (1997). *Ogoni: The struggle continues*. Geneva: World council of Churches.

Rowell, A. (1996). Sleeping with the enemy. *Village Voice* (23 January), 243.

Sule, R. A. O. (1986). The socio-economic impact of petroleum production in Nigeria, July. A paper presented at the Seminar on Environmental Pollution in NISER, Ibadan Nigeria.

CHAPTER 4

ALTERNATIVE CURRENCY NETWORKS AS UTOPIAN PRACTICE

Peter North

People will be free of all tyranny when they are truly free of enslaving moneychangers and politicians that don't represent them. (Ro and Joanna, New Zealand)

INTRODUCTION

Money is not often conceptualised as an object of protest or a tool for constructing alternative communities, economies and societies. Yet from the original utopian socialists Owen and Proudhon to contemporary alternative currency networks people have attempted to construct networks using new forms of subaltern money as a tool for building a more liberated economy and society. This chapter reviews the successes and failures of utopian money networks, arguing that although empirical success is ephemeral, the need to localise economies as a response to dangerous climate change might mean that their long-term future is brighter.

Money is not often itself an object of protest or a vehicle for constructing alternative communities and societies. The left critiques international finance as a crazy casino through which sharp-suited barrow boys and girls working for banks, rating agencies, accountancy firms and the other elements of finance capitalism are paid too much, have too much power and

Global Ecological Politics
Advances in Ecopolitics, Volume 5, 73–88
Copyright © 2010 by Emerald Group Publishing Limited
All rights of reproduction in any form reserved
ISSN: 2041-806X/doi:10.1108/S2041-806X(2010)0000005008

destabilise whole economies through their herd behaviour. These views are confirmed by the regular international finance crises that punctuate capitalisms boom and bust or by more local affairs such as the antics of private equity firms, the sub-prime mortgage market and the mobs (Argentina, 2001) or more sedate queues (Northern Rock bank, Britain, 2007) of savers looking to withdraw their savings from institutions they have lost confidence in. Those who make their living moving money about, rather than producing anything of value, are seen by the left at best as dubious, at worst parasitic. Money corrodes character and community and promotes selfishness and individualism (Leyshon & Thrift, 1997, p. 32). We are opposed to those who we think have more money than us, or we might just be jealous of them. Money can be fairly earned or dirty money, but, remarkably in many ways, we often do not problematise money itself. Money thus rarely becomes an *explicit* focus for political contestation.

Yet there is a hidden history of attempts to construct visions of a better society by designing new forms of money and either attempting to persuade elites of their value or constructing networks from below that attempt to build a new economy through use of new forms of money (North, 2007). In this chapter I examine the historical and contemporary successes and failures of groups of people who have attempted to challenge the impact of money on their lives not by overthrowing it or just by arguing for reform, but by creating local networks in which they use a form of money they have created themselves. I focus on political action, 'actually existing' local money networks, rather than the myriad writings about what is wrong with money and what might be done about it (Boyle, 2003).

I organise the discussion around conceptions of utopianism. My first reaction on hearing a presentation on local money during the depression of the early 1990s was that 'we've been here before'. Innovations in monetary forms of course go back to the very origins of money, but more concretely, political experimentation around money goes back to those Marx and Engels called the utopian socialists – Owen, Proudhon, Warren – and, it seemed to me, many of the critiques made of utopian socialism are still potentially valid. Yet, despite arguments that attempts to build more liberated forms of economic activity from below were misplaced and would inevitably either be crushed by the more powerful or blow out when the limits of people attempting to solve their problems within their own limited means were reached, the creativity, enthusiasm and optimism of local currency activists was infectious. I wanted to know more and since then have carried out research on local money networks in the United Kingdom, Canada, the United States, New Zealand, Hungary, Ireland and Argentina.

I also agreed with Marx's recognition of the ability of the nineteenth-century co-operative movement to 'practically show, that the present pauperising and despotic system of the subordination of labour to capital can be superseded by the republican and beneficent system of the association of free and equal producers' (Fernbach, 1974). Writing off local currency networks from a structural perspective would be to erase the activism of those who worked so hard for so long to set them up and run them and arrogantly label them as misplaced optimists who did not understand the way the world 'really worked'. Post-structural openness to new challenges would balance more pessimistic structural analyses.

THE HIDDEN HISTORY OF ALTERNATIVE MONEY NETWORKS AS POLITICAL PRAXIS

Marx and Engel's original conception of utopian socialism was built, to a large extent, on a critique of money reformers Robert Owen and Pierre-Joseph Proudhon. Owen established labour exchanges in a number of British cities in the 1830s through which artisans sold the goods they had produced for money based on time (Owen, 1816; Jones, 1890; Cole, 1925; Donnachie, 2000). Owen saw these as a bridge to the new co-operative commonwealth, and he invited all people of goodwill to join him on the journey. In the 1840s Proudhon developed ideas of mutual exchange based on labour theories of value with proposals for a society founded on co-operative 'Banks of the People' (Dana, 1896; Woodcock, 1962/1986). Proudhon wished to develop an economy based on the exchange of goods and services between free producers, which, he argued, would develop into one based on mutualism and real equality. In the 1850s, American Anarchist Josiah Warren ran a time bank for three years in Cincinnati and later set up two intentional communities in America ('Modern Times' and 'Utopia') which traded labour notes (Woodcock, 1962/1986, p. 391; Kanter, 1972, p. 6). They both lasted 20 years (Loomis, 2005, pp. 27–30).

Again in the United States, agitation about money erupted across the South and the West after the civil war as poor farmers forced to mortgage their next crop to merchants at usurious rates flocked to the Farmer Labour Party and the People's Party, the original Populists (Goodwyn, 1976). Before populism became associated with politicians who make crowd-pleasing speeches with no intention of delivering their promises, the US Populists developed proposals for a network of government-run sub treasuries which would provide cheap credit, and attempted to collectively buy each other out of their commitments to the moneymen. Populism came to head during the 1896 presidential contest characterised as the 'Battle of the Standards', between proposals for 'sound' and 'hard' money based on a limited and valuable commodity, gold, and for softer money based on more freely available silver. Populist Democrat Bryan declared 'you shall not crucify mankind on a cross of gold'. Bryan's defeat by the pro-Gold Standard Republican McKinley was helped by finance from guided age plutocrats and thousands of flag-waving members of Sound Money Clubs who, together with employers, argued that attacks on the soundness of the currency were a mortal threat to economic well-being, if not to the nation itself. They carried out what can only be called a reign of terror to reimpose financial stability on a nation. Railways, shops, mills, lumber companies and factories were closed down on the day of the election, with the owners saying that they would not reopen given a Bryan victory, whereas another employer told his workers that their pay would be $10 if Bryan won, $26 if the victor was McKinley. Goodyear workers were told that a vote for Bryan would be seen as an attack on the values of the company (Foner, 1955, pp. 337–342). McKinley's purge wiped out contestation over money until the next crisis of capitalism, the Great Depression of the 1930s.

In the 1930s, proposals for the construction of free societies based on open access to credit re-emerged in Social Credit. Major C. H. Douglas argued for a social dividend to be paid to all, to make up for the difference between the pay paid to workers and the price of the product the worker had produced (Douglas, 1937). Douglas argued that the depression was a crisis of under-consumption: wages were too low and needed to be boosted through government-supplied credit. Technocrats, not markets, would decide what the 'just price' was. Social Credit-inspired parties took power at provincial level in Canada, although they did not put Douglas' plans into action and quickly degenerated into rather parochial, anticommunist small business parties. In New Zealand, Social Credit had more resonance and the party had between one and three MPs from the 1960s to the 1980s (Sheppard, 1981; Zavos, 1981). The Green Shirts in the United Kingdom were a uniformed grassroots form of Social Credit, organising unemployed workers to fight fascism, carry out symbolic direct action against finance, and to agitate for nationalised credit (Findlay, 1972; Drakeford, 1997).

Douglas' ideas were generally ridiculed by elites, and he quickly came to the conclusion that 'international finance' was the real power behind a democratic façade. It did not take long for his ideas to degenerate into anti-Semitic fantasies about the power of Jewish financiers like the Rothschilds (Wall, 2003). More successful, briefly, was the rise in the issuance of local 'script' or paper money in the United States and Germany, again as a response to concerns about under consumption. Farmers, small factory owners, local government, small business associations all set up networks through which people suffering from the effects of the depression could exchange goods and services without money, before printing their own notes (Fisher, 1933). The Nazis, in Germany, and Roosevelt, in the United States, later banned script. The North American homesteading movement of the 1940s and 1950s suggested a return to the land and local food production (Loomis, 2005). In the 1960s communes grew up across North America and Europe as young people experimented, with varying degrees of success, with alternatives to the 'big system' of industrial capitalism (Kanter, 1972; Melville, 1972; Houriet, 1973; Abrams & McCulloch, 1981; Levitas, 1990; Pepper, 1990; Bahro, 1994). However, little was heard about new forms of money until the next crisis of capitalism, the restructuring of the 1980s and 1990s.

CONTEMPORARY ALTERNATIVE MONEY NETWORKS

The renaissance in alternative currency forms that we have seen around the world since the late 1980s springs from concerns, most clearly articulated by the Green movement, about globalisation and the perceived loss of local economic control associated with it (Thorne, 1996; Pacione, 1997; Bowring, 1998). Starting in 1983, Michael Linton developed a computerised exchange network which he called the 'LETSystem' through which members could exchange a form of currency they issued themselves in the form of a debit from the issuers account which would balance with a credit into the recipient's account, so the balance of the system as a whole stays at zero. It seemed a thoroughly twentieth century variation on an old concept. Inspired by the success of commercial barter networks, Linton's second innovation was to use a unit of currency linked not to the hour, but to the Canadian dollar: the 'green dollar'. Linking the value of local currency to the Canadian dollar meant that users did not have to buy into the whole philosophy of equality to of labour time in advance to join. This was seen as an advantage in the 1980s when New Right ideas were dominant and equality seemed an 'out of date' hang over from the 1960s. The LETSystem or Local Exchange Trading System (LETS) spread around the world from its origins on Vancouver Island, Canada. In the United Kingdom, LETS schemes had a more community-minded feel, using a local name for the currency like the Bobbin in Manchester, Tales in Canterbury, Favours in Bristol, Brights in Brighton. By 1999 there were 303 LETS schemes in the United Kingdom (Williams et al., 2001). Some remained small-scale networks involving 10–20 people, perhaps in a small town or neighbour-hood, whereas others grew into more substantial networks involving 100 or 200 people (e.g. in Bristol, Brighton or Stroud). One scheme, in Manchester, grew to over 500 members (North, 2006a).

Green Dollar schemes were found in Australia, Canada and New Zealand. In France, local money schemes called local exchange systems (*Systeme de Exchange Local*, or SEL – grains of salt) proliferated, whereas Germany had *Taushringe* and more recently, regional *Regiogeld* (Schroeder, 2006) and Hungary, *Talente* or *Kör* (circles) (North, 2006b). In the United States time-based local currency in paper form re-emerged in towns such as Ithaca, New York (Glover, 1995). This in turn inspired an Argentine NGO, the Programme for Local Self-Sufficiency to develop paper-based alternative currency networks that involved literally millions of users across Argentina during the first years of the twenty-first century. By 1995 Ireland had LETS schemes in Dublin, County Donegal, Banbridge County Down, Coleraine, East Clare, Cork City, the Beara peninsular in County Cork, Kiltimagh, Glenmire, County Tyrone, Westport, Bantry Bay and Sligo. Building on traditional Irish communal agricultural practices, some called the local currency networks *Meitheal Nua* (Walsh, 1994). Irish currencies included Reeks, Sods, Acorns, Skills and Cuids. Reeks in Westport, County Mayo were time based, with one Reek calculated as an average working minute (Douthwaite, 1996, p. 68). Enterprise Ulster-Connaght also experimented with a form of script system, Romas which briefly circulated in County Mayo (Douthwaite & Wagman, 1999). The Irish Department of Social Welfare funded LETS development workers, sometimes putting considerable resources into rural development: 12 MAS workers were funded on the Beara peninsular alone. Into the twenty-first century, a number of Transition Towns have developed local paper currencies (North, 2010).

The political challenge implicit in alternative currencies is that the 'money' we use is simply a social construction, a collective agreement to accept a certain form of measurement, store of value and unit of exchange. Once we accept that money is not a thing 'out there', external to us, but a social construction, it follows that we can change it: we can make collective agreements to use other forms of money. State-created money is used to discipline working people into selling their labour in what is an unequal exchange relationship. Money created from below, it is claimed, enable needs to be met irrespective of the amount of money in existence. It puts liquidity before the artificial scarcity which capitalism uses to enforce labour discipline. Money should be created not in advance – it would be worthless paper – but to meet needs, backed by the issuers' commitment to provide services in reciprocity, in the future. This money is therefore subordinate to human needs, not in charge of them. Furthermore, as local money circulates in a small geographical area, it is a tool for localising economies, reducing transport costs, and, if fully adopted, it would lead to a diversity of small economies rather than large economic monocultures, subject to financial crash (North, 2005). It is thus deeply political, even if those who promote it often deny that what they are arguing for is in any way controversial.

ALTERNATIVE MONEY NETWORKS AS UTOPIAN PRACTICE

In this chapter, I discus alternative money networks as utopian political practice for precisely this reason. Advocates of alternative forms of money often speak as if they are offering a simple, common sense solution, when they are arguing for strikes to the heart of capitalist disciplining. In 'Socialism: Utopian and Scientific' Engels (1968) argued that social change comes from mass action from below, when the capacity of the capitalist system to meet everyone's needs is exhausted. Capitalism is a necessary, if not entirely welcome, stage in human development, not something that can be wished away or avoided by some clever genius's ingenious design. For Engels, the three great utopians of the early nineteenth century, Saint-Simon, Fourier and Owen were not representatives of the newly emergent working class, but social reformers who argued that if the world was not run on rational and just lines then this is only because people have not yet understood the truth. What was required was 'the individual man of genius, who has now arisen and who understands the truth ... He might just as well have been born 500 years earlier, and then might have spared humanity 500 years of error, strife and suffering' (Engels, 1968, p. 396). In contrast, Marx argued that the 'task is no longer to manufacture a system of society as perfect as possible, but to ... discover in the economic conditions ... the means of ending the conflict' (Marx, 1852/1974). Marx and Engels were consequently sceptical about so-called practical plans for the reorganisation of society on more rational lines. Change, they argued, comes from struggle and through economic relations, not from ideas and grand designs aimed at 'reasonable' men and women.

A second element in alternative money networks that might be considered utopian is to examine the extent that Marx and Engels' critique of the project of establishing what they called 'doctrinaire experiments' like exchange banks (now local money networks) that 'renounces the revolutionising of the old world by means of the latter's own great, combined resources, and seeks, rather, to achieve its salvation behind society's back, in private fashion, within its limited conditions of existence, and hence necessarily suffers shipwreck' (Marx, 1852/1974) is still valid. Marx and Engels argued:

> Restricted ... to the dwarfish forms to which the individual wage slaves can elaborate it by their private efforts, the co-operative system will never transform society. To convert social production into one large and harmonious system of free and co-operative labour, general social changes are wanted, changes in the general conditions of society, never to be realised save by the transfer of the organised forces of society, viz. the state power, from capitalists and to the producers themselves. (Fernbach, 1974)

In short, the argument is that individuals cannot change society from below by forming small networks or communities as they do not own or control the resources they need to meet their daily basic needs for food and accommodation, let alone more complex needs. Alternative money networks contest this.

Third, Marxists argue that where co-operatively run experiments or communal forms of living are set up, the pressures of the capitalist economy are too great to be resisted indefinitely. As a system, capitalism is built on growth and competition and has a tendency to monopoly. Small-scale alternative experiments will either be defeated by political conservatism (Gibson-Graham, 2002) or find it impossible to compete in a market with larger, more efficient (read more exploitative) capitalist businesses (Kovel, 2007). Do alternative money networks suffer defeat and disgrace in similar form, or are these arguments that while true for the nineteenth century, no longer hold in world where, although many still struggle to survive, ordinary people in advanced capitalist societies often have access to resources that nineteenth-century proletarians could only dream of? My analyses of local money networks have been built on the hypothesis that we cannot assume a priori that these new utopian networks are doomed to fail. It should be a research question that can only be answered through a more rigorous empirical examination of contemporary utopian practices.

Against Marx and Engels, Martin Buber (1949) argued that in seeking the wholesale transformation of society through revolution the real utopians were Marx and Engels themselves. Buber argued that a more thorough-going, spiritual transformation of society was needed, a transformation deeper than that achievable through revolution seen as one quick push.

It was utopian to expect the state to wither away on its own, and it was no surprise that in Soviet Russia it had not withered away. What was needed was the construction of community life and feelings of collectively over some time. Buber discussed the efficacy of the nineteenth-century co-operative movement and the early twentieth-century kibbutzim of Palestine as examples of this. This suggests that alternative currency networks might be examined as the sort of experiment condemned by Marx and Engels but supported by Buber, experiments to build localised economies in which community feeling and ecological sustainability were cultivated. We will investigate both conceptions in turn.

GREEN MONEY NETWORKS AS UTOPIAN PRACTICE

The first critique is that people with limited resources cannot build liberated societies from below as they do not have the resources needed to meet basic needs, let alone more complex desires. We would therefore expect green money networks to stay small, fail to meet basic needs and quickly burn out. Although there has yet been no systematic analysis of the longevity of alternative money networks internationally, in my research I have found evidence both for and against this hypothesis. In the United Kingdom and Ireland, LETS schemes emerged through the 1992 recession and quickly spread across the two countries such that by 1999 there were 303 UK (Williams et al., 2001) and 12 Irish schemes. Some closed quickly, some lasted longer: for example Sheffield, Brighton, South Powys and Bristol in the United Kingdom and Bantry Bay in Ireland lasted over 10 years. Some green dollar networks in New Zealand have operated continuously for 20 years in places (North, 2007, pp. 126–148). Ithaca Hours in the United States grew out of a short-lived LETS system in 1996, and at time of writing (2007) was still working well (Maurer, 2005). Argentina saw a huge explosion in barter during the financial crisis of 2001–2002, with millions of participants (North, 2007, pp. 149–173). A crisis of confidence in November led to a 70–90% decline in the number of barter markets, but some did last and by 2007 had been in operation for over 10 years. Finally, in Hungary Budapest green dollar market worked well, whereas others struggled (North, 2006b).

Why the difference in performance. There are two questions: did they succeed or fail in terms of longevity, or in terms of size? The experience is that alternative currency networks *can* provide enjoyable or valued political activism, feelings of solidarity and community and real material benefits for long periods of time. A number of conditions emerge that long-lasting green money networks have in common, which might go some way towards explaining their longevity. First is the existence of at least one key and committed activist, preferably with some key helpers, who ensure that the network is run well, accounts and directories and the like come out on time and are accurate. This activist will often have strong political, environmental or religious values that enable them to see the big picture and keep them going during difficult periods. Second is that the networks that lasted generally have what utopian theorists call 'commitment building mechanisms' (Kanter, 1972, pp. 70–74). These can be ways to get members of the network together to facilitate trade such as markets, pot-luck dinners, dances, clothes sharing parties and the like. They can be mechanisms that penalise defection (leaving the network with a debt) or behaviour not supported by the group (taking and not giving, charging too much, providing poor quality services) such as debt and credit limits, public account balances, a management committee speaking to people thought to need help or causing problems or taking debtors to court). Third is a large enough and geographically dense enough network of like-minded people getting what they need and with skills to share. This can be a small network across a city or a geographically isolated rural community. 'Getting what they need' might mean a feeling of community (geographical or a like minded group of friends), providing a vision of what could be, access to alternative therapies, or basic needs. In New Zealand in particular, where members of green dollar networks had access to food grown locally, housing costs that were not too high and a part-time job, they could construct a livelihood that enabled them to live quite successfully for extended periods without having to participate fully in mainstream employment patterns. They found a network that promoted security, friendship and support, and perhaps a little vision of the good life – the latter of course a key element of utopian practice.

The extent the networks enabled the poorest again varied. In Argentina, when the barter networks were at their height in 2001–2002, interviews with participants indicated that an active member who set up a stall and who was able to produce something that others wanted or had something to sell could get by almost entirely through the alternative currency networks. They could feed and clothe themselves and their family and have enough money for luxuries such as getting their hair cut and their nails done (if they wanted), hiring a car, or buying some luxuries and presents. Often they lived off their fat by selling some non-essential possessions, meaning that poorer people could buy things that previously would have been beyond their reach. Others set up new small business, making honey, pizzas, *empañadas*, bread, biscuits, preserves, chutney and the like. However, the very poorest were excluded: they had little ability to produce, and thus to participate. Worse, when the crisis became really acute in 2002–2003 and the poorest flooded into the network, often buying up as much as they could as quickly as possible, selling it on, or offered what were thought of as substandard goods, they were castigated as 'vivos', wide boys. For a time, although, millions suffering from a crisis of capitalism were supported by currencies they produced themselves.

LETS in the United Kingdom was less successful in meeting the needs of the poorest. In 1996 I examined five LETS schemes in areas with large numbers of people unable to access fulfilling livelihoods under capitalism, in Adamsdown, Cardiff; Hattersley, Hyde, Greater Manchester; Drumchapel, Glasgow; and Bransholme, Hull (North, 1996). I found a number of problems that prevented poorer people from building liberated economic relations through LETS. First were benefit worries. Prospective members of LETS were worried that they might loose benefits if the authorities found out that they were earning LETS credits. Although the reality was that there was little evidence of benefit offices showing any interest at all in what were small amounts of 'money' that could only be spent in a very small network, the uncertainty at least was a barrier to the vulnerable joining LETS. The second problem was insecurity. It was difficult to develop reciprocal networks in environments characterised by mistrust, high levels of crime, the isolation often experienced by the vulnerable (be they lone parents, the unemployed, the sick and disabled) and unsettled circumstances. The third problem was that informal ways of making money were a more valuable and attractive alternative to LETS. Twenty pounds for fixing someone's car is untraceable – LETS records all these previously informal options.

The fourth problem was that LETS was seen as an esoteric, green, middle-class club – it was seen as something for green and political minded people, not a serious way of creating alternative livelihoods. Enjoyable and esoteric services like aromatherapy and other alternative therapies were often available on the networks, but practical or basic services – food, childcare, tradepersons – were not. The final issue was confidence and energy. This was the major barrier. Life is hard for people on low incomes, and vulnerability lowers people's confidence, pure and simple. LETS schemes in inner city areas found it hard to recruit new members from populations that felt that they had little to offer, had few skills, or that those skills they had were rusty or unsaleable. Being on low incomes, they had few resources to share. Used to the stress of getting by, they often had little energy for new, untested ideas that promised more than they delivered. The result was that recruitment was slow, the network remained small, and few services were available. Those that did join found that their needs could not be met either as no one was offering what they wanted or they would make large number of telephone calls (in itself, assuming you have a phone, your trading partner has a phone, and you can afford the calls and the time to phone round) and still not get what they wanted. The limits of poor people helping out other poor people were quickly reached, much as Marx and Engels had predicted. The result was that LETS in the United Kingdom did not take off in inner city areas to the levels hoped for. By 2007 none of the LETS schemes surveyed in 1996 are still in operation. Worse, Colin Williams and Theresa Aldridge (Williams et al., 2001; Aldridge & Patterson, 2002) found that even mature LETS had organisational problems in finding enough people to manage the scheme on a voluntary basis leading again to poor advertising and consequent slow recruitment; out of date information (old entries in directories, out of date phone numbers, entries for people who had left town months ago); difficulties in valuing work, and poor quality services. In short, LETS remained too small and too slow the meet needs. This is not a problem when all you want from LETS is access to cheap aromatherapy, but obviously not good enough if you are vulnerable and are looking to get real needs met.

The second problem identified was that utopian experiments like local money networks underestimated the opposition they would be likely to encounter from political conservatism and monopoly capital. Historically this is the case. Although Owen promoted his exchanges as an apolitical bridge to a better society, they were attacked and ridiculed by middlemen, the churches and other political opponents. American Populism was seen as a sensible reform, ferociously attacked and destroyed after 1896. European Script was closed down by Fascism. In Argentina the networks did become mass phenomena with millions of users in 2000–2002. Here again, it provoked an attack. As the crisis grew, the ruling Perónist party began to set up their own barter networks, and sometimes violently attacked independent networks. By late 2002 inflation and forgery had become widespread, the result, it was claimed, of Perónist infiltration and attempts to discredit barter or of criminal action commissioned by Perónism. Then in November 2002, a TV programme claimed to expose what it called the 'great barter rip off': food was poor quality, stolen goods were being sold, the schemes were a scam and many of the notes were forgeries. Confidence crashed overnight. When millions of people were using them in Argentina, political conservatism and monopoly capital came down on them like a ton of bricks.

But this is not the case elsewhere. Marx's critique of utopianism seems accurate for the nineteenth century, but less so now. So-called poor people can be those who actively choose non-monetised and resource poor livelihoods and have access to far more resources than the poor of industrialising England or the post-Bellum American South, or the poor of the Great Depression. Living standards in the global North are immeasurably higher for the great majority, even if the poorest and those outside the basic standards of modern complex society, homeless people, asylum seekers can suffer real levels hardship. Outside Argentina, local money networks are no threat and can be safely ignored. Furthermore, capitalism in the global North often results in jobless growth or in growth in certain, high-tech or knowledge economy sectors. Capitalism no longer needs to force independent self-provisioning peasants into the factories: the factories have closed, capital has no interest in unskilled labour, and the problem is now how surplus proletarians are to gain economic independence (we may say, again). As long as our new utopians are not claiming state benefits, the state cares little how they choose to live their economic lives. And where the network is dense enough, members who trade regularly in systems where commitment building mechanisms are strong report that they *do* feel that community feelings develop over time, as Buber suggested, within limits set by their lack of access to large productive resources (North, 1999).

GREEN MONEY IN THE FUTURE – A RESPONSE TO CLIMATE CHANGE?

Many green money schemes emerged in the 1990s as a reaction against globalisation and the recessions associated with restructuring. When the economy revived, they often declined as, understandably, people previously getting by partly through the use of local money took a job when they could. But the antiglobalisation movement and concerns about climate change mean we no longer critically regard growth as 'good'. We begin to understand that forms of growth that increase carbon emissions cut against the need to avoid 'dangerous' climate change through deep and quick cuts in carbon emissions – 80% by 2050 (Monbiot, 2006; McKibben, 2007; NEF, 2007). We begin to see things in a different light as the contemporaneous publication of IPCC report (2007), the Stern Review (2007), Al Gore's documentary 'An Inconvenient Truth' and observable extreme weather events can be conceptualised as what social movement theorists call a 'mobilising event' (Turner & Killian, 1987). Seemingly, what might not have been so clear becomes so, issues are seen in a new light, and people believe that things cannot go on as before. Action becomes not only necessary, but timely, feasible, and success seems suddenly possible. 'Now' becomes the time to solve problems that seemed endemic. We begin to understand that addressing climate change requires a fundamental restructuring of local economies so we stop moving often similar products from place to place (burning CO_2 needlessly and consuming limited fossil fuels) and focus on meeting needs as locally as possible within ecological limits (Lang & Hines, 1993; Trainer, 1995; Douthwaite, 1996; Hines, 2000; Norberg-Hodge, 2001; Shuman, 2001; Cavanagh & Mander, 2004; Woodin & Lucas, 2004; Scott Cato, 2006). Given the new salience of localisation, local currencies might be seen as appropriate as localising tools. The utopian experiments can, if this is the case, be seen as demonstration projects for what later becomes more widespread. Although beyond the scope of this chapter, the performance of contemporary utopian 'Transition Currencies' as a response to climate change will need to be followed (North, 2010).

REFERENCES

Abrams, P., & McCulloch, A. (1981). *Communes, sociology and society*. Cambridge: Cambridge University Press.

Aldridge, T., & Patterson, A. (2002). LETS get real: Constraints on the development of local exchange trading schemes. *Area, 34*(4), 370–381.

Bahro, R. (1994). *Avoiding social and ecological disaster*. Bath: Gateway Books.

Bowring, F. (1998). LETS: An eco-socialist initiative? *New Left Review* (232), 91–111.

Boyle, D. (Ed.) (2003). *The money changers: Currency reform from Aristotle to e-cash*. London: Earthscan.

Buber, M. (1949). *Paths in utopia*. London: Routledge and Kegan Paul.

Cavanagh, J., & Mander, J. (2004). *Alternatives to economic globalization*. San Francisco: Berrett-Koehler Publishers.

Cole, G. (1925). *Robert Owen*. London: Benn.

Dana, C. (1896). *Proudhon and his bank of the people*. New York: Benjamin R. Tucker.

Donnachie, I. (2000). *Robert Owen: Owen of New Lanark and New Harmony*. Phantassie, East Lothian: The Tuckwell Press.

Douglas, C. (1937). *Social credit*. London: Eyre and Spottiswoode.

Douthwaite, R. (1996). *Short circuit: Strengthening local economies for security in an uncertain world*. Totnes, Devon: Green Books.

Douthwaite, R., & Wagman, D. (1999). *Barataria: A community exchange network for the third system*. Utrecht, the Netherlands: Strohalm.

Drakeford, M. (1997). *Social movements and their supporters: The green shirts in England*. Basingstoke: Macmillan.

Engels, F. (1968). *Socialism: Utopian and scientific*. London: Lawrence and Wishart.

Fernbach, D. (Ed.) (1974). *Karl Marx: The first international and after*. London: New Left Review.

Findlay, J. L. (1972). *Social credit: The English origins*. Montreal: McGill-Queens University Press.

Fisher, I. (1933). *Stamp scrip*. New York: Adelphi.

Foner, P. S. (1955). *A history of the American labor movement IV: From the founding of the American federation of labor to the emergence of American imperialism*. New York: International Publications.

Gibson-Graham, J. (2002). Beyond global vs. local: Economic politics beyond the binary frame. In: A. Herod & M. W. Wright (Eds), *Geographies of power: Placing scale*. Oxford: Blackwell.

Glover, P. (1995). Ithaca hours. In: S. Meeker-Lowry (Ed.), *Investing in the common good*. New York: New Society Publishers.

Goodwyn, L. (1976). *Democratic promise: The populist moment in America*. Oxford: Oxford University Press.

Hines, C. (2000). *Localisation: A global manifesto*. London: Earthscan.

Houriet, R. (1973). *Getting back together*. London: Abacus.

IPCC. (2007). Climate change 2007: The intergovernmental panel on climate change fourth assessment report. Available at http://www.ipcc.ch

Jones, L. (1890). *The life, times and labours of Robert Owen*. London: Swan Sonneschein and Co.

Kanter, R. (1972). *Commitment and community: Communes and utopia in sociological perspective*. Cambridge MA: Harvard University Press.

Kovel, J. (2007). *The enemy of nature*. London: Zed Books.

Lang, T., & Hines, C. (1993). *The new protectionism: Protecting the future against free trade*. London: Earthscan Publications.

Levitas, R. (1990). *The concept of Utopia*. London: Philip Allan.

Leyshon, A., & Thrift, N. (1997). *Money space: Geographies of monetary transformation*. London: Routledge.

Loomis, M. (2005). *Decentralism*. Montreal: Black Rose Books.

Marx, K. (1852/1974). *Anti-duhring*. London: New Left Review.

Maurer, B. (2005). *Mutual life, limited: Islamic banking, alternative currencies, lateral reason*. Princeton: University of Princeton Press.

McKibben, B. (2007). *Deep economy: The wealth of communities and the durable future*. New York: Times Books.

Melville, K. (1972). *Communes in the counter culture: Origins, theories and styles of life*. New York: William Morrow and Company.

Monbiot, G. (2006). *Heat: How to stop the planet burning*. London: Allen Lane.

NEF. (2007). *The European unhappy planet index: An index of carbon efficiency and well-being in the EU*. London: The New Economics Foundation and Friends of the Earth.

Norberg-Hodge, H. (2001). Shifting direction-from global dependence to local interdependence. In: E. Goldsmith & J. Mander (Eds), *Alternatives to economic globalization*. London: Earthscan Publications.

North, P. (1996). LETS: A tool for empowerment in the inner city? *Local Economy, 11*(3), 284–293.

North, P. (1999). Explorations in heterotopia: LETS and the micropolitics of money and livelihood. *Environment and Planning D: Society and Space, 17*(1), 69–86.

North, P. (2005). Scaling alternative economic practices? Some lessons from alternative currencies. *Transactions of the Institute of British Geographers, 30*(2), 221–233.

North, P. (2006a). *Alternative currencies as a challenge to globalisation? A case study of Manchester's local money networks.* Aldershot: Ashgate.

North, P. (2006b). Constructing civil society? Green money in transition in Hungary. *Review of International Political Economy, 13*(1), 28–52.

North, P. (2007). *Money and liberation: The micropolitics of alternative currency movements.* Minneapolis: University of Minnesota Press.

North, P. (2010). *Local money.* Dartington: Green Books.

Owen, R. (1816). A new view of society, or, essays on the principle of the formation of the human character, and the application of the principle to practice. Available at http://socserv2.socsci.mcmaster.ca/~econ/ugcm/3ll3/owen/newview.txt. Retrieved on March 3, 2004.

Pacione, M. (1997). Local exchange trading systems as a response to the globalisation of capitalism. *Urban Studies, 34*(8), 1179–1199.

Pepper, D. (1990). *Communes and the green vision.* London: Greenprint.

Schroeder, R. (2006). Community exchange and trading systems in Germany. *International Journal of Complementary Currency Research, 10.*

Scott Cato, M. (2006). *Market schmarket.* Cheltenham: New Clarion Press.

Sheppard, M. (1981). *Social credit inside and out.* Dunedin: Caveman Press.

Shuman, M. (2001). *Going local: Creating self reliant communities in a global age.* London: Routledge.

Stern, N. (2007). *Stern review of the economics of climate change.* London: HM Treasury/The Cabinet Office.

Thorne, L. (1996). Local exchange trading systems in the UK – a case of re-embedding? *Environment and Planning A, 28*(8), 1361–1376.

Trainer, T. (1995). *The conserver society.* London: Zed Books.

Turner, R., & Killian, L. (1987). *Collective behaviour.* Brunswick, NJ: Prentice Hall.

Wall, D. (2003). Social credit: The ecosocialism of fools. *Capital Nature Socialism, 14*(3), 99–122.

Walsh, B. (1994). *Meitheal Nua.* Kiltimagh, County Mayo: Ecology Energy and Economics.

Williams, C. C., Aldridge, T., et al. (2001). *Bridges into work: An evaluation of local exchange trading schemes.* Bristol: The Policy Press.

Woodcock, G. (1962/1986). *Anarchism.* Harmondsworth: Penguin.

Woodin, M., & Lucas, C. (2004). *Green alternatives to globalisation: A manifesto.* London: Pluto.

Zavos, S. (1981). *Crusade: Social credit's drive for power.* Wellington: INL Print.

CHAPTER 5

ELUSIVE ESCAPES? EVERYDAY LIFE AND ECOTOPIA

Jon Anderson

INTRODUCTION

This chapter explores how the ideal of autonomous ecological living – ecotopia – is created and compromised by the everyday cultural life of mainstream society. It investigates the degree to which the structures of the mainstream are eluded, changed and subverted to create 'ecotopia', and also how this ideal is everyday compromised to survive. Drawing on empirical research undertaken at the Centre for Alternative Technology (CAT), this chapter argues that fragmented utopias are inevitable when attempting to live ecologically in twenty-first century Britain. However, the elusiveness of ecotopia offers an important opportunity to normalise these experiments in ecological living and emphasise their connections and capacity to inform mainstream society.

Faced with the increasing economic, social and environmental problems of industrial society, the lack of mainstream political will to deal effectively with them and driven by a wish for something better, many individuals actively seek to create alternatives. From the popular cliché of escaping to the country, creating community enclaves in urban areas or downsizing experiments at the individual or collective scale, people express their

Global Ecological Politics
Advances in Ecopolitics, Volume 5, 89–108
Copyright © 2010 by Emerald Group Publishing Limited
All rights of reproduction in any form reserved
ISSN: 2041-806X/doi:10.1108/S2041-806X(2010)0000005009

dissatisfaction with the current industrial paradigm by attempting to realise their own idyll, to make their future in the present and to live their dream. Such moves for utopia exist in tension with hegemonic politics and geography. This chapter is particularly interested in the environmental politics of utopian experiments, how the spaces created for autonomous ecological living – or ecotopias – are instigated, constituted and maintained. It investigates how such spaces elude and subvert the structuring parameters and ideals of the mainstream, and also how these ideal(ised) spaces are compromised through their connections with industrial society. It does so through drawing on an empirical example taken from extended research at one such ecotopian site, the Centre for Alternative Technology, Machnylleth, UK. Established in 1973 by Gerard Morgan-Grenville, the CAT began as a response to a society that was seen as imperilled by ecological instability, consumer profligacy and the atomic bomb; it was an attempt to 'head[...] off to the hills in search of arcadia, safety and the Good Life' (CAT, 1995, p. 6). CAT, 'dedicated to eco-friendly principles and a "test bed" for new ideas and technologies' (CAT, 2007a), was opened in 1975 and since then CAT has become the self-styled 'leading eco-centre' in Europe (CAT, 2007b). The research focused around 3 months participant observation within CAT's resident community and work organisation, with the author undertaking 30 in-depth interviews with a range of volunteers, employees and long-term residents of the Centre. Using this empirical data, this chapter outlines the ecological fundamentals defining the constitution of this particular ecotopia, how this space is organised and run, and the key aspects of this community and culture that help to generate and maintain an ecological lifestyle. This chapter also outlines how this ecotopian space is compromised by its interconnectivity with the spaces of mainstream society, and also by the nature of the democratic principles that underpin the site itself. From this, this chapter argues that such utopian spaces must be positioned not as autonomous zones detached and discrete from mainstream society, but crucially as an integrated, inter-dependent part of this whole. As a consequence, its participants can be framed as 'schizophrenic transhumants' (after Bey, 2007), nomadically mobile between ecotopian and mainstream spaces, contaminating and changing each space through their movements and practices. This chapter further argues that such interconnection not only has the potential to politically recuperate these ecotopian zones, but also, more radically, positions them as potential sites from which a more ecological and sustainable lifestyle can be normalised into the fabric of mainstream society.

UTOPIAN ESCAPES

'You know', Giono said to me, 'there are also times in life when a person has to rush off in pursuit of hopefulness'. (Goodrich, in Giono, 1989, p. 51)

Moves to establish utopian zones erupt from a will to create an idealised alternative to the existing societal paradigm. As Honderich posits, utopianism involves:

Critical and creative thinking projecting alternative social worlds that would realise the best possible way of being, based on rational and moral principles, accounts of human nature and history, or imagined technological prospects. Utopian thinking invariably contains criticism of the status quo. (1995, pp. 892–893, also cited in Pepper, 2005, p. 4)

Although this is not the place for a thoroughgoing review of utopia as a political and practical concept (for this see Pepper, 2005, 2007; Sargisson, 2001; de Geus, 1999, 2002), utopian spaces have been conventionally understood as zones that function as political escapes from the existing societal paradigm. Utopia functions as spaces that are at once 'internal' and 'external'; internal in the sense that they operate as mental and emotional escapes, as intellectual and fantasy sites where 'other' ways of being, organising and living can be imagined and dreamt. Concomitantly, utopia functions as external spaces; they are specific somewheres which are taken and made in line with these political blue- or green-prints to make manifest such imaginings in reality. In this way, utopia combines the mental and the material, the fantasist and the factual, and the heavenly and the heuristic.

Although intertwined, it is sometimes the case that the 'internal' dimensions of utopia are relegated to secondary importance behind the material spaces of political action. Often dismissed as simple imaginings without political purchase, internal dimensions may be seen as 'the mere building of fantasy worlds that don't and could not exist (u-topos or no place) (Best, 2000)' (cited in Pepper, 2005, p. 4). However, this aspect of utopia is perhaps just as important as more literal, external escape. As Pile argues:

it is highly unlikely that people will feel willing to resist if they feel they are useless and powerless and have no room for manoeuvre nor the capacity to change anything. Resistance, then... must also engage the colonised spaces of people's inner worlds. *Indeed, it could be argued that the production of 'inner spaces' marks out the real break point of political struggle ... maybe.* (Pile, 1997, p. 17, emphasis added)

As Pile implies, the importance of the creation of internal space, a space where the status quo can be critiqued and de-normalised, is an essential element in the formation of political resistance and should not be overlooked. Making the familiar foreign and vice versa is a crucial and empowering step in political critique (see Chase, 2003); such internal space facilitates the dismantling of 'doxa' (where one world and value system has been established as 'common sense' and 'natural', following Bourdieu, 1977) in order that unorthodox and foreign worlds can be imagined as legitimate replacements. The creation of internal space to denaturalise the doxa of hegemonic society is thus one crucial aspect in utopian experiments, yet this space exists in reciprocal relation to external sites and requires the latter to realise their transgressive potential (see Pepper, 2007; Sargisson, 2001). Translating internal dreams into external reality involves the settling or colonisation of particular material sites, specific somewheres in which alternatives can be experimented with in practice. Such sites function as 'homeplaces' (after Hooks, 1990), as platforms from which these nascent politics can develop and grow, where solidarity can be generated and marginal alternatives strengthened. When such external sites have been settled – or placed – these utopia become displaced from the core meaning of utopia itself, as Bey comments, at this stage these sites, 'cannot be utopian in the actual meaning of the word, *nowhere*, or NoPlace Place. [They are] somewhere' (2003, p. 109).

This reciprocal amalgam of internal and external space (un)settling is thus crucial to the creation of utopia. As such, this process and product has critical resonance with the concept of the 'Temporary Autonomous Zone' (or TAZ) of Hakim Bey (2003). For Bey, such zones are 'uprisings', 'guerrilla operations which liberate an area (of land, time, of imagination)' (2003, p. 99). In practice, as McKay outlines:

> The sixties-style 'tribal gathering', the forest conclave of eco-saboteurs, the idyllic Beltane of the neo-pagans, anarchist conferences, gay faery circles ... Harlem rent parties of the twenties, nightclubs, banquets, libertarian picnics – we should realise that these are already 'liberated zones' of a sort, or at least potential TAZ. (in McKay, 1996, p. 72)

The creation of utopian internal and external spaces can thus be seen as 'guerrilla operations', as intensely political in their mandate and materiality. As stated above, such moves for utopia exist in tension with hegemonic politics and geography, 'liberating' both material and mental spaces from the prevailing orthodoxy. Due to their political nature, the relationship between these spaces and the mainstream is therefore critical, and this will be discussed in depth later; however, at this stage it is worth commenting on the general siting and durability of these political actions. Bey (2003) argues that such utopia can exist only when they (un)settle spaces that are left unacknowledged by the mainstream; they exist in moments when,

> these spaces are relatively open, either through neglect on the part of the State or because they have somehow escaped notice by the mapmakers, or for whatever reason. (p. 101)

If this view is accepted, it could be assumed that utopia could be sought and found in remote, marginal spaces, away from the panoptical gaze of mainstream authorities. Indeed individuals and group do 'head off to the hills' (CAT, 1995, p. 6), and create 'hillbilly enclaves' (Bey, 2003, p. 99) for their political actions.[1] Yet even in a society saturated by CCTV surveillance, neglected sites remain in more core locations. As Hetherington states, although marginal areas can be found 'at the edge' of mainstream society, they can also be located 'at the centre', yet these 'are normally hidden from view' (1998, p. 130). In practice this potential for utopias in more central locations has been realised through the creation of networks of social centres, gatherings and conferences in urban areas (see Autonomous Geographies, 2007). Accordingly, therefore, utopia can be created not simply in conventionally marginal areas, but also in 'the folds of the map' (to use Bey's words, 2003, p. 99) right under the noses of the State itself.

The political critique inherent in the amalgam of internal and external spaces that compose utopia can take many forms. Of interest to us here are the political critiques of an environmentalist hue, creating what Callenbach, in his 1978 novel, termed 'ecotopia'. Resonating strongly with Hook's conception of 'homeplace' [if taken literally from the Greek homeplace translates as *oikos*, or Eco (home) and *topos*, or topia (place)], ecotopia are ecologically and environmentally idealised alternatives to the mainstream. There are many contemporary examples of such alternatives: some of them may be transitory (in the true sense of the TAZ, for example eco-flash mobbing, protest camps or rallies), others may be periodic or annual (for example gatherings or summer festivals), whereas many may be more durable in their nature, including eco-villages, low-impact developments, cafes, squatted centres, community facilities or other communes. The CAT is one such durable ecotopia.

SPACES INTERNAL AND SPACES EXTERNAL: CAT'S ECOTOPIA

To those trapped in the stress and ugliness of modern cities, musing about [ecotopia] ... pressed all sorts of buttons; visions of nature, nostalgia for a golden past, the simple life, release from the banality of consumer culture. Just the bare idea had a delicious ring to it. ... It is not surprising that many headed off to the hills in search of arcadia, safety and the Good Life. (CAT, 1995, p. 6)

The internal and external spaces of the ecotopian site of the CAT coalesced around a political critique of the industrial society of the 1970s. Inspired by the improvised hippy communes of the United States, CAT sought to translate the politics of the growing environmental movement into a sustainable residential community, as founder Gerard Morgan-Grenville outlines,

> About 22 years ago I took a sabbatical and went to America. I studied groups who were trying alternatives, mostly hippies. Many of them were attempting some of the technologies that CAT went on to demonstrate, but not very successfully. They were mostly muddled and disorganised, fragile. Most failed, but the important thing was they had opted out of mainstream life in order to find a way of living which respected the environment in which they lived. They also rejected Authority in principle. I found myself in sympathy with both aims. (CAT, 1995, p. 4)

Contemporary publications such as The Club of Rome's *Limits to Growth* (1972) and The Ecologist's *Blueprint for Survival* (1972) warned of the unsustainable outcomes of the industrial–military complex that championed atomic power, hard energy and environmental exploitation. Alternatives were configured around the vague notion of a 'non-industrial society', as CAT's publication 'Crazy Idealists' states, 'The [answer] seemed to be a *non-industrial* society, whatever that might mean' (1995, p. 6). With a 'hearty distrust of faceless, mass society and its mega-technologies' (*ibid.*, p. 4) CAT sought to experiment with substitutes under the rubric of 'alternative technology':

> 'Alternative Technology' was conceived as the body of genuine alternatives that would really work; it accepted the broad 'alternative' critique ... of 'counterculture', conservation and environmental groups, the 'organic' movement, cooperatives, spiritual and personal growth movements, women's liberation, de-schooling, the peace movement ... but, crucially, did not throw out the methods of science and technology, the skills that went with them, and the fundamental insight that *you have to do the sums and get the numbers right.* (CAT, 1995, p. 4, emphasis in original)

In a spirit of experimentation, CAT was thus created as a 'dance' (Harper, in CAT, 1995, p. 11) between humans and nature, between science and spirituality, and between industrial and non-industrial political culture. This broad 'dance' between micro and macro political issues has been retained through the development of the site:

> alternative technology is [now] really everything involved in saving the world. So it is funny to me, I guess because I work here as it has come to stand for everything else that we do as well which ranges from the technology side of things, to much bigger political issues about environmental policy, and even bigger issues about poverty and trade. So it is kind of everything from sort of heat pumps to poverty in Africa is what CAT is concerned about. I suppose that is what I am about as well. (Ray,[2] CAT Staff Interview)

> alternative technology could be languages, practices, far more sociable, social networks, community. So 'technology' is a kind of broader way of looking at things. It is Greek technique, of practical wisdom, so I guess there has to be a practical element to it.

Between people at CAT, you talk about all kinds of technology and they know what they mean. It is a kind of cover-all word here. (Joe, CAT Staff Interview)

For me the CAT thing is about the simplicity side of things really, I know the technology side is fantastic but I like the simplicity and it's the stripping down to the bare bones in the simplest, greenest way possible way you can ... it is doing everything with the smallest impact possible on everything that is around you really for me. Only doing what you have to do and not what you can do. (Verity, CAT Staff Interview)

Influenced by the seminal environmentalist critiques of the 1970s, the internal spaces of political critique that formed CAT dismantled the doxa of the military–industrial complex and replaced it with a 'non-industrial' politics that sought to 'respect the environment in which they live'. The alternative politics of CAT continues to include a broad swathe of ecological and communitarian ideals: from appropriate technology to downsizing, from state-of-the-science solar panels to voluntary simplicity, including the importance of human relations and community building. The internal dimensions of CAT as an ecotopian space are distinguished by this broad mix of the scientific and artistic, the collective and the individual.

In principle, the centre could have been set up anywhere, but anywhere has also to be somewhere, a unique place with its own traditions and character. (CAT, 1995, p. 20)

The creation of this internal space for intellectual and fantastic critique of mainstream society was translated into external space in an old quarry outside Machynlleth, Powys, mid-Wales. This choice of a specific somewhere to ground this ecotopia was not random. The importance of peripherality was not only important in the political sense that Bey or Abbey (1975) suggest – as beyond the gaze of the 'mapmakers' and the State – but was also important practically (and perhaps naively) as an escape from the impact and fallout of a potential nuclear attack,

we must not forget The Bomb, which at the time was a constant presence at the back of everybody's mind: if you lived in a big city you'd certainly cop it in the event of a nuclear war, while in the country – particularly in the remote west – you might stand a chance. (CAT, 1995, p. 6)

The location of the old quarry caught the imagination of the founders, as Morgan-Grenville states,

The site made a very strong impression on me. It was rare in Britain, a truly wild and abandoned place and it was also very beautiful. (*ibid.*, p. 6)

In this external space, the internal politics of this ecotopia have been formed and refined over the lifespan of CAT. The site instilled a resolve to 'disturb the habitat as little as possible' (CAT, 1995, p. 10), to limit structures to those that were 'both attractive to humans and compatible with wildlife' (*ibid.*, p. 11) and to leave '"restoration" to happen in its own way, and in its own time' (*ibid.*, p. 10). Alongside these resolutions on human–nature interactions, CAT continues to practice alternative human–human relations. As Morgan-Grenville outlined (above), CAT's political critique also included a rejection of 'Authority' in terms of societal organisation, and this element continues to significantly define the external spaces of this ecotopia.

ECOTOPIAN CULTURE, COMMUNITY AND ORGANISATION

decision-making-it's good … . It's democratic. It's not perfect. Mistakes are made. Minutes go missing. There are holes in it, but it does work. Compared to the outside world it's fantastic. (McLennan, in CAT, 1995, p. 35)

Implicit in the move for utopia and the seeking out of an alternative to the internal and external spaces of the mainstream, CAT's ecotopia has been organised around an ethic of power and agency different to that of the military–industrial complex. In line with many environmental protest and activist movements of recent decades, a spirit of do-it-yourself (DIY) culture pervades the site (McKay, 1998). Rather than power being aligned in a 'top-down', 'power over' system conventionally held in mainstream society through systems of representative liberal democracy, in this ecotopia power and responsibility are not deferred elsewhere but internalised at the individual level. This wish for autonomy, the 'rediscovery of personal responsibility in action' (Benewick & Smith, 1972), complements the broader wish to create an alternative future outside the parameters of mainstream society, looking at participants themselves to be the agents and catalysts for change.

Thus, as an alternative to a representative form of democratic organisation, CAT's decision-making framework is communal, in line with an inclusive and associative form of democracy. Paralleling a green theory of value (Goodin, 1992) such democratic decision making is decentralised, with a lack of formal hierarchies and based on broad consensus.

Foremost among [our social principles] is democracy: the idea that members of an organisation, nation or planet could feel they have a stake in it, are responsible for it and have the power to exert influence. (CAT, 1995, p. 34)

For a start, the organisation is a co-operative, so we are all involved in planning and management. We can therefore see how our individual efforts contribute to the greater whole and can take a pride in what has been collectively achieved. (CAT, 1995, p. 12)

This preference for co-operative planning and management goes hand in hand with a formal sense of equality and absence of hierarchy in decision making. Regardless of longevity or character, this commitment to communitarian ideals allows collective debate and the marginalisation of personality cults and leaders:

I expected when I came here a year ago that it was going to be 10 or 15 people who had been here since 1980 directing it and I would be a kind of outsider, and you know they have lived here for 10 or 15 years and people who, middle aged people who are running it all, but it is not at all. (Louise, CAT Staff Interview)

There are some people who are stuck in their ways and do have views on it certainly on things but they wouldn't expect their views to dictate all the time as it is generally a cooperative of the people who are running it. You may have only been here a year but you are on a committee and nobody would suggest that you should listen to the 'wise older' people who have been here for years. (Sam, CAT Staff Interview)

This form of political organisation, in line with Bey's small-scale co-operative notion of community decision-making – 'the band' or 'the party' – is free from notional hierarchies, often spontaneous and flexible, and facilitates individual freedom within a broader structure. Concomitantly, it also has the effect of empowering and inspiring the individual through the process of deliberative discussion:

We have loads of people who work here and some jobs don't give you masses of opportunity to do the debating and finding out about different options but we are trying to do more about it and debate and I think that is great. And the some of the people who are thinking or talking about it all the time are coming up with great stuff that wouldn't have entered into your mind. I go home from here still thinking about it! (Laura, CAT Staff Interview)

I can't imagine a life without constant debate and I don't know how you translate that to other people and can't imagine how other people live without constantly debating why things are done, especially in terms of environmental or political impact. I suppose I wonder whether the reasons people don't engage with environmental issues or have knowledge of them or lots of other issues to be honest is that people aren't encouraged to partake in the democratic process as they are growing up, people who don't do that don't understand. (Terry, CAT Staff Interview)

This process of decision-making is not only prevalent in staff meetings concerning education and visitor centre policy, but also in terms of the resident community. As stated above, CAT is not only a visitor centre demonstrating alternative technologies and products; but many also live on site, for both long- and short-term durations. As one respondent outlined:

> Well there are about nine different properties on site that aren't on the circuit but tucked away, and there are thirteen of us and that includes two toddlers and that included four volunteers but that changes every six months. We have had one guy who's lived here for fifteen years! (Paula, CAT Staff Interview)

The form of decision making and the anti-industrialist ideology constituting this ecotopia create a number of opportunities and technologies that enable a greener way of life for those inhabiting these residential spaces. This community, for example, has control over its own decision making:

> CAT are our landlords but in actual fact the resident community can make decisions without having to go through CAT, we have our own tenant management group and I just think it is really great. (Ruby, CAT Staff Interview)

This devolution of power to the tenants themselves results in collective decisions being made of food purchase and consumption, alongside the allocation of tasks in order to make communal living operational:

> We eat together communally on Monday and Tuesday nights and we all take turns in cooking and discuss the kind of issues we have. (Paula, CAT Staff Interview)

> We have a blackboard for anyone's suggestions for the food store, we all have different jobs, I order the wood and someone else orders the gas and someone else does the food order and then six or twelve months we will have a little shuffle around and someone else will order the food and if you have got any preferences we will put that on, we have a budget so you might not get it that week you might get it next week, and there is the staple standard things that we get each week, so it is ethical and that sort of thing. (John, CAT Staff Interview)

This set-up works well for those on low wages, and generates a sense of solidarity and community amongst the residential community that is valued and enjoyed:

> Yes well I am on a minimum wage and had to take that into consideration, but now living here communally we all have our own properties and live separately but buy our food collectively. I am living a lot cheaper by living here. (Laura, CAT Staff Interview)

> It's about just coming here and living with people who are living that lifestyle, and realising how enjoyable it is, and so living on site and living with a wood stove and living without a television and having communal meals and being around these people who discuss these issues and who are politically aware and who are politically alternative. ... I think if everybody had the opportunity to come and live with us here for a year, then they would probably go, 'Whoa, this is great and I don't actually want to live the

commercial lifestyle on my own and spend two hours on a tube going to work. This is actually not making me happy'. Maybe I am wrong and not everybody would want this lifestyle, maybe some people like going to the cinema every night whatever. (Frank, CAT Staff Interview)

In terms of practical infrastructure, the residents also benefit from more strategic decisions made by the CAT collective. The provision of low-cost housing itself – particularly beneficial due to the lower-than-average wages on offer at CAT – is a direct benefit, as these houses are serviced by off-grid heating and power that reduces the need for reliance on fossil fuel energies:

It is much easier if you live here. When I think about the first year and I was living in town there are several things that you don't have control over. Like if you are renting a place you don't have control over how the house is heated or how you source your energy. Living here is much easier because in winter the electricity comes from wind turbines and water comes from solar panels and so we are a bit spoilt and I haven't had to set that up in anyway. (Joanne, CAT Staff Interview)

Things are so much easier here ... in _____ it was much, much more difficult, it was much more difficult to get to for recycling if you didn't have a car, no door step recycling, so if you don't have a car you can't recycle, you know that sort of irony. (Beula, CAT Staff Interview)

Coupled to housing and energy provision, CAT also provides a carpooling scheme for local and regional transportation. Several cars are available for short-term use by residents and employees, negating the need for individual car purchase and use. Strategic provision of this infrastructure enables more ecological practices and performances to be enacted by the residential community. Although they may be minded to initiate these practices anyway, the structural availability of these services make their environmental values and affiliation less relevant as the use of these utilities is 'normal' practice, regardless of environmental politics. In effect, what CAT has introduced is a 'new green architecture' in its technologies and services (following Horton, 2003). This ecotopia has 'assembled ... multiple materialities, times and spaces which call forth green practices' (*ibid.*, p. 75), they have provided the 'materials, times and spaces which ... afford the performance of a green identity' (*ibid.*).

However, as outlined by one participant (above), alternative technology (or 'green architecture') is not solely about services, devices and facilities, it is also about relationships and community. Coupled to the availability of ecological infrastructure, the presence of like-minded others within the resident and work community also provide synergistic encouragement to introduce and maintain more environmentally benign lifestyles.

It was much easier, much easier really to take that radical step, because if I was living with people that I had taken my degree with or living on a housing estate in the middle of London it would not be as easy to do that kind of thing I don't think. Yes it is relatively painless and I think that CAT is more than a whole but wider than a community really, supportive and healing and forgiving really. (Lee, CAT Staff Interview)

I suppose I probably didn't think about it as much. I would recycle and do some environmental things and not think about it that much before I came here. It definitely helps having a cause community. (Rob, CAT Staff Interview)

This 'cause community' creates a sense of purpose and empowerment about the importance of the ecotopian vision,

I think that you can do things here because there are so many people with the same mindset, maybe not the same mindset but of a similar mind that are not primarily economic, for living or for working for being here, but also the amount of knowledge people have here, not just at CAT but in the surrounding area ... if I were to talk like this with people where I was brought up they would look at me as though I was on the moon, and I wouldn't get much chat. I could come here and just plug into the accumulation of knowledge, and knowing what we are capable of and what we can do and what is feasible. (Cal, CAT Staff Interview)

The thing about CAT is that it is just easier because you are in a supportive community and no-one thinks that you are a weirdo, and not that I think that people are weirdos, but people buy new and don't go to charity shops, and say what do you mean you were living without a fridge? and they think that you are completely bonkers. So it is easier to live that way, and there are other things like car share scheme in town and that is great. (Alan, CAT Staff Interview)

Thus, the combination and mutual reciprocity of the internal and the external spaces of CAT creates an ecotopian culture; it produces, to use Nelson, Treichler, and Grossberg's (1992) definition, 'a way of life – encompassing ideas, attitudes, practices, institutions and structures of power – and a whole range of cultural practices' (p. 5, cited in Mitchell, 2000, p. 14), that facilitate the performance of a green identity. This establishment of an ecotopian culture is tangible for those within it:

There is definitely a culture of swapping reusing and helping each other out something that I have not really noticed anywhere else ... there isn't a culture of people buying expensive things and I wonder if that is partly to do with it, and it would just seem almost odd if somebody would be consuming a great deal of irrelevant things and it just wouldn't fit in. So it is kind of interesting whether people consume less because they want to consume less or whether it is just the culture of living here? (Bex, CAT Staff Interview)

I have been so long out of it [mainstream culture], here people don't show off and say I have the latest hi fi or car, it is not an issue and if you happened to have one you would be more embarrassed about it, it is a different attitude. (Richard, CAT Staff Interview)

The amalgam of the internal and external spaces of the CAT have thus generated an ecotopia that has normalised a range of different philosophies and practices including an anti-industrial ideology, an absence of hierarchies and presence of direct democracy in decision making, an availability of 'green architecture' to facilitate ecological lifestyles, and the generation of a cause community and broader pro-environmental culture to facilitate the maintenance and continuing sustainability of these ecotopian space. CAT's ecotopia is not, however, without its problems. The particular way in which CAT's ecotopian space is constituted and maintained renders it susceptible to a number of tensions.

ECOTOPIAN TENSIONS AND TOLERANCES

As we have seen, CAT organises itself politically around a system of direct, deliberative democracy, with an onus on individual responsibility and personal autonomy. However, this system does not necessarily engender consensus on the purpose and objective of the Centre itself; indeed the breadth of ideas and directions inherent within the rubric of 'alternative technology' positively encourages a diversity of opinions on this issue. This diversity, and potential conflict, was evident in CAT from the outset. From its inception, the relation that CAT should have to the outside world was a point of dispute,

> There was always a tension between those who wanted to raise a drawbridge to the outside world and those who believed that what they were doing was primarily to serve others. Half the Quarry wants to relate to the outside world. (Richard St George in CAT, 1995, p. 9)

In the early stages the issue of self-sufficiency – literally 'raising a drawbridge to the outside world' – was keenly debated. Before the visitor centre being established, 'the idea was more of an experimental, largely self-sufficient community. ... The whole idea was to be as separate as possible, hence the emphasis on self-sufficiency and a kind of anti-industrial primitivism' (CAT, 1995, p. 18). However, the practical constraints of finance and the inconsistencies within the internal logic of self-sufficiency rendered this absolute goal unattainable, as current staff members outline,

> we are [now] not promoting self-sufficiency. I don't see any need for it, it makes you insular. Why do it? It makes a lot of sense for us to be self-sufficient in electricity – we've got a lot of wind, water, sun – that's fine. But to try and be self-sufficient in food when you live on a hillside in Wales is crazy. It's much more efficient to trade in good quality food

with the southeast. If you live in a highrise flat in Birmingham it's not appropriate to be self-sufficient in anything. Trade is very important. (Leslie Bradnam, in CAT, 1995, p. 23)

Self-sufficiency is dead, not because it's not green-but because it's not replicable! We now need to explore the most effective means of reducing our environmental footprints. (Paul Allen, in CAT, 1995, p. 47)

Although the visitor centre has been constructed and thus interaction and engagement with the outside world is openly encouraged – CAT's drawbridge is down and now turnstiled – the debate on CAT's relation to the outside world remains unresolved. The issue has simply been contemporarily recycled into one focused around whether the Centre's purpose is to exist sustainably or teach sustainability:

The centre's original strategy was precisely to create a workable model of a sustainable community and its supporting technologies to prove it could be done... [yet] it seemed as if doing the real thing might be incompatible with demonstrating it. This dilemma has dogged us ever since, some arguing that we should press ahead with our particular experiment, others that this was far too narrow, and that we should switch to being an education and demonstration centre focused on wider issues. And we're still arguing. (CAT, 1995, pp. 32–33)

The diversity of opinions inherent within the broad school of alternative technology, coupled to the form of continually debating democracy favoured by CAT means that key decisions in relation to the Centre's mandate and purpose are not resolved in a clear, unequivocal manner (in a way that may be possible through a conventional liberal democracy, or even a dictatorship). Rather, a system of diverse consensus is promulgated allowing tensions to exist and be explored through practice. Thus, in this particular case of demonstrating versus daily life,

instead of resolving the dilemma, we ended up doing both. The site has become a weird mixture of real functional installations that we actually use; stage sets containing educational toys; and endless signs. Does it work? It's really hard to say. ... We get remarks like: 'pathetic, incoherent, scruffy. My nine year old son could have done better. And coffee was revolting!' ... The very next ... might contain 'Brilliant! Well thought out and excellently presented. Love the coffee'. (CAT, 1995, p. 33)

Owing to this system of tolerant diversity, CAT can be considered a 'critical utopia' (after Moylan, 1986, cited in Pepper, 2005, p. 8). Rather than outlining a strict 'blueprint' or specific idealised goal for its ecotopian space, varied – perhaps even apparently contradictory – directions and objectives can co-exist in practice. Through doing so, their outcomes at the individual and collective level in terms of community sustainability – in all aspects of its tripartite union – can be considered in real time. In this sense, therefore, the 'green codes and scripts' of the Centre are broadly drawn. Horton (2003), in his work on environmental organisations, introduces the notion of 'codes and scripts' to refer to normative practices and behaviours that befit membership of a particular green group. In line with the ethic of personal responsibility, CAT's ecotopian spaces are defined by the individualisation of these codes and scripts; in other words, these codes neither emanate from an elite group nor are they base-level behaviours to which all have to comply, rather it is left to each individual to apply the general rubric of 'alternative technology' into the specific contexts of their own lives. In this way, the dilemma over the Centre's relationship to the outside world becomes replicated at the level of the individual.

INDIVIDUALISED INTERDEPENDENCES AND ELUSIVE ESCAPES: TOWARDS CONNECTIONS AND CONCLUSIONS

As we have seen, CAT's provision of green architecture makes certain environmental behaviours easy to undertake, whilst the creation of a cause community and culture encourages and empowers eco-action. The Centre's political organisation based on open discussion and personal action accommodates a diversity of experimental practices and behaviours to be undertaken under the broad rubric of 'alternative technology'. Thus, CAT's form of political organisation does not dictate or enforce any particular 'green code or script' of practice. Rather it favours the creation of a broader culture and architecture to suggest and encourage particular behaviours, as one participant describes:

> It is not that sort of place where you feel pressured into doing something because it is environmental choice. I think there is much more discussion around things, people will justify or discuss their reasons quite a lot, or it seems like that to me anyway. There doesn't seem to be the pressure to conform to their ideal but then I am very interested in that ideal anyway. (Rod, CAT Staff Interview)

Thus, in practice the ethic of individual freedom and autonomy is central to CAT's internal and external space. The Centre will encourage but not enforce certain behaviours; in practice, therefore, due to the lack of hierarchy in political organisation there is no one to stop or reprimand non-ecological behaviours when they occur. For example, during my research

smoking was still tolerated on site, if practiced discreetly, as the following
respondent commented,

> There is a bit of teasing bantering going on [about smoking], and it is not excessive, and
> there is nobody that is really hostile over it, but there is some emotion. (Laura, CAT
> Staff Interview)

During interviews the issue of carbon emissions and the personal choice to
travel by aeroplane was discussed. Although CAT as a collective minimises
air travel for business use and does not endorse carbon offsetting, individuals
are free to take their own position on the issue. Although many have debated
and discussed the pros and cons, despite the environmental effects the
majority opt to fly; the following comments are illustrative of many,[3]

> We did joke about it [not flying on vacation] but I said 'I am not stopping going on my
> holidays!' (Cal, CAT Staff Interview)

> I flew to Australia and Thailand, but now I would think about it and if I could go
> differently I would. Last year I did get the train from here to Paris instead of flying ...
> But this year I have flown twice, once to go skiing and once to Spain ... . (Holly, CAT
> Staff Interview)

This tension between the luxuries and conveniences of mainstream society
and the culture of alternative technology encouraged by CAT thus becomes
manifest at the individual level. The presence of individual freedom and the
lack of central enforcement enable individuals to opt for the alternative
choice wherever possible, but also to revert to the mainstream choice if they
prefer. In this way, the alternative message of the Centre is at risk of being
dissipated and diluted, with mainstream habits along with their negative
environmental consequences contaminating the site. As the following
example goes some way to illustrate:

> I saw an instant the other day when one of the customers walked by at the back of
> TeaChest [the staff canteen] and saw _____ eating out of a polystyrene container and they
> had a go at him, but it was just because TeaChest was closed that day and he had gone
> into town to get a snack and it came in a polystyrene container, and I thought, 'just
> leave the guy alone, it's his lunch break, he didn't make the polystyrene container and
> he was just hungry'. Maybe she just misunderstood and thought we were using them for
> staff dinners or that he had brought it here, but it was just hilarious, people just expect us
> to be perfect and holier than though and it's not that easy. (Brian, CAT Staff Interview)

It is clear therefore that the 'drawbridge' between CAT and mainstream
society is far from raised. Due to the form of political organisation at the
site, individuals and the collective itself are encouraged to adopt and
perpetuate an alternative culture, but it is not isolated nor insulated from the

pressures, appetites and attractions of mainstream society. In practice, therefore, CAT is not an independent autonomous space discrete from hegemonic society; it is *not* a true escape. Due to a range of human (and non-human) interactions, CAT has to forge a sense of alternative identity within a network of interdependency. Its practices therefore complement de Certeau's description of actions that:

> characterise the subtle, stubborn, resistant activity of groups which ... have to get along in a network of already established forces and representations ... . (de Certeau, 1984, p. 18)

In this way, the internal and external spaces of CAT should not be considered as castled moats with drawbridges that can be raised, but rather, in line with Massey, as sites within broader networks of interconnection with mainstream society. This ecotopia should thus be considered as:

> constructed out of a particular constellation of social relations, meeting and weaving together at a particular locus. If one moves in from the satellite towards the globe, holding all those networks of social relations and movements and communications in one's head, then [this] 'place' can be seen as a particular, unique, point in their intersection. It is, indeed, a *meeting* place. Instead then, of thinking of places as areas with boundaries around, they can be imagined as articulated moments in networks of social relations and understandings, but where a large proportion of those relations, experiences and understandings are constructed on a far larger scale than we happen to define for that moment as the place itself, whether that be a street, or a region or even a continent. (Massey, 1993, p. 153)

To escape to an ecotopia is therefore not to retreat to a place of complete autonomy, for due to these networks of interconnection such sites cannot exist (see Escobar & Alvarez, 1992). These sites should not be conceptualised as bounded and discrete, rather defined through,

> the particularity of linkage to that 'outside' which is therefore itself part of what constitutes the place. (Massey, 1993, p. 155)

This linkage, in the case of CAT's ecotopia, is defined through the opportunity it affords to a range of individuals – tourists, visitors, volunteers, employees, residents – to sample, experiment with, and adopt alternative technologies as part of their everyday lives. Through so doing, these individuals themselves pass through the network of interconnection, from sites that are defined by more mainstream influences, into those that are defined by an alternative praxis, and then back again. As such, these individuals – ourselves – can be considered as, using Bey's (2007) terms, 'transhumants', as nomads or 'ambulatory schizophrenics', moving between mainstream and alternative sites at different (and perhaps even the same) time(s), becoming defined by our particular linkages and connections to each of these spaces at particular times. Through these actions, such sites become connected and interpenetrated by the ideals of both alternative and mainstream worlds; their definition becomes more ambiguous as they become more individual.

Considering ecotopian spaces in this way raises important questions concerning their transgressive potential. It may be conceived that due to the interconnection between mainstream and alternative sites, the ability of these sites to offer absolute escapes from the status quo is nullified and thus their political potency negated. However, due precisely to their existence, along with the 'transhumant nomadism' of individuals within and between them, such spaces,

> encourage crossing the boundaries around the enclosed territory of ideas and social relationships in which we are situated, and [enable us to] enter ... heuristic spaces in which we would be encouraged to think in new paradigms. (Pepper, 2005, p. 7)

Ecotopia considered in this way becomes 'encounter spaces' (Percy-Smith & Matthews, 2001, p. 53), spaces of fluid interaction where examples, experiences and empowerment do not exhaust but rather enhance their and our change potential. In their own words, this situation conceives CAT's ecotopian space as, 'a bridge between conventional and alternative worlds' (1995, p. 4). If looked at negatively it may remain, 'parasitic on the very mainstream society [it is] denouncing' (*ibid.*, p. 4), yet more positively it transgresses the boundaries between these worlds, enabling movement across them and thus normalising not only the experimentation with alternative lifestyles, but also the possibility of adopting them more fully. The 'escape' offered by CAT and similar ecotopia spaces thus remains elusive, but their existence nevertheless offers vital opportunities to emphasise and enhance the sustainability and security of mainstream society.

NOTES

1. As Abbey notes, the potential utopian and thereby intensely political nature of marginal, in this case rural and wild places, should not be overlooked: 'the wilderness should be preserved for political reasons. We may need it someday not only as a refuge from excessive industrialism but also as a refuge from authoritarian government, from political oppression. Grand Canyon, Big Bend, Yellowstone and the High Sierras may be required to function as bases for guerrilla warfare against tyranny' (1975, p. 130).

2. All interviewees' names are pseudonyms.

3. There are notable exceptions amongst the CAT collective, those who have never flown and others who go to excessive lengths to take alternative transportation methods or minimise travel completely.

REFERENCES

Abbey, E. (1975). *Desert solitaire a season in the wilderness.* New York: Ballantine Books.

Autonomous Geographies. (2007). Available at http://www.autonomousgeographies.org/. Accessed on July 2007.

Benewick, R., & Smith, T. (1972). *Direct action & democratic politics.* London: Allen & Unwin.

Best, S. (2000). Scenarios of disaster, visions of liberation. *Democracy and Nature, 6*(2), 253–265.

Bey, H. (2003). *T.A.Z. The temporary autonomous zone, ontological anarchy, poetic terrorism. Second edition with new preface.* Brooklyn, NY: Autonomedia.

Bey, H. (2007). The periodic autonomous zone. Available at http://www.hermetic.com/bey/periodic.html. Accessed on June 2007.

Bourdieu, P. (1977). *Outline of a theory of practice.* Cambridge: Cambridge University Press.

Callenbach, E. (1978). *Ecotopia. A novel about ecology, people and politics in 1999.* London: Pluto Press.

Centre for Alternative Technology. (1995). *Crazy idealists? The cat story.* Machnylleth: Centre for Alternative Technology.

Centre of Alternative Technology. (2007a). *How CAT started.* Available at http://www.cat.org.uk/information/aboutcatx.tmpl?init = 4, a permanent visitor centre. Accessed on July 2007.

Centre of Alternative Technology. (2007b). *What do we do?* Available t http://www.cat.org.uk/information/aboutcatx.tmpl?init = 1. Accessed on July 2007.

Chase, S. (2003). Professional ethics in the age of globalization: How can academics contribute to sustainability and democracy now? *Ethics, Place and Environment, 6*(1), 43–78 (Short communications).

de Certeau, M. (1984). *The practice of everyday life.* London & Berkeley: University of California Press.

De Geus, M. (1999). *Ecological utopias: Envisioning the sustainable society.* Utrecht, the Netherlands: International Books.

De Geus, M. (2002). Ecotopia, sustainability, and vision. *Organization & Environment, 15*(2), 187–201.

Escobar, A., & Alvarez, S. (Eds). (1992). *The making of social movements in Latin America: Identity, strategy and democracy.* London: Harper Collins.

Giono, J. (1989). *The man who planted trees.* London: Peter Owen.

Goldsmith, E. (Ed.). (1972). Blueprint for survival. *The Ecologist, 2*(1), 1–22.

Goodin, R. (1992). *Green political theory.* London: Polity Press.

Hetherington, K. (1998). *Expressions of identity. Space, performance, politics.* London: Sage.

Honderich, E. (1995). *Oxford companion to philosophy.* Oxford: Oxford University Press.

Hooks, B. (1990). *Yearning: Race, gender, and cultural politics.* Boston: South End Press.

Horton, D. (2003). Green distinctions: The performance of identity among environmental activists. In: B. Szersynski, W. Heim & C. Waterton (Eds), *Nature performed. Environment, culture and performance* (pp. 63–77). Oxford: Blackwell.

Massey, D. (1993). *Space, place & gender.* Cambridge: Polity Press.

McKay, G. (1996). *Senseless acts of beauty.* London: Verso.

McKay, G. (1998). *DIY culture – Party & protest in nineties Britain*. London & New York: Verso.

Meadows, D. H., et al. (1972). *The limits to growth: A report for the club of Rome's project on the predicament of mankind*. London: Earth Island.

Mitchell, D. (2000). *Cultural geography: A critical introduction*. Malden & Oxford: Blackwell.

Moylan, T. (1986). *Demand the impossible*. London: Methuen.

Nelson, C., Treichler, P., & Grossberg, L. (1992). Cultural studies: An introduction. In: L. Grossberg, C. Nelson & P. Treichler (Eds), *Cultural studies*. New York: Routledge.

Pepper, D. (2005). Utopianism and environmentalism. *Environmental Politics, 14*(1), 3–22.

Pepper, D. (2007). Tensions and dilemmas of ecotopianism. *Environmental Values, 16*(3), 289–312.

Percy-Smith, B., & Matthews, H. (2001). Tyrannical spaces: Young people, bullying and urban neighbourhoods. *Local Environment, 6*(1), 49–63.

Pile, S. (1997). Introduction: Opposition, political identities, and spaces of resistance. In: S. Pile & M. Keith (Eds), *Geographies of resistance* (pp. 1–33). New York & London: Routledge.

Sargisson, L. (2001). Politicising the quotidian. *Environmental Politics, 10*(2), 68–89.

CHAPTER 6

TOWARDS A MODEL OF GREEN POLITICAL ECONOMY: FROM ECOLOGICAL MODERNISATION TO ECONOMIC SECURITY

John Barry

INTRODUCTION

Perhaps the weakest dimension of the 'triple bottom line' understanding of sustainable development has been the 'economic' dimension. Much of the thinking about the appropriate 'political economy' to underpin sustainable development has been either utopian (as in some 'green' political views) or 'business as usual' approaches. This chapter suggests that 'ecological modernisation' is the dominant conceptualisation of 'sustainable development' within the United Kingdom and illustrates this by looking at some key 'sustainable development' policy documents from the UK Government. Although critical of the reformist 'policy telos' of ecological modernisation, supporters of more radical version of sustainable development also need to be aware of the strategic opportunities of this policy discourse. In particular, the chapter suggests that the discourse of 'economic security' ought to be used as a way of articulating a radical, robust and principled understanding of sustainable development, which offers a normatively compelling and

Global Ecological Politics
Advances in Ecopolitics, Volume 5, 109–128
Copyright © 2010 by Emerald Group Publishing Limited
All rights of reproduction in any form reserved
ISSN: 2041-806X/doi:10.1108/S2041-806X(2010)0000005010

policy-relevant path to outline a 'green political economy' to underpin sustainable development.

One of the weakest and less developed areas of broadly green/sustainable development thinking has been its economic analysis. For example, what analyses there is within the green political canon is largely utopian – usually based on an argument for the complete transformation of modern society and economy as the only way to deal with ecological catastrophe, often linked to a critique of the socio-economic failings of capitalism that echoed a broadly radical Marxist/socialist or anarchist analysis – or under-developed – due, in part, to the need to outline and develop other aspects of green political theory. However, this gap within green political theory has recently been filled with a number of scholars, activists, think tanks, and environmental non-governmental organisations (NGOs) who have outlined various models of green political economy to underpin sustainable development political aims, principles and objectives.

The aim of this chapter is to sketch a realistic, but critical, version of green political economy to underpin the economic dimensions of radical views of sustainable development. It accepts the dominance of one particular model of green political economy – namely 'ecological modernisation' – as the preferred 'political economy' underpinning contemporary state and market forms of sustainable development and accepts the necessity for green politics to positively engage in the debates and policies around ecological modernisation from a strategic (as well as a normative) point of view. However, it is also conscious of the limits and problems with ecological modernisation, particularly in terms of its technocratic, supply-side and reformist 'business as usual' approach.

The chapter begins by outlining ecological modernisation in theory and practice, specifically in relation to the British state's 'sustainable development' policy agenda under New Labour. Although ecological modernisation as currently practised by the British state is 'weak' and largely turns on the centrality of 'innovation' and 'eco-efficiency', it then goes on to investigate in more detail the role of the market within current conceptualisations of ecological modernisation and other models of green political economy. In particular, a potentially powerful distinction (both conceptually and in policy debates) between 'the market' and 'capitalism' has yet to be sufficiently explored and exploited as a 'jumping off point' for the development of radical and viable conception of green political economy. In particular the role of the market in innovation and as part of the 'governance' for sustainable development in which eco-efficiency and ecological modernisa-tion of the economy is linked to non-ecological demands of green politics and sustainable development such as social and global justice, egalitarianism, democratic regulation of the market and the conceptual (and policy) expansion of the 'economy' to include social, informal and non-cash economic activity and a progressive role for the state (especially at the local/ municipal level). Here, the argument is that the 'environmental' argument or basis of green political economy in terms of the need for the economy to become more resource efficient, minimise pollution and waste and so on has largely been won. What that means is that in the developed world no one is disputing the need for greater resource productivity, energy and eco-efficiency. Both state and corporate/business actors have accepted the environmental 'bottom line' (often rhetorically, but nonetheless important) as a conditioning factor in the pursuit of the economic 'bottom line'.

However, what has been less remarked on is the social 'bottom line' and the centrality of this non-environmental set of principles and policy objectives to green politics and green political economy. In particular the argument for lessening socio-economic inequality and redistributive policies to do this have not been as prominent within green political economy and models of sustainable development as they perhaps should be. One of the reasons for focusing on the 'social bottom line' is to suggest that the distinctiveness and critical relevance of a distinctly 'green' (as opposed to 'environmental' or 'ecological') political economy will increasingly depend on developing a political agenda around these non-environmental/resource policy areas as states, businesses and other political parties converge around the ecological modernisation agenda of reconciling the environmental and economic bottom lines. It is in developing a radical political agenda around the social bottom line (without of course losing sight of the environmental and economic dimensions) that green political economy needs to focus.

It is for this reason that the final part of the chapter looks at the long-standing green commitment to re-orientate the economy towards enhancing and being judged by 'quality of life' and 'well-being'. The more recent discourse around 'economic security' is then discussed as building on and related to the quality of life perspective and is viewed as a potentially important driver and policy objective for green political economy in practice, in succinctly presenting the green economic case for a new type of economy, in which redistribution and reducing socio-economic inequality is central. The model of green political economy presented here is defined in part by its commitment to 'economic security', which has the strategic political advantage of presenting a positive and attractive discourse for sustainable development arguments, unlike the (still prevalent) negative and often disempowering discourse of 'limits to growth'. Or rather, using the language and analysis of economic security can be a more attractive and compelling way of getting to a less growth-orientated economy and consumption-orientated society and one that aims for putting quality of life at the heart of economic thinking and policy.

ECOLOGICAL MODERNISATION
IN THEORY AND PRACTICE

The New Labour government is clearly committed to an ecological modernisation approach to sustainable development. In a speech on sustainable development Tony Blair stated that 'tackling climate change or other environmental challenges need not limit greater economic opportunity...economic development, social justice and environmental modernisation must go hand in hand' (Blair, 2003).

This 'win-win' logic has also been echoed by the deputy Prime Minister John Prescott who in a speech to the Fabian Society held that:

> There is a widespread view that environmental damage is the price we have to pay for economic progress...Modern environmentalism recognises that ... an efficient, clean economy will mean more, not less economic growth and prosperity ... Treating the environment with respect will not impede economic progress, it will help identify areas of inefficiency and waste and so unleash whole new forces of innovation. (Prescott, 2003)

Like ecological modernisation discourse, New Labour sustainable development policy rhetoric adopts the language of business and orthodox economic growth, emphasising the business case for sustainability by linking environmental management with greater efficiency and competitiveness. Typical of this is the Department for Trade and Investment (DTI), which notes that 'The environment is a business opportunity...there are economic benefits in reducing waste, avoiding pollution and using resources more efficiently...Reducing pollution through better technology will almost always lower costs or raise product value/differentiation' (DTI, 2000, p. 7).

This business case for rendering orthodox neo-classical economic growth compatible with environmental considerations can also be found outside Westminister in the devolved adminstrations. In Scotland, the Scottish Exective's Enterprise Minister Jim Wallace has recently announce a 'Green Jobs Strategy', stating that:

> Economic growth and job creation can and should go hand in hand with promoting Scotland's natural environment and, through exports, sustaining good environmental practice overseas. A Green Jobs Strategy will focus our efforts on delivering sustainable

growth, which will generate employment while improving our environment and raising living standards across the country. As well as creating new business opportunities, better waste management and more efficient use of resources benefits the bottom line-raising productivity and making a big contribution to environmental targets. (Scottish Executive, 2005)

The notion that orthodox economic growth, employment investment patterns and the cross-sectoral goals of sustainable development might be in serious tension is excluded from the government's rhetoric on the environment; it is certainly not presented as a possibly problematic issue for industrial production processes or for global capitalism. Instead, environmental protection and economic growth are portrayed as a positive-sum game, a 'business opportunity', suggesting that ecological modernisation is basis upon which current debates on environmental and sustainable development policy in the United Kingdom are founded (Barry & Paterson, 2004).

Ecological modernisation as the principle 'policy telos' (Levy & Wissenburg, 2004) for environmental and sustainable development policies within the United Kingdom (but also in other European states) stresses innovative policy tools such as market-based incentives and voluntary agreements that 'steer' businesses towards eco-efficient practices, which do not undermine 'competitiveness' and ideally should create new markets, investment opportunities and technological advances. This does not rule out legislative sanctions, but ecological modernisation strongly emphasises voluntary action and 'partnership' forms of environmental governance. Having established the imperative for environmental improvement with its policies, the state also plays a key role in improving the capacity of industry to respond to that imperative through, for instance, public investment in clean technology and research and development programmes and provision of information on environmental best practice such as the recently announced 'Environment Direct' initiative contained with the latest sustainable development strategy or funded programmes in energy efficiency such as the Energy Savings Trust or programmes to encourage clean technology innovation such as the Green Technology Challenge and the Sustainable Technology Initiative. Other ecological modernisation initiatives include the state establishing or supporting new 'network organisations' tasked with promoting and encouraging 'win-win' environmental solutions to business such as the Waste and Resources Action Programme (WRAP) aimed at pump priming the market for recycled materials, or other agencies charged with informing and helping businesses (especially the small and medium sector) in respect to environmental legislation (particularly European Union directives) or other dissemination initiatives such as the

Environmental Technology Best Practice Programme and the Energy Efficiency Best Practice Programme within the DTI.

Reflecting these ideas, the policy documents *A Better Quality of Life: A Strategy for Sustainable Development for the UK* (DETR, 1999) and the DTI's *Sustainable Development Strategy* (2000) both stress the need to raise 'environmental productivity', 'to get more out of the economy from less' by using resources more efficiently. Environmental productivity is to be raised primarily by increasing the eco-efficiency of the economy through measures such as waste minimisation, recycling, energy efficiency and pollution prevention. Market-based solutions have recently become a favoured policy tool to encourage eco-efficiency in the United Kingdom, and various environmental taxes have been introduced such as the climate change levy, congestion charging in inner London, the landfill tax, aggregates tax and the fuel duty. These market-based approaches based on a voluntary and partnership approach are hallmarks of the ecological modernisation portfolio of 'policy drivers' of United Kingdom sustainable development, in comparison with the more legalistic approach of other European countries such as Germany.

One important element of such innovation is to create 'closed-loop' production, whereby waste materials are minimised and wastes themselves then become inputs to other industrial processes – central aspects of the emerging interdisciplinary science of 'industrial ecology'. The development of new markets, new commodities and services are crucial to create the possibility of continued capital accumulation and the imperative to attract foreign direct investment (FDI), whereas other markets are being restricted. This efficiency-oriented approach to environmental problems is central to understanding how ecological modernisation is both attractive to state and business elites and managers and some environmental NGOs.

But at the same time ecological modernisation processes tend to require significant state intervention. For some ecological modernisation writers, there is a reliance on a notion of an 'environmental Kuznets curve' (EKC), whereby the ecological impacts of growth go through a process where they increase but beyond a certain point of economic output start to decline.[1] For most, this is not likely to occur, except in relation to certain measures of environmental quality, without significant state intervention to enable shifts in economic behaviour (Ekins, 2000). It is thus not perhaps an accident that ecological modernisation (EM) discourse has arisen principally in social democratic countries in continental Europe where corporatist policy styles are still well established. EM as a 'policy ideology' has largely been developed in government programmes and policy styles and traditions, particularly those of Germany, the Netherlands, Sweden, Japan and the European Union (Weale, 1992, pp. 76–85; Dryzek, 1997, pp. 137–141). And while in the European countries where some of the policy outcomes associated with EM strategies, notably voluntary agreements or public-private partnerships, are often regarded as elements in a 'neo-liberalisation' of those countries, nevertheless their development still occurs within a style of policy development and implementation which is corporatist.

Corporatist arrangements are therefore usually regarded to be the most conducive political conditions for successful environmental policy reform (e.g. Young, 2000; Dryzek, 1997; Scruggs, 1999). On this view the state policy-elites act as brokers and prime movers in encouraging interest groups, trades unions, industry, consumer groups and sections of the environmental movement, to accept the agenda of EM. What then becomes interesting in the UK case we develop below is the way that globalisation acts to create potential for EM strategies in the absence of corporatist political arrangements. One argument similar to EM but couched in language more common in neoliberal countries such as the United Kingdom and the United States was popularised in an influential article by Porter and van der Linde (1995). They argue that the assumption of an economy–environment contradiction is premised on a static account of costs and fails to account for the dynamic effect which innovation has on the costs to firms of implementing environmental regulations. Thus, policies can be pursued, which promote competitiveness for firms while reducing the environmental impacts of those firms' operations. Porter and van der Linde emphasise regulation – that state regulation can create a dynamic of technical innovation by firms which is a 'win-win' scenario in economy–environment terms – but nevertheless the presumed relationship between states and firms is neoliberal rather than corporatist.

Ecological modernisation of course has its critics. Within EM discourse, advocates of 'strong' EM argue that its 'weak' variant is inadequate to deal with the challenge of ecological sustainability (Dryzek, 1997, p. 141). Critics of EM in general suggest that both versions are similarly problematic. In particular, the reliance on a set of technological fixes to solve what are widely seen as political problems is often seen as a key weakness, and one of its principal limitations when compared to its sister discourse of sustainable development which has explicit political bargains about limits and global justice built in, even in its relatively conservative versions (Langhelle, 2000). The focus on efficiency gains is often seen as wildly optimistic where all current experience suggests that in most areas, efficiency gains per unit of consumption are usually outstripped by overall increases in consumption.

This is another way of saying that the notion of an EKC, which underpins claims for the potential compatibility of growth and environmental sustainability, is implausible; drawing as such arguments do on a narrow set of processes and measures of environmental quality (Ekins, 2000). But ecological modernisation discourse is explicit about not attempting to limit overall levels of consumption. Indeed, one of the main points of this chapter is to suggest that if ecological modernisation is to be used as basis for developing a realistic but critical model of green political economy, ecological modernisation needs to be integrated with a model of sustainable political economy in which consumption is also addressed within the context of a far more radical economic vision which focuses on economic security and quality of life, rather than orthodox economic growth, and associated policies to increase formally paid employment, attract FDI and fully integrate local and national economies into the global one.

ECOLOGICAL MODERNISATION AND THE UNITED KINGDOM'S SUSTAINABLE DEVELOPMENT STRATEGY

The recently launched New Labour's sustainable development strategy, *Securing the Future: Delivering the United Kingdom Sustainable Development Strategy* [Department of Environment, Food and Rural Affairs (DEFRA), 2005], a follow-up in the 1999 strategy document, *A Better Quality of Life* (DEFRA, 1999) is a timely publication to take stock and assess the role of ecological modernisation within official government thinking on the transition to the a more sustainable economy and society.

Of particular interest is Chapter 3 of the Strategy, 'One Planet Economy: Sustainable Production and Consumption'. While containing some positive features, not least the over-arching idea of living within a sustainable 'ecological footprint', greater support for ecological innovation and rsource productive technoologies, enabling us to 'achieve more with less' and in relation to the key but challenging issue of consumption, the report while woefully inadequate, does at least place the issue of tackling and adddressing consumption alongside the more long-standign productive focus of United Kingdom sustainable development strategy. The strategy document studiously avoids what many would see as the real issue with consumption – that is how to reduce it rather than simply focusing on making it 'greener' or lessen its environmental impact. The report notes that 'there will also be a need for households, businesses and the public sector to consume more efficienty and differently, so that consumption from rising incomes is not accompanied by rising environmental impacts or social injustice. The challenge is big. But so too are the opportunties for innovation to build new markets, products and services' (DEFRA, 2005, p. 51). At no point in the report is the question of reducing or maintaining consumption discussed, or relating consumption and patterns of consumption to quality of life or well-being.

The extent of government action or policy in respect to consumption amounts to a series of 'processes' such as

- building an evidence base around the environmental impacts arising from households and how patterns of use can be influenced
- woking on a new information service – 'Environment Direct'...
- through a refocused Environmental Action Fund...
- delivering a large-scale deliberative forum to explore public views on sustainable consumption and lifestyles...
- the new Round Table on Sustainable Consumption (DEFRA, 2005, p. 52).

Of these, perhaps most hope lies in the deliberative forum and the round table in riasing the central but complex and difficult issue of reducing consumption and not simply changing current patterns of consumption per se, which leaves the quantity of consumption unchanged or is premised on increasing consumption. Before going on to look at the way in which the document articulates an ecological modernisation view, it is worth briefly looking at the role of consumption within ecological modernisation as the dominnat viuew of sustainable development within government thinking.

One of the limitations with ecological modernisation as many authors and critics have pointed out (Barry, 2003a) is its focus on the production side of economic activity and its impact on the environment – leading to its main focus on finding ways of increasing resource efficiency. What is missing from the ecological modernisation agenda is a concern with sustainable consumption to balance with sustainable production patterns and technologies. Indeed, I would suggest that the integration of serious consideration as to how to tackle consumption into the ecological modernisation framework holds out the possibility of a positive and more robust model of green political economy which is more consistent with basic green political and normative goals (particularly, as indicated in the concluding sections of this chapter, ecological modernisation can be framed within an overarchign policy approach to sustainable development aimed at producing 'economic security' and 'well-being' rather than orthodox 'economic growth').

The thinking behind Tim Jackson's recent report for the Sustainable Development Research Network entitled *Motivating Sustainable Consumption* (Jackson, 2005) seems to have influenced the Strategy's focus on providing deliberative fora and government leading by example in terms of public procurement, as the main policy contribution towards addressed sustainable consumption.

The conclusions of his report are as follows:

> Changing behaviour is difficult. The evidence in this review is unequivocal in that respect. Overcoming problems of consumer lock-in, unfreezing old habits and forming new ones, understanding the complexity of the social logic in which individual behaviours are embedded: all these are pre-requisites for successful behaviour change initiatives. But in spite of all appearances this complex terrain is not intractable to policy intervention. Policy already intervenes in human behaviour both directly and indirectly in numerous ways...a genuine understanding of the social and institutional context of consumer action opens out a much more creative vista for policy innovation than has hitherto been recognised. Expanding on these opportunities is the new challenge for sustainable consumption policy.
>
> In following up on these possibilities, Government can draw some clear guidance from the evidence base. In the first place, leading by example is paramount. The evidence suggests that discursive, elaborative processes are a vital element in behaviour change – in particular in negotiating new social norms and 'unfreezing' habitual behaviours. This shift from 'deliberation' to 'elaboration' as a working model of behavioural change can be seen as a key message of this study. (Jackson, 2005, p. 132–133)

He goes on to point out that there is perhaps some hope to be found in more participatory community-based approaches to changing patterns of consumption along more pro-environmental lines. According to Jackson

> In particular, the relevance of facilitating conditions, the role of lock- in and the critical importance of the social and cultural context emerge as key features of the debate. The role of community in mediating and moderating individual behaviours is also clear. There are some strong suggestions that participatory community-based processes could offer effective avenues for exploring pro-environmental and pro-social behavioural change. There are even some examples of such initiatives which appear to have some success. What is missing from this evidence base, at present, is unequivocal proof that community-based initiatives can achieve the level of behavioural change necessary to meet environmental and social objectives. (Jackson, 2005, p. 133)

This does seem to suggest that there is a role not just for deliberative, community-based processes (as indicated in the DEFRA strategy document) as enabling processes to overcome the obstacles to more sustainable patterns of consumption, but also of the possible role of community-based initiatives for delivering sustainable consumption itself. Here, the role of the social economy and community-based enterprises can be seen as important loci for sustainable consumption as well as sustainable production, suggesting a happy marriage between the three bottom lines of sustainable development within this sector (Barry & Smith, 2005). Jackson concludes that:

> It is clear from this that behaviour change initiatives are going to encounter considerable resistance unless and until it is possible to substitute for these important functions of society in some other ways. In this context, motivating sustainable consumption has to be as much about building supportive communities, promoting inclusive societies, providing meaningful work, and encouraging purposeful lives as it is about awareness raising, fiscal policy and persuasion. This is not to suggest that Government should be faint- hearted in encouraging and supporting pro-environmental behaviour. On the contrary, a robust effort is clearly needed; and the evidence reviewed in this study offers a far more creative vista for policy innovation than has hitherto been recognised. (Jackson, 2005, pp. 133–134)

Whether or not the British state's existing ecological modernisation approach to sustainable development (with its focus on resource efficiency and greening production within a conventional economic model that seeks to promote economic growth and competitiveness) can be integrated with a focus on sustainable consumption remains to be seen, and the current DEFRA sustainable development strategy can be seen as indicating some tentative steps in that direction. However, I suggest that the government's approach to sustainable consumption as a whole will probably be a version of its approach to private car transport – encouraging people to buy (and manufacturers to produce) more fuel-efficient and more ecologically responsibly produced cars, while doing little to regulate their use or provide attractive public transport alternatives to reduce their over-use (Barry & Paterson, 2004).

The judgement of environmental groups such as Friends of the Earth (FoE) is that the New Labour government has produced 'more green smoke than the Wizard of Oz'. FoE in a press statement in December 2002 claimed that

> Despite promising to cut traffic levels in 1997, the Government has done precious little to achieve this. The cost of motoring has fallen under Labour, whilst the cost of using buses and trains has risen. The Government abandoned the fuel price escalator following protests from motoring groups. Labour has offered only luke-warm support to the few local authorities that have introduced congestion-charging. Billions of pounds of road-widening schemes were announced last week – even though the Government stated in its 1998 Transport White Paper 'people know we cannot build our way out of congestion with new roads'. The Government has admitted that road congestion is unlikely to improve by the end of the decade. Since Labour came to power in 1997, road traffic is estimated to have grown by 7 per cent. There has been inadequate funding for transport alternatives to the car. (FoE, 2002)

A clear indication of the ecological modernisation approach adopted in the DEFRA report is the linking of economic competitiveness, innovation and the environment, building on the Government's previous 2003 Innovation review, which identified the environment as a key driver of innovation (DEFRA, 2005, p. 44). This focus on innovation, resource efficiency and so on should be welcomed and is a key part of the ecological modernisation agenda in general, and the ecologically modernising state in particular (Barry, 2003a).

A central aspect of the state in ecological modernisation is its 'enabling', co-ordinating and supporting role, in terms of encouraging technological innovation and greater economic and ecologically efficient use of resources and energy. Through subsidies and research and development assistance for renewable energy, or investment in fuel cell technology, to forms of environmental regulation, setting emissions standards, environmental taxes and other regulatory mechanisms: 'Regulation can be used to drive the process of industrial innovation with environmental and economic gains realised as a result' (Murphy & Gouldson, 2000, p. 43). Indeed, much of the 'modernisation' aspect of ecological modernisation rests on the central emphasis on innovation, both technologically and in production processes and management and distribution systems.[2] Smart production systems, 'doing more with less', applying novel scientific breakthroughs (e.g. in renewable energy, biotechnology and information and communication technology such as nanotechnology) and developing and utilising 'clean' technologies, are all hallmarks of the modern, dynamic, forward-looking, solutions-focused character of ecological modernisation. Although the state 'enables' and supports innovation, it is left to the private sector to develop, test and market these new ecologically efficient innovations and production methods.

However, although the issue of consumption is not (yet) integrated within ecological modernisation thinking, a related and perhaps more damning critique from a robust or radical conception of sustainable development is that ecological modernisation is explicitly viewed as contributing to rather than challenging or changing the orthodox economic policy objective of growth in the formal economy as measured by GNP/GDP. In short, ecological modernisation – at most – deals with the effects rather than the underlying causes of unsustainable development.

FROM ECONOMIC GROWTH TO ECONOMIC SECURITY

The critique of conventional economic growth has been a long-standing position of green thinking and radical conceptions of sustainable development. Indeed, I would suggest that any plausibly 'green' conception of political economy must articulate. That is, for a model of political economy to be classed as 'green', this critique of conventional, neo-classical economic growth as the main economic policy objective of any state or society is a sine qua non. Now although there are many debates as to understandings and measurements of 'economic growth' (does growth refer to increases in monetary value or does it refer to physical/resource measures?), a 'post-growth' economy is one that has featured prominently within green political and economic discourse, most usually associated with the environmental benefits of a less growth-orientated and programmed economic system.

A major report by the International Labour Office Economic *Security for a Better World* [International Labour Organisation (ILO), 2005] found that economic security coupled with democracy and equality were key determinants of well-being and social stability. According to this report:

> People in countries that provide citizens with a high level of economic security have a higher level of happiness on average, as measured by surveys of national levels of life-satisfaction and happiness ... The most important determinant of national happiness if not income level – there is a positive association, but rising income seems to have little effect as wealthy countries grow more wealthier. Rather the key factor is the extent of income security, measured in terms of income protection and a low degree of income inequality. (ILO, 2005)

Such findings give empirical support to long-standing green arguments stressing policies to increase well-being and quality of life, rather than conventionally measured economic growth, rising personal income levels or orthodox measures of wealth and prosperity.

In particular, the report confirms the long-standing green critique of economic growth as necessarily contributing to well-being. It states that, 'there is only a weak impact of economic growth on security measured over the longer-term. In other words, rapid growth does not necessarily create better economic security, although it sometimes can do if it is accompanied by appropriate social policies' (ILO, 2005). Of particular note is that many of the policies the ILO recommends to accompany an orthodox growth objective go against the neo-liberal/Washington consensus model – premised on increasing the openness national economies to one another, integrating them into the global market and prioritising trade and FDI as the main determinants of domestic economic growth. The ILO report makes the point that:

> For developing countries national level of economic security is inversely related to capital account openness, implying that it would be sensible for developing countries to

delay opening their capital accounts until institutional developments and social policies were in place to enable their societies to withstand external shocks. In other words, countries should postpone opening their financial markets until they have the institutional capacities to handle fluctuations in confidence and the impact of external economic developments. (ILO, 2005)

At the same time, that a democratic political system has no necessary connection with ever increasing levels of material consumption is a touchstone of green democratic arguments (Barry, 1999), and indeed, democratic and egalitarian principles are at the heart of sustainable development (Jacobs, 1999). More important to a democratic polity is a well-developed 'democratic culture', a shared sense of citizenship, plurality and socio-economic and political equality. Plurality and equality are more significant than prosperity as preconditions for an ongoing and vibrant democracy. In other words, a shift away from 'economic growth' and orthodox understandings of 'prosperity' should be taken as an opportunity by green theory to redefine basic political and economic concepts. It asks us to consider the possibility that human freedom and a well-organised and well-governed polity does not depend, in any fundamental sense, on increasing levels of material affluence. Indeed, there may be a trade-off between democracy and orthodox economic growth and a related government policy heavily or exclusively focused on improving material well-being.

According to a study by Lauber (1978) in the late 1970s, there is evidence to show that the relatively democratic and liberal, and consequently less powerful, British state was an important determinant of the stagnation and decline of its economy since the second world war. Relying on the comparative studies of Schonfield (1965), he states that, 'the governments that have been most successful in the pursuit of the new [economic] goals have been those which had few doubts about the extensive use of non-elected authority, for example, France. The more 'timid' governments were less successful' (Lauber, 1978, p. 209). Having 'modernisation' and the pursuit of orthodox economic growth as one's highest goal can lead to non-democratic, illiberal forms of state action, or policies and styles of governance that at the very least are at odds with a pluralist democratic system.

It needs to be recalled that the 'free market' revolution ushered in by the likes of Thatcher in the United Kingdom and Regan in the United States were also accompanied by a centralisation and strengthening of the state, and an redrawing of the relationship between state and civil society which privileged the former over the latter. The 'free market and strong state' are both still with us, increasingly integrated under economic globalisation and those governments – such as New Labour – that embrace and promote a broadly neo-liberal version of globalisation (Barry & Paterson, 2004).

The ILO report quoted earlier provides other evidence of the dangers of economic growth policies that undermine economic security. The report finds that:

> the global distribution of economic security does not correspond to the global distribution of income, and that countries in South and South-East Asia have a greater share of global economic security than their share of the world's income... By contrast, Latin American countries provide their citizens with less economic security than could be expected from their relative income levels. Indeed, being insecure has resonance in people's attitudes, which at times can be detrimental to their ideas of a decent society. In a recent survey taken by the Latino barometro in Latin America, 76% of the people surveyed were concerned about not having a job the following year, and a majority said that they would not mind a non-democratic government if it could solve their unemployment problems. (ILO, 2005)

So, not only states but also citizens can contemplate and act in non-democratic ways in pursuit of orthodox economic modernisation and economic growth objectives. If one values democracy and its values of pluralism, freedom, equality and so on, then one has to seriously question any putative or enforced connection between its maintenance and further development and orthodox policies aimed at economic growth. The ILO report goes on to note that 'economic insecurity fosters intolerance and stress, which contribute to social illness and ultimately may lead to social violence' (ILO, 2005).

Beyond a certain threshold, greater increases in the latter may be accompanied by decreases in the former. A less materially affluent lifestyle may be consistent with enhanced democratic practice since the decrease in complexity, social division of labour, inequality and hierarchy, allows the possibility of greater participation by individuals in the decisions that affect their lives and that of their communities. For example, a shift away from economic growth as a central social goal would undermine the justification of socio-economic inequalities on the grounds that they are necessary 'incentives' to achieve economic growth. At the same time, as early proponents of the steady-state economy pointed out, the shift from a society geared towards economic growth, to a society where material growth is not a priority may lead to more extensive redistributive measures (Daly, 1973). This redistributive aspect to the sustainability critique of excessive material development echoes the socialist critique of the disparity between formal political equality and socio-economic inequality within capitalism.

Indeed, the findings of the ILO report strengthen not only sustainability arguments concerning the non-democratic and non-well-being contribution of economic growth policies but also the dangers of authoritarian positions.

Over 150 years ago Alexis de Tocqueville suggested that 'General prosperity is favourable to the stability of all governments, but more particularly of a democratic one, which depends upon the will of the majority, and especially upon the will of that portion of the community which is most exposed to want. When the people rule, they must be rendered happy or they will overturn the state: and misery stimulates them to those excesses to which ambition rouses kings' (de Tocqueville, 1956, pp. 129–130).

This assumption of the positive correlation between material affluence and the stability of a democratic political order is one which is closely associated with 'modern' political traditions such as liberalism and Marxism.[3] In this section, it is the negative corollary of this assumption, that is that material scarcity creates the conditions for political instability and a shift to authoritarianism that will be examined. What can be called a 'Hobbes-Malthus' position underpins the 'eco-authoritarian' school of green thought (Barry, 1999), which in the literature is most closely associated with Ophuls (1977), Hardin (1968, 1977) and Heilbroner (1980). The eco-authoritarian implication of the link between scarcity and political arrangements has been forcefully made by Ophuls. He begins from the assumption that:

> The institution of government whether it takes the form of primitive taboo or parliamentary democracy... has its origins in the necessity to distribute scarce resources in an orderly fashion. It follows that assumptions about scarcity are absolutely central to any economic or political doctrine and that the relative scarcity or abundance of goods has a substantial and direct impact on the character of political, social and economic institutions. (Ophuls, 1977, p. 8)

Calling the affluence experienced by western societies over the last two hundred years or so 'abnormal', a material condition that has grounded individual liberty, democracy and stability (p. 12), he concludes that with the advent of the ecological crisis, interpreted as a return to scarcity (following 'the limits to growth' thesis), 'the golden age of individualism, liberty and democracy is all but over. In many important respects we shall be obliged to return to something resembling the pre-modern closed polity' (p. 145).

These eco-authoritarian arguments can be countered if one focuses not on economic prosperity or growth as the main connection between democracy and individual freedom and social and political stability, but on economic security. In part, what this implies is that economic growth policies to be effective in promoting the goal of economic security need to be connected to redistributive and other policies. In particular, as well as supporting policies promoting job security (and job/skill satisfaction),[4] and ones promoting income security within employment (such as minimum wage legislation), greens have also been long-standing advocates for income security outside the formal employment sphere, through a universal, rights-based provision of a basic citizen's income.

CONCLUSION: INTEGRATING ECOLOGICAL MODERNISATION, INNOVATION AND ECONOMIC SECURITY?

Although viewed by itself ecological modernisation is a reformist and limited strategy for achieving a more sustainable economy and society, and indeed questions could be legitimately asked as to whether the development of a recognisably 'green' political economy for sustainable development can be based on it, I nevertheless contend that there are strategic advantages in seeking to build upon and radicalise ecological modernisation. Although there are various reasons one can give for this, in this conclusion, I will focus on two – one normative/principled the other strategic.

From a strategic point of view, it is clear that, as Dryzek and his colleagues have shown (Dryzek, Downes, Hunold, Schlosberg, & Hernes, 2003), if green and sustainability goals, aims and objectives are to be integrated within state policy, these need to attach themselves to one of the core state imperatives – accumulation/economic growth or legitimacy (Barry, 2003b). It is clear that the discourse of ecological modernisation allows (some) green objectives to be integrated/translated into a policy language and framework which complements and does not undermine the state's core imperative of pursuing orthodox economic growth. Therefore if in the absence of a Green Party forming a government or being part of a ruling coalition, or even more unlikely of one of the main traditional parties initiating policies consistent with a radical understanding of sustainable development, the best that can be hoped for under current political conditions is the 'greening of growth and capitalism' that is ecological modernisation.

On a more principled note, the adoption of ecological modernisation as a starting point for the development of a model/theory of green political economy does carry with it the not inconsiderable benefit of removing the 'anti-growth' and 'limits to growth' legacy which has (in my view) held back the theoretical development of a positive, attractive, modern conceptualisation of green political economy and radical conceptualisations of sustainable development. Here the technological innovation, the role of regulation driving innovation and efficiency, the promise that the transition to a more sustainable economy and society does not necessarily mean completing abandoning currently lifestyles and aspirations – strategically important in generating democratic support for sustainable development. Equally, it does not completely reject the positive role(s) of a regulated market within sustainable development. However, it does demand a clear shift towards making the promotion of economic security (and quality of life) central to economic policy. Only when this happens can we say we have begun the transition to a sustainable development path.

NOTES

1. The EKC approach is the principal site where an attempt is made to demonstrate (rather than assert) the potential to combine environmental improvements with economic growth (Ekins, 2000; Cole, 2000). The basic assumption of the EKC analysis is that continued economic growth passes a point beyond which environmental degradation begins to decrease (Ekins, 2000, pp. 182–183).

2. 'Innovation is central to ecological modernisation of production because it is through innovation and change that environmental concerns can begin to be integrated into production' (Murphy, 2001, p. 9).

3. Classical liberals such as Tocqueville assumed a relationship between an affluent economy and political democracy. One aspect of Tocqueville's thought turns on the idea that 'a flourishing economy is essential to the stability of democracy, since it gives defeated politicians an alternative, which makes them more likely to accept defeat rather than attempt to illegally to hold on to office' (Copp et al., 1995, p. 3). Classical Marxism, on the contrary, assumed a connection between 'emancipation' and material abundance. The roots of the different understandings of the connection between the two may lie in the inter-relationship between the logics and the legacies of the Industrial and French Revolutions, understood as expressing the core values of modernity, one relating to economic abundance and the other to political democracy.

4. Another of the ILO report's findings was that one of the seven forms of work-related security, skills security was 'inversely related to well-being when jobs are poorly attuned to the needs and aspirations of people, especially as they become more educated and acquire more skills and competencies. At present, too many people are finding that their skills and qualifications do not correspond to the jobs they have to perform, resulting in a "status frustration" effect' (ILO, 2005). One of the clear implications of this is that the mantra that job creation per se is all that matters is one that does not necessarily support economic security and the promotion of well-being. From a purely economistic and orthodox position

promoting economic growth, employment creation is completely indifferent to the quality or the types of jobs that are being created. On this orthodox economic view, short-term, low-paid, low-skilled jobs ('McJobs' or jobs in call-centres for example) are to be judged as the same as skilled, highly-paid jobs with high levels of job satisfaction and job security.

REFERENCES

Barry, J. (1999). *Rethinking green politics: Nature, virtue and progress*. London: Sage.

Barry, J. (2003a). Ecological modernisation. In: E. Page & J. Proops (Eds), *Environmental thought*. London: Edward Elgar.

Barry, J. (2003b). Holding tender views in tough ways: Political economy and strategies of resistance in green politics. *British Journal of Politics and International Relations, 5*, 4.

Barry, J., & Paterson, M. (2004). Globalisation, ecological modernisation, and new labour. *Political Studies, 4*, 54.

Barry, J., & Smith, G. (2005). Green political economy and the promise of the social economy. In: P. Dauvergne (Ed.), *International handbook of environmental politics*. Cheltenham: Edward Elgar.

Blair, T. (2003). *Sustainable development helps the poorest*. Available at http://www.labour. org.uk/tbsd/. Retrieved on June 13, 2005.

Cole, M. (2000). *Trade liberalisation, economic growth and the environment*. Cheltenham: Edward Elgar.

Copp, D., et al. (1995). Introduction. In: D. Copp, J. Hampton & J. Roemer (Eds), *The idea of democracy*. Cambridge: Cambridge University Press.

Daly, H. (Ed.) (1973). *Toward a steady state economy*. San Francisco: Freeman.

Department of Environment, Food and Rural Affairs. (1999). *A better quality of life*. London: HMSO.

Department of Environment, Food and Rural Affairs. (2005). *Securing the future: Delivering the United Kingdom sustainable development strategy*. London: HMSO.

Department of Environment, Transport and the Regions. (1999). *A better quality of life: A strategy for sustainable development for the UK*. London: HMSO.

Department of Trade and Industry. (2000). *Sustainable development strategy*. Available at www.dti.gov.uk/sustainability/strategy/. Retrieved on June 1, 2005.

de Tocqueville, A. (1956). Democracy in America. In: R. Heffner (Ed.), New York: Mentor Books.

Dryzek, J. (1997). *The politics of the earth*. Oxford: Oxford University Press.

Dryzek, J., Downes, D., Hunold, C., Schlosberg, D., & Hernes, H. K. (2003). *Green states and social movements*. Oxford: Oxford University Press.

Ekins, P. (2000). *Economic growth and environmental sustainability: The prospects for green growth*. London: Routledge.

Friends of the Earth. (2002). *Government failing to tackle transport crisis*. Available at http://www.foe.co.uk/pubsinfo/infoteam/pressrel/2002/20021217170949.html. Retrieved on January 8, 2003.

Hardin, G. (1968). The tragedy of the commons. *Science, 168*.

Hardin, G. (1977). *The limits to altruism*. Indianapolis: Indiana University Press.

Heilbroner, R. (1980). *An inquiry into the human prospect* (2nd ed.). New York: WW Norton.

International Labour Organisation. (2005). *Security for a better world.* Available at http://
    www.ilo.org/public/english/protection/ses/index.htm. Retrieved on October 10, 2004.
Jackson, T. (2005). *Motivating sustainable consumption.* London: Sustainable Development
    Research Network.
Jacobs, M. (1999). Sustainable development as a contested concept. In: A. Dobson (Ed.),
    Fairness and futurity. Oxford: Oxford University Press.
Langhelle, O. (2000). Why ecological modernisation and sustainable development should not be
    conflated. *Journal of Environmental Policy and Planning, 2*(4), 303–322.
Lauber, V. (1978). Ecology, politics and liberal democracy. *Government and Opposition, 13,* 2.
Levy, Y., & Wissenburg, M. (2004). Sustainable development as a policy telos: A new approach
    to political problem-solving. *Political Studies, 4,* 54.
Murphy, J. (2001). *Ecological modernisation: The environment and the transformation of society.*
    Research Paper No. 20, OCEES, Oxford.
Murphy, J., & Gouldson, A. (2000). Environmental policy and industrial innovation: Integrating
    environment and economy through ecological modernisation. *Geoforum, 31,* 1.
Ophuls, W. (1977). *Ecology and the politics of scarcity.* San Francisco: Freeman.
Porter, M., & van der Linde, C. (1995). Toward a new conception of the environment-
    competitiveness relationship. *Journal of Economic Perspectives, 9*(4), 97–118.
Prescott, J. (2003). Environmental modernisation. Speech to Fabian Society/SERA Conference.
Schonfield, A. (1965). *Modern capitalism.* Oxford: Oxford University Press.
Scottish Executive. (2005). *Proposals for green jobs strategy.* Available at http://www.
    scotland.gov.uk/News/Releases/2004/06/5656. Retrieved on June 26, 2005.
Scruggs, L. (1999). Institutions and environmental performance in seventeen democracies.
    British Journal of Political Science, 29(1), 1–31.
Weale, A. (1992). *The new politics of pollution.* Manchester: Manchester University Press.
Young, S. (Ed.) (2000). *The emergence of ecological modernisation: Integrating the environment
    and the economy?* London: Routledge.

CHAPTER 7

GREEN POLITICS AND ANTHROPOLOGY

Michael O'Kane

INTRODUCTION

In recent years there has been much discussion about the relevance of the discipline of anthropology to the various emergent discourses on the environment. Among those researching in the area, reason for concern has been confirmed by a failure to make themselves heard as experts over the growing din of the other branches of social research passionately pleading the case for the relevance of their respective disciplines. This is evidenced to some degree by the lack of anthropological literature in the field of environmentalism and comes into stark relief when compared with the extensive treatment of the area given by the political sciences. This chapter seeks to focus on reactions by anthropologists to this dearth of environmentally concerned research within the discipline over the past decade. The debate over the issues raised by this discussion has evolved principally between a small number of dedicated anthropologists, and although it is now spilling out into the wider anthropological community, it is from these scholars work that a path forward has been constructed.

Anthropology traditionally has strong links to the study of the environment through its focus on human interaction in environmental context. This basic connection is depicted by Milton, who says: 'If one accepts the anthropological cliché that culture is the mechanism through

Global Ecological Politics
Advances in Ecopolitics, Volume 5, 129–149
Copyright © 2010 by Emerald Group Publishing Limited
All rights of reproduction in any form reserved
ISSN: 2041-806X/doi:10.1108/S2041-806X(2010)0000005011

which human beings interact with (or, more controversially, adapt to) their environment (Ingold, 1992, p. 39), then the whole field of cultural anthropology can be characterised as human ecology' (p. 4). In the light of this, it is pertinent to ask why anthropology has not come to prominence in the study of environmentalists and environmentalism? Brosius (1999, p. 278) addressed this by noting significant differences between 'the ecological anthropology of the 1960's and early 1970's and what some are calling 'the environmental anthropology' of the present'. In mentioning ecological anthropology, Brosius is referring to the meticulous work carried out by anthropologists studying the impact of human communities within the ecosystems they inhabit/ed. These anthropologists used concepts such as carrying capacity and systems theory to discern, among other things, the relationship between ecological variables and cultural adaptations governing patterns of resource use. They were interested in bringing anthropology into line with the natural sciences in an attempt to legitimise culture as an empirical phenomenon. Brosius regards this as an inappropriate direction for anthropology, in hindsight, and brands it 'scientism'. Accordingly, he states that:

> One does not have to be a post-structuralist to recognize the valorisation of anthropology as a science, long a prominent element in our disciplinary self-identification (recall Radcliffe-Brown's efforts to establish a 'natural science of society'), reached a kind of rhetorical apogee in 1960s-1970s ecological anthropology as we borrowed one concept after another-ecosystem, adaptation, niche, carrying capacity-from ecology. (Brosius, 1999, p. 300)

According to Brosius and other like-minded anthropologists, this approach constituted a relegation of notions of culture to a series of competing strategies aimed solely at enhancing the chances of physical survival for the species. It is not clear as to whether or not the alternative approach was born out of the work of ecologically oriented anthropologists or as a response to it; however, a divergent stream did come to prominence in the 1960s and 1970s. This has come to be known as 'environmentalism'. Brosius (1999, p. 278) argues that environmentalism refers broadly to the field of 'discursive constructions of nature and human agency'. He makes the point that the study of environmentalism should encompass much more than an analysis of the different social movements involved and their various trajectories over time and space. As stated earlier in text, he feels that at the crux of environmentalism is the ongoing discourse about human beings and their place within nature. As a postmodernist thinker and an anthropologist, Brosius declares that the relevance of anthropology in this field of investigation is due to its unique concentration upon the phenomenon of culture. He urges anthropologists to see environmentalism as a 'rich site of cultural production' (*ibid.*, p. 277) and stresses that 'a whole new discursive regime is emerging and giving shape to the relationships between and among natures, nations, movements, individuals, and institutions' (*ibid.*). It should be noted here that, although Brosius is thinking about environmentalism in terms of his work with discourse theory, the assertion of a more holistic approach by anthropologists to the study of environmentalism is not dependent upon the use of that branch of social theory. Discourse theory, which came to prominence with MacDonell's (1986) work Theories of Discourse, has been aptly described by Torfing (1999, p. 3) as 'a constructivist and relationalist perspective on social identity perspective on social identity combined with an insistence on the heterogeneity of discourse'. Given this, Brosius' interest in the discursive constructions regarding nature comes as no surprise. What should be appreciated here is not the fact that anthropologists using discourse theory have become interested in environmentalism but that, as 'a rich site of cultural production' (Brosius, 1999, p. 277), environmentalism offers anthropologists of all theoretical persuasions many avenues of worthwhile investigation. The following discusses the different directions in which anthropology has been taken by the study of environmentalism over the past decade.

KAY MILTON: CULTURAL ANTHROPOLOGY

Kay Milton has made a number of important contributions to this area of anthropological investigation over recent years. In 1993 she edited a work, entitled *Environmentalism: The View from Anthropology*, which attempted to position anthropology more centrally within the multi-disciplinary study of environmentalism. Her introduction contains O'Riordan's (1981, p. xi) assertion that environmentalism preaches 'a philosophy of human conduct' and is also 'a state of being' (cited in Milton, 1993, p. 1). This, for her, is a crucial observation as it allows anthropologists to see environmentalism as a social commitment undertaken by social actors in complex multi-sited cultural settings. Milton (1993, p. 2) goes on to express the belief that environmentalism is, in the main, 'a quest for a viable future, pursued through the implementation of culturally defined responsibilities'. Obviously, these responsibilities vary between cultural settings but, as Milton observes, they originate from the recognition that environmental problems are caused by human interaction with the environment. She feels that the key to a viable future lies in a better understanding of human activity (*ibid.*). Milton also raises the issue of the potential conflict faced by anthropologists concerning anthropological research and environmental advocacy. Although not calling for all anthropologists to become advocates for the environmental cause, she does outline three main ways in which anthropological knowledge could further the cause of environmentalism. The first of these is through an approach centred upon human ecology but would only be of merit if the initial premise was that all human interactions with the environment took place 'through the medium of culture' (*ibid.*, p. 5). As with Brosius, Milton recognises the pitfalls of the ecological determinism of the 1950s and 1960s while also being aware of the dangers of cultural determinism which, in extreme cases, 'can appear to deny the very existence of objective reality' (*ibid.*, p. 4). Therefore, the benefit of this approach lies mainly in its attempt to investigate the way in which people culturally perceive their interactions with the environment. The second approach concerns the cross-cultural interpretation of the 'meanings imputed to reality' which are the building blocks of cultural understanding (*ibid.*, p. 5). Milton feels that this would be invaluable when formulating broad reaching environmental policies such as those implemented by the United Nations and the European Union. An understanding of the cultural meanings and symbolism at work in particular cultural contexts would greatly assist the linkage of local, regional and global action concerning environmental initiatives. Third, Milton notes that environmentalists could be well served by the anthropological study of environmentalism itself (*ibid.*, p. 6). Importantly, in keeping with O'Riordan's notion of environmentalism as a philosophy of human conduct, she identifies it as a 'social commitment' gaining momentum through 'the development and expression of ideas' (*ibid.*, p. 6). It is in the analysis of what constitutes the environmentalist social commitment and the evolution of environmental theory that anthropology may further the cause of environmentalism. Again, the notion of discourse features prominently in Milton's work and she defines it as follows:

A discourse is an area of communication defined purely by its subject matter. In this sense, environmental discourse is communication about the environment, and environmentalist discourse is communication about the protection of the environment. There is no indication here that a particular mode of communication is being used, or that a particular way of understanding is being generated. (*ibid.*, p. 167)

She describes environmentalism as a trans-cultural discourse that, not being rooted in any specific culture, spans the local through to the global and now has become a specific cultural discourse existing within, although not bounded by, other cultural systems. Thus, environmentalism is perceived by her to transcend many traditional geographical and conceptual boundaries such as east/west, north/south, first world/third world and left/right. As Milton describes it, environmentalism incorporates 'all culturally defined environmental responsibilities, whether they are innovative or conventional, radical or conservative' (*ibid.*, p. 11). Furthermore, in her view environmental discourse does not merely articulate perceptions of the environment, it contributes to their formulation. In this way, the whole spectrum of thought is included in Milton's analysis because a pro-environmentalist stance is not required for discourse to be considered environmental (*ibid.*, p. 8). If we also take into account Brosius' description of environmentalism provided earlier, we see that anthropologists have begun to discern environmentalism as being expressed through a myriad of social and cultural relationships and situations. Milton explains this well when she writes:

> In this framework, social movements and political ideologies become specific cultural forms through which environmental responsibilities might be expressed and communicated. Instead of environmentalism being seen as a category of social movement or ideology, these forms of cultural expression become types of environmentalism (*ibid.*, p. 8).

Milton's Environmentalism and Cultural Theory (1996) extends and develops the ideas from her earlier work. Here she contends that anthropology is going through a time of fundamental theoretical change in relation to the concept of culture (Milton, 1996, p. 11) and that this is evidenced by three different trends within the discipline. The first of these trends is what Milton describes as 'dissatisfaction with the cultural relativist perspective which has characterized anthropology in the post-structuralist era' (*ibid.*). This harks back to her earlier (1993) discussion of environmentalism and advocacy within anthropology but indicates that, in her judgement, anthropologists are now less inclined to entertain notions of cultural relativity when confronted with their burgeoning ability to contribute directly to environmental debates. The second trend she identifies is 'a widespread reaction, both within and outside anthropology, against the Cartesian dualisms of mind-body, thought-action, nature-culture, which are seen as obstructing progress in anthropological theory' (Milton, 1996, p. 11). These dualisms, or dichotomies, were seen by Milton to have outlived their usefulness 'as a framework for understanding the human condition' (*ibid.*, p. 12). She singles out the nature–culture dichotomy as particularly unhelpful and notes that this is an area within which anthropological investigation has much to offer (*ibid.*). The third trend Milton points to is the increasing focus by anthropologists on the way in which cultural exchange is taking place in the modern world. Anthropologists have always been interested in how cultural influences are spread and Milton notes that, given the advantages of modern technology, the current high rate of cultural exchange 'has led social scientists to ask whether it is appropriate to speak of a "global culture" (*ibid.*). This is, she asserts, a direct challenge to the anthropological methodology of cross-cultural comparison. According to her, anthropology has only just begun to look at the cultural connotations of the world system theorised by scholars such as Wallerstein (1979), Nash (1981), and Chirot and Hall (1982) and is in danger of being marginalised in the debates about globalisation that have sprung from them. She goes on to urge anthropologists to refrain from assuming the relevance of the concept of globalisation to the analysis of environmentalism but rather to see the problems that surround it (Milton, 1996, p. 13). This argument is crucial in understanding Milton's overall conception of anthropology's position within the study of environmentalism. She notes that 'the debate on the environment has adopted the concept of the global as both 'motive and motif' (*ibid.*) and makes no secret throughout her book that anthropological perspectives on culture are invaluable in the attempt to gain a clearer notion of what constitutes the 'global'.

Regarding anthropological perspectives on culture, Milton identifies a broad and a narrow view at work within anthropological theory. The broad view of culture, most common in the 1950s, encompassed 'actions, ideas and material objects' (*ibid.*, p. 17). She believes that this view was only appropriate while 'anthropologists were mainly concerned with describing and understanding whole ways of life, "whole systems" (*ibid.*) as the discipline attempted to understand cultures as constituting discreet systems in their own right. The obvious flaw regarding the inclusion of material objects being the inability of this definition to cope with the flow of artistic and technological ideas through and across cultures. By the late 1950s and early 1960s, anthropologists were beginning to 'distinguish between what people do and what they think, feel and know' (*ibid.*, p. 18). In other words, ideas were being separated from actions and material objects in an attempt to redefine culture. Milton argued that the benefit of this 'was that it opened up the possibility of studying the relationship between them' (*ibid.*). Thus, at this point anthropologists were now simply interested in not only how people reacted within their societies but also how they used culture to change them. The notion of cultural relativity developed as a consequence of this new, narrow definition of culture as culture now began to be perceived as a way of knowing rather than a way of life. Milton pointed out that this had both positive and negative connotations for the study of culture. On the one hand it affected a significant decrease in discrimination and ethnocentrism, whereas, on the other, its preoccupation with the contextual nature of culture problematised cross-cultural transmission to such an extent that that notion became theoretically impossible (*ibid.*, pp. 19–20). Additionally, it sparked off a debate concerning advocacy within the discipline that still exists to this day. Some anthropologists, inspired by the new degree of dignity afforded to indigenous cultures by cultural relativity, became advocates for the people they studied while others, equally inspired by the cultural relativist standpoint, opposed advocacy as they perceived it as active interference by anthropologists into subject communities. By 1996, Milton argued that perceptions of culture among anthropologists had again shifted. The post-structuralist distinction between the mental and the physical was now seen as a continuation of the mind–body dualism that had been prominent in the 1950s. She stated that 'In an attempt to eliminate the dualism, the term 'culture' is being used less to refer to what people know and think, and more to refer to the process by which that knowledge and those thoughts are generated and sustained' (*ibid.*, p. 22).

Thus, the main thrust of Milton's discussion concerning the concept of culture is that it has begun to be seen as something that 'exists in peoples minds ... consists of perceptions and interpretations (and) ... is the mechanism through which human beings interact with their environment' (*ibid.*, p. 66). This has, in more recent decades, given rise to a more interpretive and less scientistic perspective. As Milton explains:

> Anthropologists have not given up the effort to explain cultural features, and some regard this as their ultimate goal, but since the 1970's many have seen their task as interpretive rather than explanatory (see Geertz, 1973). Their role has been to reveal how cultural perspectives make sense, by showing how they are related to the activities of those who hold them, and how their various components – assumptions, values, norms, goals – relate to one another. (Milton, 1996, p. 102)

Milton employs this more interpretive and hermeneutic approach to culture to investigate environmentalism as a 'cultural phenomenon' of global proportions (*ibid.*, p. 142). She singles out Robertson's definition of globalisation because she feels it has the capacity to provide a framework in which the study of environmentalism as a cultural phenomenon can be seriously undertaken. Robertson's definition, states that 'Globalization as a concept refers both to the compression of the world and the intensification of consciousness of the world as a whole' (Robertson, 1992, p. 8 cited in Milton, 1996, p. 164). Milton understands the first part of this definition to refer to the process of linking the disparate parts of the world by economic, political and technological means and bringing each part under the influence, to greater and lesser degrees, of the others. She understands the second part of the definition to refer to the way in which people are becoming aware of this interconnectedness and the changes that this awareness is bringing to people's perceptions about themselves, their own condition and that of others. In short, Robertson, for Milton, emphasises the cultural nature of globalisation and asserts that an awareness of this has been absent in, for example, the earlier theories of Wallerstein (1974, 1980), Saurin (1993) and Giddens (1990) (Milton, 1996, pp. 144–154). I contend that Robertson's approach reveals that it is possible to see that relationships between east and west, north and south and first world and third world are not simply relationships where the more powerful and affluent sector influence the lesser while remaining unaffected. Here, for instance, Robertson indicates that the third world influences the first world significantly and that the power of the north has not made it invulnerable to the needs and demands of the south. I should point out here that neither Robertson nor Milton portrays these relationships as being between equals. They simply stress that the suppositions surrounding them have been unchallenged for too long. Thus, Milton advocates a role for anthropology in the study of environmental activism that is based around the notion of discourse and globalisation. For her, environmentalism is a trans-cultural discourse played out within and across the cultures of the globe but never rooted in any one of them. In this way environmental movements, and the discourses they gave rise to, can be studied by anthropologists as cultural expressions of a wider cross-cultural phenomenon.

BERGLUND: ANTHROPOLOGY AND ENVIRONMENTALISM

Eeva Berglund is another anthropologist who wishes to establish anthropology as a legitimate participant in the study of environmentalism. Like Milton, Berglund notes the lack of anthropological involvement in this field. As she contends, it seems 'curious that so little attention has been paid by anthropologists to the ways in which people around the world have joined the chorus of voices who are constituting as well as contesting, the notion of the global environmental crisis' (Berglund, 1998, p. 4). In her book, *Knowing Nature, Knowing Science: An Ethnography of Environmental Activism*, Berglund (1998, p. 4) explores the role of what she terms 'techno-science' in environmental discourse. Her fieldwork was conducted in a German city of approximately 220,000 people which she dubbed 'Mittelstadt'. Situated near the eastern border of the former German Democratic Republic, Mittelstadt is the site of three different sustained actions by environmentalists that provided Berglund with the central case studies for her research. The first case involved a protest against the continued use of a landfill site containing toxic waste that was leaching into the local water supply. The second protested against the construction of a high speed motorway running through the local vicinity, whereas the third opposed the construction of high-voltage overhead power lines. Her research was inspired by her observation that, within the ongoing debates concerning the environment, the theories and conclusions of the 'natural' sciences are frequently used to establish credibility and authority. Furthermore, in many instances participants with opposing viewpoints, yet using the same data, draw vastly different conclusions. Importantly, Berglund was aware of the fact that, in modern western – or, alternatively, northern or industrial – societies, the language and symbolism of 'techno-science' carries much weight and authority as a direct consequence of the enormous influence still exerted within these societies by Enlightenment thinking (*ibid.*, p. 6). However, science, she argues, is beginning to lose its sheen of invulnerability because, subject to multiple interpretations within the very public field of environmentalism, it becomes disputed terrain in a 'contest between believing and knowing' (*ibid.*, p. 10). This contest about the meaning and veracity of scientific knowledge was crucial to her research as an anthropologist interested in letting the social actors involved in her study speak for, and define themselves, in relation to their lived experience. As she sees it, her insights are gained by conceiving environmentalism as 'a heightened awareness of the negotiability of human relationships' (*ibid.*, p. 7). Science and its discourse, 'techno-science', operate for her within this context as a conduit through which the struggle between believing and knowing is waged.

Although Berglund, in mapping out the field of inquiry, acknowledges the significant contributions of social theorists such as Beck (1992), Giddens (1990, 1991), Bauman (1993) and Melucci (1992), her work addresses the lack of adequate case studies with which to augment and further the theoretical debates underway in the social sciences. Like Milton, Berglund feels that this is legitimately the realm of anthropological investigation given its pre-occupation with cultural interpretations of reality and the comparative nature of its analysis. She argues that this is so even though there is a dualism within the discipline in relation to the treatment of science (Berglund, 1998, p. 12). On the one hand, anthropologists have traditionally placed great emphasis on the way in which human beings interact with and within their environments, but this has been predicated on an ecological determinism which portrayed culture as little more than a reactive coping mechanism. For instance, much of the ecologically based anthropology of the previous era involved the study of exotic cultures that were analysed as complex whole systems engaged in adapting human populations to environmental necessities. Thus, the emphasis placed on the information given by those being studied was often devalued in the face of the theories of modern science. On the other hand, anthropologists have sought to redress this problem in recent decades by taking a much more relativistic stance towards culture and the legitimacy of the different forms of knowledge derived from it. There has been a sustained push within the discipline to write both the subjects of investigation, and the investigators, back into ethnographies with both being seen as social actors in specific contexts.

Berglund's approach to participant observation gives full recognition to her identity as both a researcher and an activist. She declares that the 'many insights I have gained through environmental politics have come through taking up a series of perspectives squarely within the world I describe, even as having access to scholarly analyses distinguishes my experience from that of activists' (*ibid.*, p. 13). Hence, Berglund's knowledge or reflexivity about being an activist and a scholar led her to seek to engage more closely with her research subjects and more insightfully with academic theory. However, more than simply adding case studies to an existing body of theory and empirical findings, Berglund seeks to redress the determinism inherent in the work of some of the more prominent social theorists.

Taking Ingold's criticism of social science's predilection for the creation of categories in which to place social and cultural phenomena (*ibid.*, p. 13), she reserves particularly harsh criticism for Douglas and Wildavsky's (1982) social organisational grid theory in which the form of social organisation present determines the moral order of the day within each society. Interestingly, Milton (1996, p. 97) is also uncomfortable with this deterministic approach on the grounds that it denied the possibility of change on any meaningful scale. For Berglund (1998, p. 179), their work 'seemed like an almost trivial intellectual indulgence around eminently non-trivial issues', and she feels that the placing of themselves within the most morally superior category 'valuing resilience and an open mind' (*ibid.*) was inspired by arrogance rather than any intellectual endeavour. This arrogance, she asserts, is a reoccurring theme within the work of western intellectuals as they consistently fail to see themselves as bounded by culture in the same way that they suppose other people to be (*ibid.*, p. 80). In many previous anthropological works, the focus has been on the exotic 'other' with culture being something experienced by those 'others' but escaped by those who study it. Finally, through her study of the role played by modern western science in environmentalism, Berglund illuminates the ways in which people in modern western societies use different kinds of knowledge, many of them culturally specific, to understand their place in the world. Let us now return to Brosius and his article in Current Anthropology (1999) mentioned at the start of this chapter. I have paid close attention to this article and the comments that it generated as it provides an overview of the engagement by anthropologists in the field of environmentalism, which includes aspects of the past, present and future. It also explores this engagement in such a way as to contextualise the above discussion principally concerning Milton (1993, 1996) and Berglund (1998).

BROSIUS AND ENVIRONMENTAL RESEARCH

One of the most striking things about the anthropological study of environmentalism in recent times is the prominence of discourse as a method of analysis. As we have seen, Milton, Berglund and Brosius have all employed this term and its mode of analysis in their research, but it is Brosius most of all who provides us with a rationale for this strategy. His approach is based 'on the premise that discourse matters and that an environmental discourse can be manifestly constitutive of reality (or rather a multiplicity of realities)' (Brosius, 1999, p. 278). This is an approach that recognises the fact that struggles within the field of environmentalism have been, will be and are being fought through discursive means. Whosoever can dictate the flow of information through discourse has an almost unassailable advantage in controlling the wider debate, and Brosius is well aware of the different agencies and institutions concerned with doing just that for many reasons (*ibid.*). As to how these competing centres of discourse construction may be dealt with by researchers, he contends that:

> Indeed, any attempt to understand the socio-cultural movement aspects of environmentalism must necessarily frame them within a larger set of questions about this

wider discursive domain and examine the complex relationships which exist between historical and contemporary forms of domination, existing or emerging structures/ institutions, the politics of representation, processes of discursive production, and emerging forms of political agency. (*ibid.*, p. 278)

Thus, Brosius perceives the discursive aspects of culture to be the most productive way of understanding environmentalism as a cultural phenomenon. I should note here again that, although discourse theory is useful in the study of environmentalism, it is not the only valid approach. In fact, significant proportions of this thesis are intended to illustrate how a broad approach combining a number of theoretical points of view provides a range of analytical possibilities worthy of further study by anthropologists. However, for the moment, I shall remain within the realms of Brosius' discussion. Brosius feels that anthropologists have become interested in environmentalism, after a long hiatus preceding the decline of ecological anthropology as a prominent field within the discipline, for three main reasons (*ibid.*, p. 279). The first two he does not dwell on. They are, first, the discipline had been caught in the momentum created by other branches of the social sciences such as sociology, human geography, cultural studies and the political sciences and, second, the emergence of environmental groups within sites of fieldwork already under study. The third, a series of overlapping recent theoretical trends, he discusses more fully. He feels that the most noticeable of these is the move by anthropologists to redress essentialisations of indigenous people by various civil rights groups interested in 'proving' their authenticity (*ibid.*).

Given that Brosius has spent much of his academic career studying and working with indigenous people, particularly the peoples of the Sarawak in East Malaysia, this tendency to essentialise both habitat and inhabitant by human rights and environmental organisations must have struck him forcefully and had a profound effect on his own research. Brosius believes that the way in which anthropology has sought to redress the consequences of its late engagement with environmentalism has been to re-engage with the cultural critique of 'otherness' in what Marcus and Fischer (1986, p. 111) have called 'repatriation of anthropology as cultural critique' (cited in Brosius, 1999, p. 279). This 'repatriation', asserts Brosius, was accompanied by, among other things, a renewed interest in the discourse/power/ knowledge interconnections discussed by Foucault (1972, 1980, cited in Brosius, 1999, p. 279); innovative approaches to the study of resistance predicated on a reassessment of humanity's positioning within or outside nature (Brosius, 1999, p. 279); the rise of 'science studies' as a new field of investigation examining 'the bases of scientific knowledge about nature' (*ibid.*); globalisation studies; and finally, an effort to understand the environment as a locus for inequality within the field of political ecology (*ibid.*, p. 280). Brosius positions his own work in the context of a growing number of anthropologists studying environmentalism in relation to 'globalization and the trans-nationality of these movements and discourses' (*ibid.*, p. 280). As Brosius relates, these anthropologists are interested in the intersection of local concerns and global discourse (*ibid.*, p. 281), and the way in which each is brought into the others sphere and becomes legitimated in the quest for information and funding. As he writes, anthropologists are now paying attention to how, within environmental movements, environmental discourses are 'deployed, appropriated, transformed, circulated, and recirculated by variously positioned actors, as well as the ways in which environmental imperatives are framed and deployed with respect to claims about local authenticity, national sovereignty, or global significance' (*ibid.*, p. 281). Indeed, he understood this kind of anthropology to be part of environmental praxis because anthropologists are bringing a critical perspective to environmentalism that can be used to refine the existing body of knowledge already in use by activists.

As part of this critical perspective, Brosius cites the further investigation of the significance of particular topologies, north-south and local-global, within environmentalism. He is particularly concerned that, just as topologies have been created within which to locate the environmental paradigm, so specific categories of inhabitants have been created to inhabit these spaces (*ibid.*, p. 282). He feels that this is problematic when we consider that certain populations may become conceptually bounded by their habitat in a way that inhibits broader analysis through a comparative methodology. The example provided by Brosius is the valorisation of certain groups within the human populations living in the rainforests. The way in which indigenous people have been portrayed in environmental campaigns has led to the widespread popular belief that only they, as 'guardians of biodiversity', 'belong' in the forest while others, such as 'peasants and migrants from urban areas' (*ibid.*, p. 282) do not. Brosius also calls for notions of temporality to be integrated into the study of environmentalism. He makes the point that dynamism is an important aspect of any debate and that environmental discourse has evolved rapidly. As the creation of knowledge concerning the environment and environmentalism becomes more widespread the debates that employ this knowledge become more complex. They are multifaceted, theoretically sophisticated, and are continually being influenced by the most recent developments (*ibid.*, p. 283). This also raises for Brosius the issue of momentum concerning environmentalist actions, and he cites the campaign for saving the Sarawak forest as an example. During the early stages the campaign built up such momentum that those involved believed at times that success was certain but then suffered disappointment when that momentum was lost (*ibid.*). I feel that the notion of momentum in environmental campaigns is a particularly relevant concept when we take into account the political processes through which many environmental organisations have chosen to operate. Here it is important to note that Brosius identifies the deeply temporal nature of environmentalism. I have found notions of temporality to be essential in the descriptions and analysis of my own fieldwork and have attempted, wherever necessary, to incorporate this within my work. One has only to look at the speed of the rise of environmental movements to appreciate the significance of this notion. Indeed, temporality does not only figure in the rise and fall of different environmental movements and campaigns, it also effects their form while in existence. Brosius feels that this is visible in the way in which most environmental debates seemed to progress through an initial emphasis on consciousness raising, typified by the actions of the more radical direct action group. The next phase is marked by the adoption of a more mainstream approach to promote and sustain long-term strategies.

Of particular resonance with my own research is Brosius' call for a deeper analysis of the effects of national political cultures on environmental movements. He notes that anthropologists have generally failed to include the nation-state in a meaningful sense within their ethnographies and puts this down to a disciplinary preference for either, a narrow focus on the locality of fieldwork, or a linkage of local realities to 'the transnational realm' (*ibid.*, p. 285). He notes the identification of national political cultures with their physical surroundings and suggests that notions of national ownership can not be ignored in the study of environmentalism. Indeed, national political cultures affect vast areas of government planning and policy which in turn affect their physical, social and cultural landscapes. He cited Tsing (1993) and Rosaldo (1989) as two leading proponents of this area of study and proposes that anthropologists 'have been so fixed on local social movements, transnational NGOs, and globalization processes that we seem to have forgotten about the need to understand how national political cultures might mediate between these' (Brosius, 1999, p. 285).

In concluding the article, Brosius posits that environmentalism is 'a series of transformative discourses' (*ibid.*, p. 287) in which anthropologists have become legitimately engaged. Given this, he warns, anthropologists must be constantly aware of the effects that their participation might have on the actors they study and acknowledge that these effects may not necessarily be beneficial. He was concerned that anthropologists might become so single-minded in pursuit of their research goals and the advancement of the field of inquiry that they could jeopardise environmental movements, especially third-world social movements also involved in struggles of resistance, by providing their opposition with intricate knowledge of their organisational structures and activities. Brosius calls on his fellow anthropologists to ask themselves 'why' they were studying environmentalism in the first place and to be conscious of the 'politics of representing these [environmental] movements' (*ibid.*, p. 287). Brosius' article inspired a number of comments from fellow anthropologists engaged in the study of environmentalism. These comments span the full range of issues he broaches, of which I have abbreviated or omitted according to my needs, and offer suggestions on future research foci and constructive criticism concerning Brosius' own understanding of the field. The following is not intended to be a full exploration of each of the correspondents' views but, rather, a discussion of the points made in these replies that resonate most with my research goals and material. The issues addressed will be chosen to give the reader a sense of the direction taken by this thesis within the broader field of environmentalism. The relationship between anthropology and environmentalism will be held in mind.

COMMENTS ON BROSIUS

The first of these comments to be addressed concerns the issue of what Bavaskar calls temporality. Baviskar (in Brosius, 1999), in addressing Brosius' comments on the way in which environmental debates are fluid and dynamic over time, warns that an over emphasis on the effects of temporality and dynamism in environmental debates would negate any meaningful analysis drawn from these discussions. He explains this by arguing that meaningful analysis demanded there be definite heuristic boundaries within which to examine data, make assumptions and formulate theory. If the passage of time erodes all certainty, then the analysis of data becomes impossible except in retrospect. Accordingly he wrote 'The heuristic need for stable topologies, reference points, and boundaries cannot be denied. This need is felt not only by members of environmental movements but everyone engaged in meaningful action. Practice demands working assumptions, temporary certitudes, and acts of faith. Where do we anchor practice if our conceptual shores keep shifting'? (Baviskar in Brosius, 1999, p. 288).

This statement, in addition to tying the practice of both environmentalism and anthropology to the necessity of a degree of temporal and conceptual stability, also reminded Brosius that, in that necessity, anthropology is no different than other social sciences. Baviskar praises Brosius' 'pithy review of themes in environmental anthropology' and observes that the 'dilemma of interrogating categories even as one continues to use them is not exclusive to environmental anthropologists but shared with everyone who is sensitive to the political implications of academic practice' (*ibid.*, pp. 288–289). As Brosius does not specifically address these comments by Baviskar in his reply, I will not speculate as to his position vis-à-vis excessive emphasis on temporality, but it does appear to me to be a useful concept if applied thoughtfully. Similarly, Berglund finds much to commend it because of Brosius' discussion of momentum and environmental campaigns. For her the concept presents the possibility of seeing 'patterns in the highs and lows of activism which scholars would be better placed than those at the centre of the political action to document' (Berglund in Brosius, 1999, p. 289). She suggests that, due to the ease with which large bodies of information can now be sent across temporal and spatial divides, the activism inherent within environmental movements has the ability to move at speeds that could outstrip current research methods generally associated with the social sciences. In any case she poses the question as to whether this offers anthropologists an opportunity to make their expertise 'count' in the field (*ibid.*, p. 290). Additionally, she stresses the importance of finding patterns by stating her belief 'that anthropological insight can be extended to searching for systematicity across contexts without totalizing' (*ibid.*). Here Berglund advocates a move towards a theoretical middle ground in which the postmodernist preoccupation with context does not rule out the possibility of commonality across socio-cultural divides with respect to experience and organisation in environmentalism. She states 'There are huge similarities not only in the platforms but in the dilemmas faced by environmentalists' (*ibid.*). This theoretical middle ground would, according to her, involve a new kind of ethnography that was 'only contingently place-bound' (*ibid.*) and could thus operate within a locus that included 'regional, national, and global networks' (*ibid.*). Notably, Berglund makes the statement:

> I would be delighted if more fieldwork-based material on environmentalism as a political commitment were available with the help of which I could begin to consider anthropology (along with disciplines such as cultural geography and media and communication studies) as compelling in its claims about environment-focused anxieties.

The concept of momentum suggests one promising way for discerning connections between unique situations and systemic outcomes. (*ibid.*, p. 290)

Escobar began his comments by identifying Brosius as a poststructuralist who focuses on 'social movements as privileged spaces for the production and contestation of discourses of nature and culture' (Escobar in Brosius, 1999, p. 291). He commends Brosius on this focus as he feels that the study of social movements, as an area, has been insufficiently addressed by anthropologists in the past but holds the key to a future meaningful engagement with environmentalism for the discipline. In his words, social movements 'are the key actors in the production of environmental discursive regimes and should thus be a primary focus of anthropological investigation' (*ibid.*). However, he notes that Brosius, during his discussion of the disjunction between the anthropological approaches of the 1960s and 1970s and today's post-structuralism, ignores the contribution of those anthropologists whose work is not largely informed by notions of discourse or power. To address this oversight, Escobar calls for a 'renewed dialogue' between the various environmental and ecologically based forms of anthropology practiced throughout the discipline. He does not stop there. Importantly he notes that:

This need for dialogue also applies, in a different way, to the majority of Marxist and political-economy approaches that have made only superficial overtures towards the poststructuralist concerns with power, knowledge, and discourse. These themes would also have to be mapped into Brosius' landscape of discursive regimes on the nature/culture interface. (*ibid.*, p. 292)

Escobar also detects two trends emerging from anthropology's engagement with environmentalism. The first is the growing contribution to debates concerning sustainability and conservation made by anthropologists studying NGOs and 'grassroots' movements. The second is the increasing number of anthropologists articulating the discourses of environmentalism and struggling to theorise its social movements as evidence of 'an entire political ecology' (*ibid.*). He feels that these trends could be important factors in generating within anthropology a re-examination of the role of less traditional facets of the discipline, such as applied anthropology and anthropology based around advocacy and public policy formulation. These may well be taken to a more sophisticated theoretical-political basis than previously established (*ibid.*). In his comments, Hornborg finds common ground with Escobar with respect to the exclusion of non-discourse-based anthropological research in Brosius' essay. He points out that, in theorising environmentalism through recourse to discourse models, the socio-economic realities on which many of the debates concerning the environment rest have been neglected. He states that money and the abstractions of economics are cultural vehicles of exploitation and should be quintessential targets for anthropological analysis and critique (cf. Hornborg, 1998, 1999). Such cultural categories intervene in very tangible ways in the 'physical and biotic' environment (Hornborg in Brosius, 1999, p. 294). When seen in the light of the comments made by Berglund and Escobar, this is a telling comment by Hornborg with regard to the future direction of anthropology's engagement with environmentalism. Hvalkof understands Brosius article to be, on a fundamental level, a call for the re-politicisation of anthropology through purposeful contextual ethnography 'that is so much needed in our postmodern era of relative truths' (Hvalkof in Brosius, 1999, p. 295), whereas Stonich calls for theoretical and methodological perspectives in anthropology to include 'ways to integrate the political (broadly conceived to include power and power relations) and the material into our studies' (Stonich in Brosius, 1999, p. 298).

BROSIUS ON BERGLUND

In reply, Brosius says Berglund makes a valuable contribution to the article by leading discussion about momentum in a direction that he had not previously contemplated. This prompts him to write 'I share her concern for 'seeking systematic pattern(s) as a principle for scholarly practice...without totalizing' and, in a time of reactionary anti-environmentalism, see the value in this as a form of engaged scholarly practice' (Brosius, 1999, p. 299). Additionally, he agrees with Escobar and Hornborg's comments concerning his preoccupation with discourse and notes that, although it is a popular approach to environmentalism in anthropology, discourse theory is but one of many valuable theoretical tools at anthropologists' disposal (*ibid.*, p. 300). He also reiterates his concern that anthropologists be aware of their responsibilities to those whose lives their research effects. He refers to the way in which detailed ethnography can easily be used by forces antithetical to environmentalist causes, nevertheless he feels that the discipline has much to offer in the evolution of environmentalism regarding both advocacy and theoretical advancement (*ibid.*, p. 302). As for the benefits to be gained by the discipline through the study of environmentalism, Brosius declares: 'For those of us engaged in anthropological studies of contemporary environmentalism, it is the very diversity of perspectives among and between various kinds of actors and the shifts that we continually see in their perspectives and positioning that makes this such a compelling topic of research' (*ibid.*, p. 303). The earlier discussion provides us with a map upon which we can trace the history of anthropology's engagement with environmentalism and the consequences of this engagement for the discipline as a whole up until the recently. The discipline has undergone several periods of change and seems to be fast approaching another. The functionalism of the 1950s gave rise to the structuralism of the 1960s and early 1970s which, in turn, resulted in a move away from structural analysis in favour of anti-metanarrative perspectives characterised by a deeply contextual focus on narrative. This has been accompanied by a parallel shift from scientific-ecological notions of culture, in which culture often seemed little more than a codification of survival strategies, to an understanding of culture as the medium through which human beings comprehend their physical and social environment. The anthropological study of culture has now been reconstituted as more than what we think and why we think it – it is also the study of how we think. The study of environmentalism has had major, and in some cases unexpected, consequences for anthropology. One of the most significant of these is that the discipline has been compelled to seriously consider globalisation and its effects on the theoretical and methodological fundamentals of anthropology. This has allowed anthropologists in the field to once again recognise the need for larger frameworks within which to place their observations while also seeing the dangers of over contextualisation arising from excessive relativism.

Anthropologists engaged with environmentalism in its many forms seem to be leading the discipline out of its recent trajectory in which extreme cultural relativism and deconstructionism had begun to isolate it from the other social sciences. Anthropology now seems capable of attaining a new relevance within the social sciences based on cross-cultural methodology and knowledge combined with a deepening analytical and reflexive grasp of globalisation. Thus social anthropology can now play its part, along with the other social sciences, in furthering our understanding of modernity and its discontents. Over the past decade, many anthropologists working in the field of environmentalism have used the study of discourse to investigate cultural phenomenon. In this context, environmental discourse contains both global and local aspects and incorporates many other discourses in its articulation. These two developments, the move away from the extremes of cultural relativism and the focus on global discourses, constitute major changes within the discipline but perhaps the greatest change is still to come. There is a clear call, within the ranks of those anthropologists engaged in the study of environmentalism, for a broader canvass upon which to portray their descriptions of those they observe. Milton (1996, p. 164), using Robertson's definition, encourages globalisation to be seen as a phenomenon in which the interconnectedness of political, economic and technological spheres is more relevant than ever before to anthropological analysis. As a series of interacting discourses deeply embedded in globalising processes, environmentalism can not be analysed adequately without recourse to a greater framework than cultural relativism provides. Brosius (1999, p. 278) notes that any future serious analysis of social movements linked to environmentalism needs to take into account the wider picture of history, power relations and political agency to be worthwhile. Berglund takes this a step further when she calls openly for a search for patterns within environmentalism in order to create a space for comparative analysis-this she refers to as systematising without totalising (*ibid.*, p. 289).

Escobar urges the resumption of meaningful dialogue between anthropologists employing Marxist and political economy approaches and researchers utilising discourse theory (*ibid.*, p. 292). Hornburg calls for a greater emphasis to be placed in socio-economics in the future and Hvalkof (*ibid.*, p. 295) and Stonich (*ibid.*, p. 298) both point to the need to repoliticise anthropology. The question before us now, having identified the need for a broadening of the theoretical foundations that underpin the study of environmentalism, is how will this be achieved? One possible answer has been supplied by Berglund (1998, p. 188) who, in discussing environmentalism as manifested in social movements located within her research site, writes:

> Like all social movements, environmentalism in Mittlestadt forges a space in which to discuss expectations, desires and access to decision making. Despite its ostensibly technical character then, environmentalism, like developmentalism (Watts 1995) is not only cultural; it is ideological.

REFERENCES

Bauman, Z. (1993). *Postmodern ethics*. Massachusetts: Blackwell, Oxford and Cambridge.

Beck, U. (1992). *Risk society: Towards a new modernity*. London: Sage.

Berglund, E. (1998). *Knowing nature, knowing science: An ethnography of environmental activism*. Cambridge, UK: White Horse Press.

Brosius, P. J. (1999). Analyses and interventions: Anthropological engagements with environmentalism. *Current Anthropology, 40*(3), 278–309.

Chirot, D., & Hall, T. D. (1982). World-system theory. *Annual Review of Sociology, 8*, 81–106.

Douglas, M., & Wildavsky, A. (1982). *Risk and culture: An essay on the selection of technical and environmental dangers*. Berkeley: University of California Press.

Foucault, M. (1972). *The archaeology of knowledge*. Translated by A. Sheridan Smith. New York: Harper Colophon.

Foucault, M. (1980). *Power/knowledge: Selected interviews and other writings, 1972–77*. Translated by C. Gordon. New York: Pantheon.

Geertz, C. (1973). *The interpretation of cultures*. New York: Basic Books.

Giddens, A. (1990). *The consequences of modernity*. Cambridge: Stanford University Press and Polity Press.

Giddens, A. (1991) *Modernity and self-identity: Self and society in the late modern age*. Cambridge: Polity Press.

Hornborg, A. (1998). Towards an ecological theory of unequal exchange: Articulating world-system theory and ecological economics. *Ecological Economics, 25*, 127–136.

Hornborg, A. (1999). Money and the semiotics of ecosystem dissolution. *Journal of Material Culture, 4*(2), 143–162.

Ingold, T. (1992). Culture and the perception of the environment. In: E. Croll & D. Parkin (Eds), *Bush base: Forest farm: Culture, environment and development*. London: Routledge.

Macdonell, D. (1986). *Theories of discourse: An introduction*. Oxford: Basil Blackwell.

Marcus, G., & Fischer, M. (1986). *Anthropology as cultural critique: An experimental moment in the human sciences*. Chicago: University of Chicago Press.

Melucci, A. (1992). Liberation or meaning? Social movements, culture and democracy. *Development and Change, 23*(3), 43–77.

Milton, K. (Ed.) (1993). *Environmentalism: The view from anthropology*. London: Routledge.

Milton, K. (1996). *Environmentalism and cultural theory: Exploring the role of anthropology in environmental discourse*. New York: Routledge.

Nash, J. (1981). Ethnographic aspects of the world capitalist system. *Annual Review of Anthropology, 10*, 393–429.

O'Riordan, T. (1981). *Environmentalism* (2nd ed.). London: Pion.

Robertson, R. (1992). *Globalization: Social theory and global culture*. London: Sage.

Rosaldo, R. (1989). *Culture and truth: The remaking of social analysis*. Boston: BeaconPress.

Saurin, J. (1993). Global environmental degradation, modernity and environmental knowledge. *Environmental Politics, 2*(4), 46–64.

Torfing, J. (1999). *New theories of discourse: Laclau, mouffe, and zizek*. Oxford, UK: Blackwell Publishing.

Tsing, A. (1993). *In the realm of the diamond queen: Marginality in an out-of-the-way place*. Princeton: Princeton University Press.

Wallerstein, I. (1974). *The modern world-system: Capitalist agriculture and the origins of the European world economy in the sixteenth century*. New York: Academic Press.

Wallerstein, I. (1979). *The capitalist world economy*. Cambridge: Cambridge University Press.

Wallerstein, I. (1980). *The modern world system II: Mercantilism and the consolidation of the European World Economy, 1600–1750*. New York: Academic Press.

CHAPTER 8

ENVIRONMENTAL DISPUTES IN FRANCE

Darren McCauley

INTRODUCTION

French environmental actors have suffered from long-term exclusion from policy-making. However, an increasingly precarious environmental movement continues to diversify its actions. The French political setting is also undergoing processes of decentralisation and Europeanisation. Moreover, French state–group relations are unravelling within a multi-level opportunity system *as well as* a continually transforming domestic environment under the pressure of European Union (EU) processes, polices and institutions. Drawing from empirical evidence on biodiversity conflicts, it is argued that the debate should move from a state-centric to a group/movement-centric approach.

The study of French state–group relations encounters seemingly innumerable conceptual models describing inclusive or exclusive forms of decision-making. This chapter underlines the inadequacies of traditional models while advocating the repositioning of such studies from a state-centric to a group-centric approach in an increasingly multi-level opportunity system. It will concentrate primarily upon French environmentalism as an understudied movement that finds itself between models of exclusion and inclusion. Environmental groups have indeed suffered from long-term exclusion from policy-making. However, the multi-faceted impact

Global Ecological Politics
Advances in Ecopolitics, Volume 5, 151–169
Copyright © 2010 by Emerald Group Publishing Limited
All rights of reproduction in any form reserved
ISSN: 2041-806X/doi:10.1108/S2041-806X(2010)0000005012

of the EU creates opportunities for inclusion in local, national and supranational decision-making. State-centric models provide minimal assistance in bridging this conceptual gap. This chapter presents evidence from the activities of a regional environmental group in the area of biodiversity. It is, therefore, argued that combining notions of social movement theory and Europeanisation can offer a group-centric perspective in a multi-level system of governance.

There have been few works (Dunkerley & Fudge, 2004; Tarrow, 1995; Warleigh, 2001) that have combined some element of social movement theory with Europeanisation. The concept of political opportunity provides a framework for understanding how the EU has changed present opportunity structures at *both* the supranational and the national level. Equally originating from social movement theory, resource mobilisation theory allows us to reposition our analysis firmly on the perspective of groups within an ever-changing multi-level political opportunity structure. It is argued that these approaches should embrace both the appearance of a multi-level political opportunity system *and* the transformative power of EU processes and actors in the domestic context.

This chapter analyses the experiences of a regional environmental group (FRAPNA – *la Fédération Rhône-Alpes de la Nature*) within the EU's cornerstone program on biodiversity, NATURA2000 (N2000). Addressing the need for a European wide programme on the protection of birds and natural habitats, N2000 has resulted in the establishment of regional level 'N2000 contracts' alongside a powerful financial instrument called LIFE-Nature. New forms of regional-level institutionalised group–state interaction (so-called *comités de pilotages*) have emerged as a direct result of the contracts. In accordance with resource mobilisation theory, it is revealed that groups can mobilise at different times, in several ways and on different levels throughout the policy cycle of N2000. From this perspective, it is argued that we should also take account of *group specific* factors (such as strategies and resources) within a European context in the analysis of French environmental groups.

The chapter, first, introduce French environmentalism within processes of Europeanisation. Traditional models of state–group relations (in particular pluralism, corporatism and policy networks) are then presented as inadequately state-centric and basically inapplicable in its purist form to the French case. As a well-established excluded movement in France, environmental actors are habitually restricted to a 'protest model' understanding of state–group relations. In the light of a growing diversification of environmental actors and action, it will therefore outline a group-centric approach that could bridge the gap between traditional models of exclusion and inclusion. This approach will be demonstrated through a case study on FRAPNA in N2000. Last, the chapter discusses the consequences of this approach for French environmentalism in an increasingly Europeanised context.

FRENCH ENVIRONMENTALISM

There are two major groups of interest representation in France. First, the 'occupational' groups (trade unions, business, farmers etc.) are seen to be the most active, with sophisticated networks of power and influence with government. The 'promotional' groups (environment, feminist, consumer groups) have evolved quickly in recent years, but remain much less powerful (Bell, 2002, pp. 129–140). The environmental movement in France is categorised under the first wave of new social movements in the late 1960s. The 'green movement' refers to a large group of actors who promote wide-ranging concerns of ecology, conservationism, environmentalism, even regionalism and pacifism. Like other new social movements, the environmental movement has consisted of large numbers of small groups (Szarka, 2002).

The emergence of this movement led to a period in time referred to by Prendiville (1994, p. 10) as the 'crazy years'. This characterisation originated from a series of protests in 1968 that eventually resulted in the collapse of the De Gaulle government. At its height, violent clashes between student protesters and the police took place in several areas of Paris. 'May 1968' became known as a watershed moment that led to the replacement of conservative morality by more liberal values. The subsequent period (1970s) witnessed an explosion in the number of 'promotional' groups. At the spearhead of this movement, protests against the installation of nuclear plants emerged throughout France as a direct consequence of more pronounced Left-wing social overtones inspired by 'May 1968'.

The anti-nuclear movement mobilised more protests in France than any other country. French environmental groups (FFSPN, FNE, la societe nationale de protection de la nature) sprang up in the 1970s, initially in an attempt to stop the construction of nuclear plants. As part of the less reputable (and less researched) 'promotional groups' (feminists, anti-racism), French environmental associations have, nevertheless, had little success on imposing their will on government. As is common among movements that find their origins in the new social movements of the 1970s, environmental organisations have been largely forced into state relations based on pre-emption, incorporation, contestation and direct action. State–group relations have been impeding to environmental groups even though the EU has changed the political landscape in France (Cole, 1998, pp. 187–189).

These groups have, moreover, adopted different strategies than the new social movements of the 1970s. Contemporary social movements no longer focus on mass protests such as the 1968 student uprising (Appleton, 2000). Festivals, petitions, civil disobedience and other media-directed events are tools that are being increasingly employed by relevant groups. Additionally, associations prefer participatory forms of mass mobilisation. They bring together a large number of groups on an *ad hoc* basis. Contemporary movements tend to operate within a fragmented system of alliances without the domination of one single group. The French environmental movement could, therefore, be referred to as a 'space or aggregation of interest' (Waters, 1998, p. 183). As a result, the support base of each individual group is liable to be more diverse and less predictable.

THE OVERBEARING FRENCH STATE

As an idea that can be traced back as far as Jean-Jacques Rousseau, interest group pressure is seen, historically, as being illegitimate (Cohen-Tanugi, 1991). The traditional role of the French state is classified as *Jacobin*, which stipulates that elected governments are mandated with the will of the people directly, without the mediation of other interests (Hazareesingh, 2002). Effectively banning interest group representation after the French Revolution, le Chapelier Law of 1791 was the legislative expression of the political culture of Jacobinism in France. Although there has been a history of certain privileged government-group relations, the predominance of Jacobin traditions have led to a deep distrust of interest groups (Knapp & Wright, 2001, pp. 300–302). Interest group politics has been traditionally shaped by the mistrust of interest groups, low rates of group representation and the fragmentation of interest groups (Elgie & Griggs, 2000, pp. 147–148).

The traditional Jacobin distaste for interest groups is only partly relevant for contemporary state–group relations. There are three important reasons for this change. First, a transformation has occurred mainly through the loosening of state control of civil society. Second, there has been a modernisation of public administration that has ensured freedoms of access to information. More recently, the multi-faceted influence of the EU has been largely accredited with this change (Hayes, 2002; Szarka, 2002). Although French pressure group activity would appear to be weaker in France than in the north European democracies, the traditional image of France as a state that pays no attention to associational life is becoming increasingly irrelevant to understanding the reality of French politics.

With regard to conceptualising a relevant theoretical model, this mixture of a traditionally exclusive and an increasingly open state has reinforced the 'exceptional' status of French state–group relations. The model of French 'exceptionalism' may be defined as the situation where the policy-making style in France is different from the equivalent style in any other country. As such this model might equally be known as the model of French specificity, or the model of French distinctiveness (Elgie & Griggs, 2000). It is, therefore, contended that the French case cannot be easily fitted into the traditional pluralist or corporatist models of state–group relations.

EXAMINING RESOURCES AND OPPORTUNITIES

There are two distinctive strands of social movement theory that perceive environmental movements as based on either fundamentalism or pragmatism. The former believe that environmental groups are driven by anti-establishment values that lead to unconventional and direct forms of action (Thompson, 2003; Tarrow, 2001). The later conceptualises environmental groups as actively promoting their cause to government through more conventional lobbying techniques (Dreiling & Wolf, 2001; Richards & Heard, 2005). The traditional dichotomy surrounding new social movement research relies on separating those groups who oppose the political order, from those who embark on a pragmatic reform of the political system. This leads to a distinction between 'environmental movement organisations' that focus on inclusive forms (lobbying, participation on committees) of interaction with the state and 'direct action groups' (Barry & Doherty, 2001). However, this dichotomy is overstated and misplaced (as demonstrated by the FRAPNA case study later). Environmental groups undertake, in fact, a series of activities (both fundamental and pragmatic) to achieve multiple objectives (Dalton, Recchia, & Rohrscheider, 2003, p. 747).

The diversification of contemporary environmental groups reinforces the need for a group-centric perspective towards state–group relations in France. Social movement theory provides, above all, a framework for studying group behaviour and interaction with the state (Kriesi, 2004). It has the ability to shed light on how and why groups are mobilised and detail how they interact with the state through two revitalised concepts: resource mobilisation theory and political opportunity structures.

Resource mobilisation theory posits that sufficient levels of resources are needed for initial and sustained mobilisation. Freeman (1979, p. 167) simply asserts that 'the group can do no more than its resources ... permit'. Focusing on resource mobilisation theory prioritises, in effect, the study of 'movement organisations over movements' (Eyerman & Jamison, 1991, p. 21). It concentrates on the rationality of movement groups through emphasising a range of 'resources', which is conceptualised both from a classical (labour and capital) and a modern (experience, information, beliefs and networks) perspective. The principal hypothesis maintains the activity of any group is increased when it acquires more resources. As a result, the groups with more resources can exert more effort for all types of political action. Poorer resourced environmental groups are more likely to perform more confrontational activities (Dalton et al., 2003, p. 756).

Political opportunity can simply be defined as 'institutional incentives and/or constraints upon ... (group) action' (Appleton, 2000, p. 59). Collective action involves, therefore, rational actors who attempt to realise certain objectives within an ever-changing larger political apparatus. In contrast to resource mobilisation theory, this approach does not reveal the direct causes for the mobilisation or actions of an environmental group. Political opportunity offers a framework for understanding the 'cues that signal movement actors toward possible venues for action' (Dreiling & Wolf, 2001, p. 37). These cues from the political environment are, of course, interpreted differently by various organisations. Political opportunity allows us to explore what prompts a movement activist to respond to a changing political environment.

BIODIVERSITY CONFLICTS: N2000 AND LOCAL ENVIRONMENTAL ACTORS

With 40% of Europe's flora located in France, and over 100 endangered species of mammals, politics on the protection of nature have represented a core element of French environmental policy: the *natural history* tradition (Duhautois & Hoff, 2004). In contrast, the protection of nature has traditionally been low on the EU environmental policy agenda. Other areas such as chemicals, air, waste and water quality had a more immediate relationship to building the single market (McCormick, 2001, p. 237).

However, the EU unanimously approved the Habitats Directive (92/43/EEC) in 1992 to complement the Birds Directive (79/409/EEC). As a result, the N2000 network was created with the aim to contribute to the preservation of biodiversity throughout the EU. It is, essentially, a framework for designating zones for special protection (ZSP) in each member state in accordance with the Habitats and Birds Directives. This case study offers empirical evidence from the experiences of FRAPNA, a regional environmental group located in the Rhône-Alpes region.

The Ministry for the Environment organised the first stage (1992–1995) of N2000 by compiling scientific inventories and identifying the most relevant sites for protection. This Inventory of Natural Areas of Ecological, Fauna and Flora (37 ZSPs in total) was then sent to the Commission under the obligations established by N2000. The second stage (1995–1998) focused on a consultation exercise with scientists and environmental associations undertaken by the European Commission to decide upon which ZSPs would make up the N2000 network. The third stage (1998+) involved the preparation, establishment and maintenance of ZSPs by each member state in accordance with N2000 (Rémy & Mougenot, 2002, p. 315). From this perspective, we underline that the first, second and third stages of N2000 are translated in policy terms to phases of *agenda-setting, decision-making* and *policy implementation*, respectively.

The establishment of N2000 in France has been an arduous process. The procedures that were drawn up by the Ministry for the Environment for the implementation of the project were actually suspended for almost two years (1996–98). The Ministry largely neglected the consultation process believing that it would take too long. As a result, it endured significant opposition from various actors from French civil society (Alphandéry & Fortier, 2001; Thompson, 2003). Above all, delays in establishing N2000 originate from a multitude of misunderstandings among different sectors as to the objectives and implications of the project. Each policy area (agriculture, transport, fisheries) adopted individual standpoints as to what implementation of N2000 should actually involve (Julien, 2000, p. 363).

Empowering the 'Local' through Contracts and Finance

Under the requirements of N2000, the Ministry created a network of contracts (*les contrats Natura 2000*), for a renewable period of five years. Focused uniquely at sub-national level, these contracts were established between the local authorities, environmental associations and various other actors. The contract includes monthly meetings of a special committee (*un comité de pilotage*, consisting of the local authorities and other actors including environmental associations), to assess their work in achieving the aims set out in the *document d'objectifs* (set by central government and the N2000 scheme) (Le Grand, 2004a, pp. 48–58). Therefore, instead of the national association, it was the regional/local environmental groups that played a decisive role in the establishment of N2000. From this perspective, N2000 has largely restructured domestic political opportunity structures in favour of regional environmental groups.

LIFE (The Financial Instrument for the Environment) was designed by the European Commission to encourage the development of environmental projects in member states. We are currently in the third cycle (2000–2007) of LIFE offering 957 million euro in total. LIFE–Nature, LIFE–Environment and LIFE–Third countries are the three thematic components of the larger LIFE programme. The specific objective of LIFE–Nature is to contribute to the establishment of the N2000 project. All other environmental issues are funded through LIFE–Environment (in non-accession/candidate countries). Funding is distributed on a project basis within the N2000 framework. Therefore, financial and technical assistance is only offered at the regional/ local level where the specific project is due to be implemented. Therefore, involvement in the preparation and maintenance of a N2000 ZSP is accompanied by significant resources. I examine in particular two local groups that have essentially responded differently at various stages of European policy processes.

As the main non-environmental group in focus, FRC Rhône-Alpes is an offshoot from the larger association – *la Fédération Nationale des Chasseurs* (FNC). It effectively represents the principle opposition from the viewpoint of N2000 supporters. It is the largest and only national association for the representation of hunting interests in France. FNC benefits from a complex network of member organisations at departmental and regional level. There are over one million registered hunters (more than any other member state) accounting for over 2 billion euros. Generally, opposition between environmentalists and the FNC network has become a regular occurrence in France. Environmental activists have periodically sought either delays or postponements in the hunting season for over 20 years (Bronnner, 07 August 2005). In terms of N2000, the regional members of FNC have been involved in protests against the establishment of sites in France. Basically, the introduction of these sites threatens their members' ability to pursue hunting in such areas.

Case study selection on the regional level was based on the largest (in terms of members) and most active (in terms of site involvement) group in the FNC federation of associations. Equipped with 18 full-time personnel, FRC Rhône-Alpes represents over 30,000 registered hunters. It has been active in eight sites of importance without participating in sites of particular importance. In contrast, only two of these sites have managed to establish a contractual agreement and resulting LIFE status for financial assistance.[1] The same criteria were applied to the largest and oldest French environmental umbrella association – *France Nature Environnement* (FNE). FRAPNA, the largest group associated to FNE, controls a regional office of 15 full/part-time employees while representing 7,000 members. The vast majority of smaller groups received finance, information and skills through the larger regional group. Some groups only employ one or two people rendering resource examination more difficult. FRAPNA is involved in the protection of 22 sites of importance,[2] as well as 3 sites of particular/special importance[3] under the N2000 programme (all with established steering committees and contractual agreements).

FRC Rhône-Alpes: Limited Resources, Limited Strategies

The main influence of the N2000 project on FRC centres on issues of information and repertoires of action. FRC has benefited from officially close collaboration with its national umbrella association FNC. With well-established links to the Agricultural Ministry, FNC provides information on the overall N2000 implementation process. Most notably, FNC became a member of the national 'monitoring committee' on hunting and biodiversity issues that has convened annually since 2003. Consequently, FNC and its members are kept afloat with on-going project re-examination on a national basis. Moreover, regulatory information provided by EU institutions and the French Agricultural Ministry has allowed FRC to closely monitor the legislative responsibilities of national government. The N2000 project has equally influenced the action repertoires of FRC. Since 1996, it has participated in a series of protest activities against the establishment of N2000 sites in Rhône-Alpes: public demonstrations, lobbying authorities and campaigns against the 'Eurocrats' (these are explored later in text).

Although FRC has been involved in two established regional steering committees with full LIFE financial assistance, N2000 did not have a substantial effect on this hunting organisation. Financial and organisational capacity, the other two factors in the category 'material resources', have

been modestly influenced through its participation in the N2000 programme.[4] In terms of human resources, there was only little evidence to
suggest such an influence. Although the organisation did not encounter any
directly linked increase/decrease in staff size or skills, there was evidence of
enhanced experience in the organisation of dealing with EU related projects
and legislative procedures[5]. Crucially, there was no evidence of any
ideological change in this regional hunting association. FRC Rhône-Alpes
maintained a highly confrontational approach to the establishment of sites
throughout the N2000 implementation lifespan. It is argued that the
inability of N2000 and its resource potential to change this factor restricted
this association's mobilisation.

In terms of strategies, FRC has also limited its activities to focus uniquely
on 'substantive' approaches (Hayes, 2002). It is argued that the inability
of the Commission (through N2000 and LIFE) to change the FRC's
(in particular 'moral') resources has resulted in fewer forms of mobilisation.
Their 'substantive' strategy was initiated in 1996 when this association
took part in a series of protests against N2000. Opposition was instigated
by French representatives of private forests in Rhône-Alpes (and other
regions) who became increasingly discontented with the methods used by
local government in compiling inventories. Under initial guidelines,
3.5 million hectares (almost a quarter of French forestland) was to be
included in the N2000 inventory. Fearful of the potential disruption to
hunting practices, FNC and its regional associations (including FRC
Rhône-Alpes) joined this movement against the implementation of N2000 in
France. It is evident that hostility to N2000 became embedded into the
actions of FRC ever since.

The first action in this 'substantive' strategy was to secure the opposition
of local mayors and regional state actors. Gérard Collomb, the Left-wing
mayor of the biggest city in Rhône-Alpes (Lyon), has frequently expressed
his concerns over the scope of this biodiversity project. In 2005, a
representative declared that 'Natura 2000 poses the most serious problem
for town and country planning for thirty years'.[6] Protests became the second
activity through which FRC attempted to underline its hostility. Between
2002 and 2005, it participated in four major demonstrations against the sites
for protection. This ideological opposition must be considered within a
broader agricultural response to the 'environmentalisation' of rural land. In
this way, N2000 was a project that forced farming and hunting communities
to acknowledge the damage caused to biodiversity by their actions. More
specifically, ownership of their land was symbolically threatened by this
European project as it became the concern of French authorities.

The environmentalisation of rural land through N2000 engendered a long-standing division between rural and urban life. Crucially, the EU became the main target for imposing this 'environmentalisation' upon hunting rights. This was even apparent in early protests in 1996, when one protester remarked 'if there is a decision to take, it's up to the French Parliament not the European ... you can count on us'[7] (Chassain, 15 April 1996). Later protests focused on slowing down the implementation process. Although FRC was officially involved in eight N2000 sites post 1998, it essentially attempted to hamper the development of any steering committee or contractual agreement. In one example, a representative from FRC commented 'we are not against the protection of endangered species...just the form it takes'.[8] The DIREN underlined that the contractual nature of agreements 'frightened' these local stakeholders with an essentially 'anglo-saxon' tool imposed by 'Eurocrats' (Durand, 15 January 2005).

FRAPNA: Increased Resources, Multiple Strategies

In contrast to the experiences of FRC, involvement in the N2000 project has had a major effect on the resources of FRAPNA. In terms of material resources, this environmental group benefits, first, from regular information exchanges with FNE. It ensures a continual flow of reports and communiqués between the Environment Ministry, its national and regional offices on this issue. As an integral player in implementation, FRAPNA trades its regional expertise in the form of site data with the Ministry (through FNE) for up-to-date information on national and other regional experiences. Second, the LIFE instrument has provided this environmental group with 50 times more financial assistance than FRC. It is estimated that this association has benefited from 224,000 euros in total.[9] In contrast to the hunting association, FRAPNA has dedicated the vast majority of its work to the establishment and maintenance of sites.

This capital has, therefore, been used for maintaining an effective program of protection for the designated ZSPs. In relation to organisational and human resources, this financial aid has also helped to develop its internal capacity through purchasing relevant equipment, as well as partial funding for specialist employees. Similarly, the group has increased (and partially restructured) its labour force for the protection of certain zones.[10] In terms of cultural resources, FRAPNA has been involved in legal proceedings against the state for not upholding certain responsibilities under the programme.[11] More often, the group has attempted to negotiate (more so lobby) regional government actors (in particular the *prefet*) on such areas of tension. In stark contrast with FRC, the contractual framework of N2000 has, more generally, institutionalised greater cooperation between state authorities, FRAPNA and other regional stakeholders. The environmental group welcomed the development of rigorous contractual agreements and financial aid as a tool for promoting environmental values.

In contrast to FRC, this regional group has focused on four forms of mobilisation strategy: 'sensitising, procedural, substantive and *re-sensitising*'. In terms of a 'sensitising' approach, this association was involved alongside LPO Rhône-Alpes (*la Ligue pour la Protection des Oiseaux*) in the first N2000 test sites (six in total between 1995 and 1998). It effectively had an opportunity to input their experiences into the final structure for implementation. Its 'substantive' approach developed during the same period when state and non-state actors were encountering a number of problems. Similar to FRC, FRAPNA became discontented with the methods used by local government in compiling inventories. In contrast to the ideological reservations of FRC, this association desired a more ambitious and inclusive process to setting up N2000 in France. Consequently, it was able to pursue this 'substantive' strategy in the form of several protests in Lyon for expanding the N2000 networks.

This attempt at 'sensitising' and 'substantive' strategies was supplemented with a coherent 'procedural' approach to exploiting contractual and financial incentives. Both protests from FRC and FRAPNA (for different reasons) during the period 1996–1998 had encouraged the establishment of *les contrats Natura 2000*. Since this phase, FRAPNA has placed volunteers in the conservation of all 25 ZSP in the Rhône-Alpes area. It has had one representative on the largest committee – *le comité de pilotage régional de Rhône-Alpes*. It meets biannually to discuss progress on the establishment of all the special interest zones in this region. Moreover, N2000 contracts and smaller steering committees with LIFE financing have been successfully established in 18 sites. Unlike FRC, the group collaborates with other stakeholders in contractual agreements on the preservation of such sites. Each committee must publish documents on their aims and objectives, as well as their annual results. Under article R 214–32 in *Code Rural*, non-compliance with contractual agreements established in these committees can result in the official suspension of financial aid (Truilhe-Marengo, 2005).

Indeed, FRAPNA has benefited from this article as a lever for '*re-sensitising*' the implementation process through directly appealing to the European Commission. Two sites (FR8201653 and FR8201696) were temporarily suspended throughout 2003 due to the committee's inability to agree upon the demarcation of the zones in question. The text of the two Directives (Habitats and Birds) does not include any instructions on management or the appropriate action to be taken. Ultimately, the French government suffers during such a suspension for delayed implementation. The European Commission applied pressure on France for the slow implementation of N2000 on several occasions since 1998 (European Commission, 2002). Moreover, the Commission has twice pushed back and redefined implementation deadlines. Both FR8201653 and FR8201696 were restarted in 2004 with different demarcations to the original implementation outline.[12] FRAPNA (alongside other regional representatives) tried to use this measure to review and reshape ('re-sensitise') the implementation of N2000.

DISCUSSION

The case study on N2000 underlined the value of resource examination to understanding the mobilisation capabilities of civil society actors. This section reveals two important conclusions from the study. First, the European Commission (through N2000 and the LIFE instrument) had a substantial influence on the resource base of FRAPNA. Overall, it significantly changed its material, human, cultural, moral and network categories throughout the project. The second conclusion focuses on the resulting influence of these resources on the *amount and venue* of groups' strategies. FRAPNA was clearly able to pursue a greater number of strategies than its regional counterpart. In addition to sensitising, substantive and procedural strategies, the experiences of this association also revealed that it can *seek* (even if unsuccessful) to have a *re-sensitising* influence on EU institutions and decision-making. From this perspective, increased resources allowed FRAPNA to avoid the regional and national level through directly contacting the European Commission. FRAPNA sought to apply pressure on the French government to reshape specifications on policy implementation. Consequently, the European Commission adapted zone allocation in France, as well as establishing new deadlines. Benefiting from the substantial resources offered through the LIFE–Nature financial instrument, FRAPNA succeeded in 'using' EU-level opportunities for re-shaping the implementation process (Jacquot & Woll, 2003).

This study confirms that environmental groups are adopting different strategies than those associated with the NSM of the 1970s. Contemporary groups no longer focus uniquely on mass protests, such as the 1968 student uprising. In terms of direct action repertoires, petitions, civil disobedience, and other media-directed events are tools that are being increasingly employed by groups. In contrast to more recent observations (Fillieule, 2004), the case study on N2000 revealed that associations are equally involved in mass mobilisation as well as lobbying activities. In the case of FRAPNA, it was involved in direct protests against the government on the establishment of N2000. Within two years, its members played an integral consultative role in local committee meetings that shaped the policies development in France. In this way, movement research fundamentally (Barry & Doherty, 2001; Dreiling & Wolf, 2001; Tarrow, 1995) over-stereotypes groups as fundamentalists or pragmatists.

A group-centric approach (rather than movement) to examine the activities of environmental groups allows the researcher to appreciate intra-group diversity. Moreover, a longitudinal policy-based approach teases out how one actor can alter its strategies over time. This study has underlined the integral explanatory variables of resources and opportunities within this framework (see McCauley, 2007 for an in-depth discussion on the explanatory power of resources in the same policy field). Overall, it is argued that French environmental groups are increasingly defined by a heterogeneous response to cross issue shared values. As underlined throughout, the multi-strategic reaction of such actors is, above all, shaped by fluctuating resource capacity levels. The next section, therefore, re-analyses the approach to exploring the group–state relations in France.

Europeanisation and French Environmentalism

The present case study on FRAPNA partly supports research conducted by Grossman (2004), Rootes (2004), Tarrow (1995) and Warleigh (2001). It clearly emphasised the dominant role of national and local opportunities for the activities of FRAPNA. Nevertheless, this group did use supranational opportunities in the form of the Commission (albeit on a particular issue – i.e. inconsistently). In this way, the case study demonstrates that groups have 'windows of opportunity' throughout a European policy process that they can exploit with 'adequate resources'.

However, we must not limit our understanding of Europeanisation to supranational opportunity structures. This chapter reinforces the point that Europeanisation is, in fact, a two-way process. It is a matter of reciprocity between two moving features (the EU and member states). The EU influences groups as part of a wider series of changes at the national level. Europeanisation has transformed the relations between state and group at the EU, national and regional levels because it modifies national opportunities and threats to each actor. As a result, this process encourages a change in the objectives, resources and behaviour of environmental interest groups (Fairbrass & Jordan, 2002, pp. 139–143). The ability of groups to maximise these supranational structures is, therefore, shaped by the opportunity structures that are available at the national level (Ward & Lowe, 1998, p. 2).

We should, in fact, view Europeanisation as both 'pressure' (as explained above) and 'usage' (Jacquot & Woll, 2003, Radaelli, 2004). By introducing the sociological perspective of 'usage', we provide further understanding of Europeanisation. As demonstrated in the FRAPNA case, the term 'usage' underlines that national actors actively transform opportunities or constraints presented by the introduction of the EU and integration process into concrete political action. This term refers, secondly, to the habitual nature that such a process takes after a period of time (such as the N2000 policy cycle). From this standpoint, European integration can only happen if an actor seizes these national/EU opportunities or constraints. Europeanisation is, therefore, considered to be a non-linear and dynamic process, where actors proactively (as opposed to reactively) seek to maximise their new national and supranational environment.

Models of State Interaction

Commentators continue to struggle with the nature of state–group relations in France. The seemingly exceptional circumstances posed by the French case have led numerous authors to elaborate specific frameworks. Domination-crisis, endemic/open and Marxist models have all been unsuccessful in fully explaining the relationship between the French state and interest groups. Perhaps this failure is best summed up by the 'untidy reality model'. It admits overtly that the best description for such relations would simply be 'complex and untidy'. However, a myriad of authors maintain that this complexity is best understood as variations on both traditional and more recently applied approaches in this area. It is argued here that these attempts have also failed to adequately describe state–group relations in France.

We still find ourselves unsatisfied with both traditional and more recent attempts to understand French state–group relations. This chapter argues that we need to include concepts found in social movement theory to our understanding of state–group interaction. The 'protest model' has traditionally expressed basic notions of social movement theory in the French case. From locating a French inclination for protest to explaining 'le mouvement altermondialiste', the protest model has sought to include largely 'excluded' groups in the analysis of state–group relations. Under the first wave of new social movements, this model has also attempted to include French environmentalism within its analysis. Environmental associations in France have, indeed, experienced little success in dealing with an imposing state. Although this model introduces new perspectives, it cannot adequately explain state–group relations outside notions of exclusion and protest.

This chapter argues for the abandonment of such models in preference for the group-centric perspective employed in the case study. Group–state relations are essentially studied within the context of resources and political opportunity. Europeanisation is firstly perceived as a pressure resulting in the redistribution of power in national politics. From this top-down/downloading perspective, power will be defined as being located within country specific opportunity structures, configuration of actors and interaction context (Kriesi, 2004). In turn, these factors influence the resources available to environmental movement organisations and direct action groups. Second, Europeanisation is a pressure, 'which leads in turn to the active "usage" of political opportunity structures' (Jacquot & Woll, 2003). Essentially, pressure leads to environmental groups exploiting new domestic and/or supranational opportunities and/or new resources.

CONCLUSION

This chapter argues, above all, that we can bridge the gaps in our understanding of French state–group interaction by combining several notions within both social movement theory and Europeanisation. 'Resource mobilisation' depended traditionally on very rationalist perspectives of group resources. A collection of authors (particularly Hayes, 2002) has allowed us to re-apply political opportunity to state–group relations in France. Moreover, the multifaceted influence of the EU has worryingly been under-developed in this area. It is argued that we must move beyond perceiving the EU as simply an opportunity structure. Europeanisation is a distinct two-way process between two ever-changing entities.

Traditionally embedded between state-centric models of inclusion and exclusion, the study of French environmentalism demands a group-centric approach. Through combining concepts within social movement theory and Europeanisation, we can arrive at a more comprehensive understanding of non-state mobilisation and its relationship with the French state.

NOTES

1. These two sites were included under the financial arrangements of LIFE03 NAT/F/000100 and LIFE05 NAT/F/000135.
2. Further details on these projects can be acquired from the Environmental Ministry.
3. The three projects are FR8210017 'Hauts Plateaux du Vercors', FR8210058 'Iles du Haut Rhône' and FR9310036 'Les Ecrins'.
4. FRC received a total of 4,700 euros from involvement in these two LIFE designated sites. In terms of organisational resources, there is no evidence of any specialist N2000 posts or equipment in contrast to the FRAPNA experience.
5. This conclusion resulted from a series of interviews with staff at FRC. A growing familiarity with EU information sources increased understanding with some representatives.
6. During an interview (10 September 2005) with a representative from *la Mairie*: 'Natura 2000 pose le plus grave problème d'aménagement des territoires depuis trente ans'.
7. «S'ily a une décision à prendre, c'est au parlement français de le faire, pas au parlement européen. Vous pouvez compter sur nous».
8. «Sur le fond, on ne peut pas être contre la protection des espèces menacées. Sur la forme, c'est autre chose».
9. We have not been able to ascertain precise figures for LIFE financing in the case of FRAPNA. This conclusion is based on interviews with representatives and figures from LIFE-Nature on a project basis.
10. In particular, FRAPNA create a N2000 dedicated team (initially five strong and primarily scientists) in 1999.
11. Its involvement in a high profile case against France in 2001 was its only notable success. A coalition of environmental actors (lead by LPO) succeeded in bringing legal proceeding against the state for its 'under-ambitious' approach to site designation and implementation (Cour de Justice Européenne, 2003).
12. FRAPNA representatives presented these two examples as victories over agricultural associations, as the new demarcations were very close to those proposed by FRAPNA.

REFERENCES

Alphandéry, P., & Fortier, A. (2001). Can a territorial policy be based on science alone? The system for creating the Natura 2000 network in France. *Sociologia Ruralis, 41*(3), 311–328.

Appleton, A. (2000). The new social movement phenomenon: Placing France in comparative perspective. In: R. Elgie (Ed.), *The changing French political system* (pp. 57–75). London: Frank Cass.

Barry, J., & Doherty, B. (2001). The greens and social policy: Movements, politics and practice? *Social Policy and Administration, 35*(5), 587–607.

Bell, D. S. (2002). *French politics today.* Manchester: Manchester University Press.

Cohen-Tanugi, L. (1991). Légitimité et Réglementation: Les Réticences Françaises. *Problèmes Politiques et Sociaux, 662*, 54–57.

Cole, A. (1998). *French politics and society.* Prentice Hall: Simon and Schuster International Group.

Dalton, R., Recchia, S., & Rohrscheider, R. (2003). The environmental movement and the modes of political action. *Comparative Political Studies, 36*(7), 743–771.

Dreiling, M., & Wolf, B. (2001). Environmental movement organizations and political strategy. *Organization & Environment, 14*(1), 34–57.

Duhautois, L., & Hoff, M. (2004). *La flore de France, enjeu majeur de la politique de conservation de la nature.* Orléan Cedex 1: Institut Français de l'Environnement (IFEN).

Dunkerley, D., & Fudge, S. (2004). The role of civil society in European integration: A framework for analysis. *European Societies, 6*(2), 237–254.

Elgie, R., & Griggs, S. (2000). *French politics: Debates and controversies.* London: Routledge.

European Commission. (2002). *XXth report on monitoring the application of community law.* Luxembourg: Information Office.

Eyerman, R., & Jamison, A. (1991). *Social movements: A cognitive approach.* Cambridge: Polity Press.

Fairbrass, J., & Jordan, A. (2002). The Europeanization of interest representation: The case of United Kingdom environment policy. In: A. Warleigh & J. Fairbrass (Eds), *Influence and interests in the European Union: The new politics of persuasion and advocacy* (pp. 138–157). London: Europa.

Fillieule, O. (2004). *Local environmental politics in France: The case of the Louron Valley 1984–1996.* Grenoble: CNRS/CRESAL.

Freeman, J. (1979). Resource mobilization and strategy: A model for analyzing social movement organization actions. In: M. Zald & J. McCarthy (Eds), *The dynamics of social movements: Resource mobilization, social control, and tactics* (pp. 167–190). Cambridge: Winthrop Publishers.

Grossman, E. (2004). Bringing politics back in: Rethinking the role of economic interest groups in European integration. *Journal of European Public Policy, 11*(4), 637–654.

Hayes, G. (2002). *Environmental protest and the state in France.* Basingstoke: Palgrave.

Hazareesingh, S. (2002). *The Jacobin legacy in modern France.* Oxford: Oxford University Press.

Jacquot, S., & Woll, C. (2003). Usage of European integration – Europeanisation from a sociological perspective. EIoP (European Integration online Papers). Available at http://eiop.or.at/eiop/texte/2003-012a.htm

Julien, B. (2000). Voicing interests and concerns – NATURA 2000: An ecological network in conflict with people. *Forest Policy and Economics, 1*(3), 357–366.

Knapp, A., & Wright, V. (2001). *The government and politics of France.* London: Routledge.

Kriesi, H. (2004). Political context and opportunity. In: D. Snow, S. Soule & H. Kriesi (Eds), *The Blackwell companion to social movements* (pp. 67–90). Oxford: Blackwell Publishing.

Le Grand, J. (2004). *Pour une mise en valeur concertée du territoire Natura 2000* (Vol. 1). Paris: Ministère de l'écologie et du développement durable.

McCauley, D. (2007). Environmental mobilisation and resource-opportunity usage: An examination of WWF-France, FNE and LPO. *French Politics, 5*(4), 333–353.

McCormick, J. (2001). *Environmental policy in the European Union.* London: Palgrave.

Prendiville, B. (1994). *Environmental politics in France.* Oxford University Press: Oxford.

Radaelli, C. (2004). Europeanisation: Solution or problem? European Integration online papers (EIOP). Available at http://eiop.or.at/eiop/texte/2004-016a.htm

Rémy, E., & Mougenot, C. (2002). Inventories and maps: Cognitive ways of framing the nature policies in Europe. *Journal of Environmental Policy and Planning, 4,* 313–322.

Richards, J., & Heard, J. (2005). European environmental NGOs: Issues, resources and strategies in marine campaigns. *Environmental Politics, 14*(1), 23–41.

Rootes, C. (2004). Is there a European environmental movement? In: J. Barry, B. Baxter & R. Dunphy (Eds), *Europe, globalization and sustainable development* (pp. 32–56). London: Routledge.

Szarka, J. (2002). *The shaping of environmental policy in France.* New York: Berghahn.

Tarrow, S. (1995). The Europeanisation of conflict: Reflections from a social movement perspective. *West European Politics, 18*(2), 223–251.

Tarrow, S. (2001). Contentious politics in a composite polity. In: D. Imig & S. Tarrow (Eds), *Contentious Europeans: Protest and politics in an emerging polity* (pp. 233–251). London: Rowman & Littlefield.

Thompson, D. (2003). Protest politics and violence in the French countryside in the 1990s: An expression of Euroscepticism. *Modern and Contemporary France, 11*(3), 293–306.

Truilhe-Marengo, E. (2005). Contractualisation, reglementation: quelle articulation entre les outils de gestion des sites Natura 2000. *Revue Juridique de l'Environnement, 5*(2), 131–146.

Ward, S., & Lowe, P. (1998). National environmental groups and Europeanisation: The British lobby and the attraction of Europe. *Working Papers in Contemporary History and Politics, 21,* 1–46.

Warleigh, A. (2001). 'Europeanizing' civil society: NGOs as agents of political socialization. *Journal of Common Market Studies, 39*(4), 619–639.

Waters, S. (1998). New social movement politics in France: The rise of civic forms of mobilisation. *West European Politics, 21*(3), 170–186.

CHAPTER 9

ECOTOURISM AND SUSTAINABILITY IN THE TOURISM SECTOR

James Hanrahan

Is scath a cheile a mharienn na daoine.

It is in the shelter of one another that people do live. (Anon.)

INTRODUCTION

Sustainable development may best be achieved by enhancing the commitment of local communities. Stewart and Hams (1991) argue that the requirements of sustainable development cannot merely be imposed but that active participation by local communities is needed. However, the terms 'community', 'host community' and 'participation' can be interpreted in a myriad of ways. Before entering a full discussion of host community participation in tourism planning, it is first necessary to explore the various potential interpretations of these terms and to define their meaning and function. This chapter therefore clarifies some of the issues surrounding the terms community, host, host community and participation. The major typologies and available models in relation to host communities' participation in sustainable planning for tourism are also reviewed.

Global Ecological Politics
Advances in Ecopolitics, Volume 5, 171–220
Copyright © 2010 by Emerald Group Publishing Limited
All rights of reproduction in any form reserved
ISSN: 2041-806X/doi:10.1108/S2041-806X(2010)0000005013

COMMUNITY PROBLEMATIC

According to the tenets of Agenda 21, sustainable development will only be achieved through planned democratic, cooperative means, including community involvement in decisions about the environment and development. This concept is not new and increasingly many consultants, policy writers and academic commentators continue to advocate community involvement in tourism planning (Young, 1973; Bosselman, 1979; Krippendorf, 1982; D'Amore, 1983; Murphy, 1985; Gunn, 1988; Keogh, 1990; McIntosh & Goeldner, 1990; Inskeep, 1991; Getz & Jamal, 1994; Bramwell & Sharman, 1999; Oppermann & Weaver, 2000; Mason, 2003; Reisinger & Turner, 2003; Mason, 2003; Boyd & Singh, 2003; Murphy & Murphy, 2004). The associated implementation of sustainable tourism is reliant on a number of key factors, one of which is host community participation. This was reinforced with 6 out of the 12 aims for sustainable tourism focused on community, with aim 6 dedicated to local control:

> To engage and empower local communities in planning and decision making about the management and future development of tourism in their area, in consultation with other stakeholders. (UNWTO, 2005, p. 9)

This requirement is specifically supported within the 'Action for More Sustainable European Tourism' (European Commission Enterprise and Industry, 2007, p. 5) and in the mandate of Local Agenda 21(LA 21). This requires local government to make community involvement central in the implementation of strategic development initiatives and programmes. Agenda 21 requires

> every local authority to consult its citizens on local concerns, priorities and actions regarding the environment, development and other (e.g. social) issues, to encourage local consideration of global issues, and to encourage and foster community involvement. (Jackson & Morpeth, 1999, p. 3)

In order to analyse host communities' participation in sustainable tourism planning, it is necessary first to explore definitions of community and second to discuss the relationship communities may have with tourism.

The term host community is problematic as it assumes the existence of community. In fact the term community has long been contested within the tourism literature. Despite its ambiguity, the concept continues to retain an intuitive appeal. According to Delanty (2003), current theory highlights how social and political scientists, historians and philosophers have been divided on their use of the term community, leading many to question its usefulness.

But virtually every term in social science is contested, and if we reject the word community, we will have to replace it with another term. This problem of defining the term is further accelerated by the current growth and expansion of the cyber or virtual community. Indeed there is increased discussion on the virtual community in the wider literature (Castells, 2001; Delanty, 2003; Shields, 1996). Theory suggests the emergence and now development of technologically mediated communities where the cyber or virtual communities are bringing about new kinds of social groups that are polymorphous, highly personalised and often expressive. They however can also take more traditional forms, reconstituting families and rural areas and even political movements (Delanty, 2003). The emergence of electronic-planning (e-planning) for tourism in the European Union certainly recognises the growth of this element of community. It is therefore essential that this research clearly outlines the context in which the term community will be used in order to assess sustainable tourism planning. A rather simplistic approach to community was taken by Jamal and Getz (1995) when they examined collaboration in tourism planning. They state the term community refers to 'a body of people living in the same locality'. However, others (Porteous, 1989; Joppe, 1996; Sproule & Suhandi, 1998; Mayo, 2000; Delanty, 2003) have argued the term cannot solely be defined in geographic terms, and that its definition is therefore much more complicated. For instance, Delanty argues:

> Contemporary community is essentially a communication community based on new kinds of belonging. No longer bound by place, we are able to belong to multiple communities based on religion, nationalism, ethnicity, lifestyles and gender. (2003, p. 194)

This understanding reinforces the argument that communities can comprise specific groups from different geographical areas, for example, tenants and landowners, farmers and organic farmers, bed-and-breakfast owners, hotel owners, planners, politicians and even new and old residents. Different interest groups within the community, according to many tourism scholars (Sproule & Suhandi, 1998; Murphy, 1999; Gunn, 2002; Mowforth & Munt, 2003; Mason, 2003; Inskeep, 1991), are likely to be affected variably by change associated with tourism. How these groups then respond to change is influenced by kinship, religion, politics and the strong bonds that have developed between community members over generations. What must also be highlighted is, depending on the particular issue, the community may be united or divided in thought and action (UNFAO, 1990).

The current debate on community argues that 'community' does not simply exist but may also emerge periodically to represent opposition or resistance to some extent (Dalton & Dalton, 1975; Anderson, 1983; O'Carroll, 1985;

Porteous, 1989; Delanty, 2003; Murphy & Murphy, 2004). Thus, community can also represent the mobilisation of interest groups seeking to achieve some predefined goal. Delanty (2003) states that for sociologists, community has traditionally designated a particular form of social organisation based on small groups, such as neighbourhoods, small towns or a spatially bounded locality. Anthropologists have applied it to culturally defined groups. In other usages, community refers to a political community, where the emphasis is on citizenship, self-government, civil society and collective identity. Philosophical and historical studies have focused more on the idea of community as ideology or utopia. What must be understood is these different usages of the term are unavoidable and have reflected the changing society we live in and the forces that act upon it.

Therefore, it is evident that although communities can have much in common, they are still a very complex phenomenon that cannot be conceptualised simply in geographic terms. Therefore, the complexity and issues of the term community have further ramifications for planners, as pointed out by Jackson and Morpeth (1999, p. 6):

> Review of even some of the notions involved suggest that without some recognition of the detail and issues, many of the otherwise well conceived community schemes associated with sustainable development initiatives will be doomed to failure, or will result in tokenism in terms of embracing the level and potential of community involvement envisaged by Agenda 21.

This chapter is primarily concerned with analysing the level of host community participation in sustainable tourism planning at the local authority level in Ireland and it is not intended to be a theoretical discussion on the existence of community. However, the problematic of defining a community and its implication in relation to community involvement in planning is recognised (Gunn, 2002; Cohen, 1988; Sproule & Suhandi, 1998; Keogh, 1990; McIntosh & Goeldner, 1990; Inskeep, 1991; Getz & Jamal, 1994; Bramwell & Sharman, 1999; Jackson & Morpeth, 1999; Murphy, 1999; Gunn, 2002; Mowforth & Munt, 2003; Mason, 2003; Delanty, 2003; Murphy & Murphy, 2004). Early into this field was Hillery (1955) with his survey of 94 different definitions of the term and his conclusion that the only element they all appeared to have in common was a conviction that community in some way dealt with people. Cohen (1985) argued in his book 'The Symbolic Structure of Community' that community is to be understood less as a social practice than as a symbolic structure. This argument seems to be reflected in Anderson's (1983) work on 'Imagined Communities'.

This inevitably led to a view of community as shaped by what separates people rather than by what they have in common. Furthermore, O'Carroll (1985) suggested that 'community' can be conceptually coherent if we distinguish clearly between the 'communal' and the 'local', and restrict 'community' purely to that meaning for which Bell and Newby (1976) proffer the term 'communion'. Thus, 'community' would then refer only to a type of effectual relationship between individuals, with no preconceptions about the basis on which this might rest. Tovey (1984, p. 152) strongly contradicts this argument, pointing out that community would rapidly become a superfluous and uninteresting concept. These different uses of the term are unavoidable. However, Delanty (2003) argues that a closer look reveals that the term community does in fact designate both as an idea about belonging and a particular social phenomenon, such as expression of longing for community, the search for meaning and solidarity, and collective identities.

It must be argued at this stage that it seems evident that while the problems associated with defining community in tourism have been more than highlighted, little or insufficient attention has been given by tourism academics to the detailed definition of the term 'community' in terms of tourism planning, and more detailed analysis is needed from the academic community. Furthermore, it must be stated that this research is primarily concerned with what may be apparently happening under the label of 'community' in relation to tourism planning in Ireland, if anything. To facilitate this analysis and to assist the more complicated definition of 'host community', the following definition of community will be used in this chapter:

> 'Community' is self-defining in that it is based on a sense of shared purpose and common goals. It may be geographical in nature or a community of interest, built on heritage and cultural values shared among community members. (Joppe, 1996, p. 475)

With this definition in mind, it allows us to move from the problematic geographic definitions of community and embrace the notion of e-communities/ virtual communities, or as Delanty (2003) prefers, communication communities, while accepting communities are ultimately metaphysical systems that tend to outweigh even their physical and anthropological constructs. The understanding that communities are symbolic constructs is perhaps rudimentary with respect to any attempt to launch tourism in various social settings (Boyd & Singh, 2003, p. 30). It is however necessary for the purpose of this chapter to understand that 'community' needs to be discussed in relation to the relatively modern term of host community that will be discussed and clarified here in relation to participation in sustainable tourism planning.

Host Community

Again it appears through an analysis of the literature that in relation to tourism planning there are insufficient detailed comprehensive definitions of the term 'host'. Even the most prominent definitions seem weak and vague in terms of allowing consistent empirical analysis. One of the few definitions found in literature is given below:

> The host is a national of the visited country who is employed in the tourism industry and provides a service to tourists such as hotelier, front office employee, waiter, shop assistant, custom official, tour guide, tour manager, taxi and bus driver. (Reisinger & Turner, 2003, p. 34)

This definition is clearly problematic, as it does not include the unintentional host who may not be working in the tourism industry. The tourists may simply unintentionally compete for parking with a resident with whom they have little interaction, or meet a community member walking on the beach or in the local pub who may in fact act as a host to the tourists. According to Medlick (2003, p. 86) these residents of tourism destinations are also considered as part of the host community.

The reason for the lack of definitions may lie in the growth of tourism research that has witnessed an expansion of terminology associated with tourism (Gunn, 1988; Keogh, 1990; McIntosh & Goeldner, 1990; Getz & Jamal, 1994; Bramwell & Sharman, 1999; Oppermann & Weaver, 2000). One such term is host community, which may be somewhat misleading as it implies that there are guests to complement the supposed host. Mason (2003) argues that tourists are not always welcome and a more appropriate term could be:

- Local community,
- Resident community or
- Destination community.

However, as the term host community has been broadly accepted by tourism academics and is commonly in use in the tourism literature, this research will employ the term host community. Other factors that seem to complicate matters is that the host community can in fact act as an attraction or tourism product for tourists. The cultural manifestations of the community, including dance, music, temples, craft and festivals, build up important attractions for the tourist (Murphy, 1985; Gunn, 1988; Keogh, 1990; McIntosh & Goeldner, 1990; Inskeep, 1991; Getz & Jamal, 1994; Bramwell & Sharman, 1999; Oppermann & Weaver, 2000; Boyd & Singh,

2003; Mason, 2003). Various forms of contact between host and tourist bring a myriad of benefits but also in some cases conflict. These need to be understood if planners are to actively engage the host community in sustainable tourism planning.

Forms of Tourist–Host Contact

Tourist–host contact can take many forms, it may merely consist of a friendly greeting on the street or business transaction in a café or at a tourist attraction. de Kadt (1979) has identified three major contact situations between tourists and hosts:

- When tourists purchase goods and services from residents,
- When tourists and residents find themselves side by side at an attraction and
- When the two parties come face to face during the process of information exchange.

The contact between host and tourist can have both positive and negative outcomes: it may result in mutual appreciation, acceptance, respect, tolerance and attraction (Dann, 1978; Bochner, 1982; Murphy, 1985; Reisinger & Turner, 2003); develop positive attitudes (Mathieson & Wall, 1982); reduce ethnic prejudices, stereotypes and racial tension (Cohen, 1971) and generally improve the social interactions between individuals from different cultures. This interaction may also lead to cultural education, enrichment and pride (Li & Yu, 1974; UNESCO, 1976).

However, the same tourist–host contact may also develop negative perceptions, attitudes, stereotypes, prejudices and increase tension, hostility, suspicion and in some cases, violent attacks (Bochner, 1982; Mathieson & Wall, 1982). Differences in national origin, cultural values and cultural gaps generate clashes of values, conflict and disharmonies (Peck & Lepie, 1977; de Kadt, 1979; Boissevain, 1979; Cooke, 1982; Mathieson & Wall, 1982; Choy, 1984; Hall, 1984; Murphy, 1984; Reisinger & Turner, 2003). It may be possible also to have division among the community in relation to tourism with some individuals or groups being against tourism (Mathieson & Wall, 1982; Gunn, 2002; Mowforth & Munt, 2003) and other members becoming advocates for tourism (Inskeep, 1991; Mason, 2003; Page & Dowling, 2002), while other members of the host community may not be concerned at all (Keogh, 1990; McIntosh & Goeldner, 1990). With this in mind, it is necessary to discuss the make up of the host community.

Host Community as a Heterogeneous Group

When discussing the term host community, the current literature suggests that it is wrong to assume that host community is a homogenous entity. In fact it is just as heterogeneous as the tourists (Doxey, 1975; Knopp, 1980; Murphy, 1985; Long & Richardson, 1989; Lankford, 1994; Cooke, 2000; Mason, 2003; Boyd & Singh, 2003). A host community can be made up of indigenous first nation peoples, long-term colonial residents and recent domestic and new migrants. This is then coupled with the obvious demographic segmentation of age, gender and lifecycle. Furthermore, within the host community there will be various groups made up of varying value positions. For example, within a rural community you may have a gun club and a local bird-watching group. According to some scholars (Reisinger & Turner, 2003; Mason, 2003; Murphy & Murphy, 2004), the host community is likely to have individuals and groups with several different value positions, political persuasions and attitudes to sociocultural phenomena, including tourism.

A spatial definition of host community seems sensible as it allows the people in a specific geographic area to be discussed within the context of the tourist–host relationship. However, as suggested earlier, this is very simplistic and may possess certain obvious problems as some communities extend past geographic boundaries. The same issue arises when attempting to define community by the values and behaviour it shares. According to Mason (2003), this approach is problematic as many geographic settlements are made up of majority and minority groups in any one community. Hence, geographic settlements include many tourist destinations; exhibit variations of community in terms of ethnic background, length of residency, age of residents and income. Swarbrooke (1999, p. 125) divides host communities in terms of:

- Elites and the rest of the population;
- Indigenous residents and immigrants;
- Those involved in tourism and those not involved;
- Property owners and property renters;
- Younger people and older people;
- Employers, employees and self employed;
- Those with private cars and those relying on public transport;
- Affluent and less well off residents; and
- Majority communities and minority communities.

Clearly these deviations highlight the heterogeneous nature of the host community. To ensure effective participation from the host community in tourism planning it is necessary for planners to understand and embrace the heterogeneous nature of community (Murphy, 1985; Mason, 2003). With these divisions in mind it is necessary to look deeper into the purpose and function of community. Murphy and Murphy (2004) suggest in their review of community definitions that community has three general dimensions: social functions, spatial area and external recognition. The 'social function' has been described by Murphy and Murphy as people working together to create a place of their own, such as a neighbourhood. These social functions have been described as follows:

> Interest in community is based on the practical grounds that people increasingly are coming together to identify their needs and through cooperative actions improve their social and physical environment. (Dalton & Dalton, 1975, p. 13)

This social cohesion can take on a community development approach,

> which encourages citizen participation, with or without government assistance, in efforts to improve the economic, social and cultural conditions of the locality, with emphasis on self-help. (Dalton & Dalton, 1975, p. 1)

This social function dimension of community has a strong link with the role of community in sustainable tourism planning. A sociological definition of community highlighted by Murphy and Murphy (2004) as being particularly relevant to community tourism is:

> An aggregation of people competing for space. The shape of the community, as well as its activities are characterised by differential use of space and by various processes according to which one type of people and/ or type of social function succeeds another in the ebb and flow of structural change in a completive situation. (Warren, 1977, p. 53)

This definition recognises the ecological principles that conceptualise change as an outcome of competition that is highlighted in Murphy's (1984) ecological model of tourism planning, where he recognises that residents have to compete with tourists for basic community resources such as space (parking, restaurants) and facilities (public transport, housing). This does not exist in isolation however as all too often there are opposing interest groups that also fulfil the social function of community.

The 'spatial function' of community does not generally exist in isolation of the social function or 'external recognition function' of community. Small coastal villages dependent on tourism are often obvious to planners. In larger more urban settings, planners generally attempt to identify neighbourhoods in a manner that retains the social characteristics and dynamic of a community (Gunn, 1988; Inskeep, 1991; Murphy & Murphy, 2004). However, the task of describing and locating a community on a map can prove to be a more difficult process. More often the problems emerge not in determining where the core of the spatial community is but where does it end and another begin. Interestingly, on a spatial level, community seems to react if its territory or comfort zone is threatened. This is encapsulated by the term 'limited liability' which is given to the neighbourhood level because participation in the community is a voluntary choice. Most people of the area will participate in organisations and political interest groups but some will not be activated unless their particular street or territory is threatened.

The common terms used to describe such community groups that have primarily developed to stop a particular development they find undesirable are 'NIMBY' (Not In My Back Yard) and 'NOTE' (Not Over There Either). Such spatial functions of community are not uncommon in relation to tourism development. It is paramount then that such spatial functions of community are recognised by the tourism industry and associated planners. A third dimension of community is external recognition, as communities generally need some form of recognition externally by society. Although a group can band together and create a strong sense of belonging, even with an internally recognised spatial context, it is of limited utility unless these two dimensions have been recognised and acknowledged by some external agency (Murphy & Murphy, 2004). The media quite often provides external recognition for a community; however, it is also important to realise that this can also be achieved by open and inclusive planning processes.

Host communities are heterogeneous and the vested interests of these groups may be varied and complex and have various dimensions: social functions, spatial area and external recognition. It must also be recognised that host communities are not just passive recipients of tourism. The residents of tourist destinations may also have a significant stakeholder's role in the tourism industry. They may be actively involved in the provision for tourism, for example, ghillies, musicians, bed-and-breakfast owners. As the involvement of the host community has gained more momentum in the tourism planning debate, the involvement and inclusion of the term 'stakeholders' has emerged, and this needs some attention. Although the host community is an important component of stakeholders in tourism planning, it is also noted that not all stakeholders are part of the host community. Stakeholders can be defined as any person, group or organisation that is affected by the cause or consequence of an issue. According to Bryson and Crosby (1992, p. 65), these include all individuals, groups, or organisations directly influenced by the actions others take in relation to tourism in the community. The citizens living in a community with tourism will often find they have multiple roles and views regarding the industry. Murphy and Murphy (2004) suggest that in many communities residents with no apparent link to the industry could in effect be indirect stakeholders, since so many of their local governments invest in tourism-related services such as piers, parks and parades.

It is seen as increasingly important for tourism planning in destinations to involve the multiple stakeholders affected by tourism, including environmental groups, business interests, public authorities and community groups (Williams, 1996; Bramwell & Lane, 2000; Murphy & Murphy, 2004). The theory suggests, though it is often difficult, costly and time-consuming, to involve a range of stakeholders in the tourism planning process; this involvement may have enormous benefits for sustainability. In particular, participation by multiple stakeholders with varying interests and sometimes conflicting perspectives might encourage more consideration for the associated social, cultural, environmental, economic and political issues affecting sustainable development (Bramwell & Lane, 1999; De Araujo & Bramwell, 2000; Mason, 2003; Murphy & Murphy, 2004). Furthermore, Bonilla (1997) and Timothy (1998) argue that participation in tourism planning by many stakeholders can help promote sustainable development by increasing respect for the environment, harmony and equality.

COMMUNITY PARTICIPATION IN TOURISM

One of the criteria essential to the conditions of sustainable tourism planning is participation of the host community. Tourism literature has well documented the evolution and ground swell of opinions that communities should be actively involved in planning for tourism (Gunn, 1972; Doxey, 1975; Knopp, 1980; Murphy, 1985; Long & Richardson, 1989; Lankford, 1994; Cooke, 2000; Mason, 2003; Reisinger & Turner, 2003; Murphy & Murphy, 2004). One of the first texts on tourism planning was produced by Gunn who advocated the use of forums to ensure public participation:

> By means of forums with community leaders and constituencies, designers can foster open discussion of the desired goals of tourism development. (1972, p. 66)

However, it is important to realise communities also provide a basic motive for tourists to travel, to experience the way of life, products and festivals of different communities. In the early 1980s Murphy argued that if tourism makes use of a community's resources then the community should be a key player in the process of planning. Furthermore, Murphy (1985, p. 17) argued that

> As tourism relies upon the involvement of local people, as part of the tourism product, then if the industry is to be self-sustaining, it should involve the community in decision making.

The potential benefits of host community involvement in tourism planning are substantial. It gives planners an improved understanding of the relevant impacts of tourism within the community (Doxey, 1975; Haywood, 1988; Murphy, 1985; Mason, 2003). In his paper 'Responsible and responsive tourism planning in the community' Haywood argues:

> As a democratic and egalitarian movement, and as a fundamental instrument of constructive social and political change, public participation has the potential for providing new 'social bargaining tables' that can turn conflicting views into truly integrated awareness of wider implications of debated issues. (1988, p. 108)

The argument that the quality of community life can be enhanced by orientating tourism planning towards resolving probable conflicts, mitigating negative impact and moving towards desirable alternatives while allowing planners to integrate tourism and gain acceptance by the majority of the community through participation is reinforced throughout the literature (Murphy, 1985; Ritchie, 1988; Simmons, 1994; Pearce, Moscardo, & Ross, 1996). This argument is supported by Tosun (2000, p. 615) who states:

> It is believed that a participatory development approach would facilitate implementation of principles of sustainable tourism development by creating better opportunities for local people to gain larger and more balanced benefits from tourism development taking place in their localities.

Host community participation has thus evolved in its relationship with tourism and is now seen as a method of improving the image and professional basis of tourism development and planning (Pearce et al., 1996; Tosun, 2004) while also respecting and meeting the needs of the host community (Murphy, 1985; Tosun, 1998) as well as supporting a more democratic approach to planning with the host community (Syme, MacPherson, & Seiligman, 1991; Simmons, 1994; Tosun, 2004).

There has been a significant shift towards participation in recent years and today a once-marginal activity has become the mainstream work of many NGOs, development agencies, and tourism consultants. In fact the 1990s was seen as a decade of participatory development and according to Henkel and Stirrat (2001, p. 168), 'it is now difficult to find a development project that does not claim to adopt a 'participatory' approach involving 'bottom-up' planning, acknowledging the importance of 'indigenous' knowledge and claiming to 'empower' local people'. Through the evolution and development of LA 21, participation has become part of the apparatus of development, an inseparable process. Swarbrooke (1999) suggested the rationale for community involvement in tourism as follows:

- It is part of a democratic process;
- It provides a voice for those directly affected by tourism;
- It makes use of local knowledge to ensure decisions are well informed and
- It can reduce potential conflict between tourists and members of the host community.

This rationale put forward by Swarbrooke is supported by LA 21 in relation to sustainable development and community involvement. It is also important to consider this within the context of this chapter.

LA 21 emerged from the 1992 Rio Earth Summit, and it challenges local authorities, according to Jackson and Morpeth (1999), not only to adopt policy goals encompassing sustainable development but also to incorporate participative, collaborative processes that involve local communities in defining their own sustainable futures. However, it is important to note, as Boyd and Singh (2003, p. 19) argue, that although mechanisms for accomplishing this have been proposed with the intention of facilitating judicious use of common endowments for the benefit and perpetuation of community values and for the promotion of community health and well being, putting these mechanisms in place is a daunting task.

Assuming the host community may be involved in tourism planning, what conditions are necessary to ensure effective participation? According to Mason (2004), the successful involvement of a community in tourism planning will depend on a number of particular factors being present:

- The nature of the political system at national and local level;
- The degree of political literacy of the local population;
- The nature of the particular tourism issue;
- The awareness of the tourism issue in the community;
- The history of involvement (or lack of it) in tourism-related issues and
- The attitudes and behaviour of sections of media.

Mason's factors seem to ignore the problematic associated with the term community in that it is accepted and utilised, but is not defined or used consistently. It also does not indicate the amount of time or resources needed to be present to achieve successful community involvement.

These limitations and problems are not unnoted, the association of participation with 'empowerment' and 'sustainability' and the multi-beneficial direct and indirect impacts identified as arising from it have tended to place it on a pedestal (Mowforth & Munt, 2003). Host community participation in tourism planning is fundamentally about degrees of citizen power and influence within the policy-making process, and as such embodies a relationship between the state (bureaucrats and politicians) and the public (rest of us) (Bahaire & Elliot-White, 1999). As this chapter focuses on the level of host community participation in sustainable tourism planning, the limitations to participation must be discussed and the whole notion of assessment of degrees of participation must be critiqued.

Participation Not a Panacea

Participation however has also been under attack in the literature (Rahnema, 1992; Cooke & Kothari, 2001; Mowforth & Munt, 2003). Participation it is argued should be subject to critique and must be alive to the possibility that it has the potential for unjustified exercise of power (Cooke & Kothari, 2001). According to Brandon (1993), phrases such as 'targeting local people' and 'eliciting community-based participation' rest on gaining community support for projects. Literature has not questioned the good intentions or ethical and theoretical values that lie behind participation, but it is the uncritical manner in which participation is conceptualised and practised that has attracted attention, debate and critique. The problems with participation seem to centre on the manner in which participatory exercises have been conducted and the way in which it has been subsumed into contemporary planning practices. Cleaver (2001) argues that a new faith in participation arises from three key tenets:

- That participation is inherently good;
- That good techniques can ensure success and
- That considerations of structures of power (and politics) should be avoided.

With Cleaver (2001) arguing that participation is in fact an 'act of faith in development' (p. 37), Henkel and Stirrat (2001) suggest that what the 'new orthodoxy boldly calls empowerment' has special resonance in what Michel Foucault (1980) calls 'subjection,' where the technical framework, approach and means of participation in Participatory Rural Appraisal (PRA) is preordained and fixed.

Ultimately, critics (Taylor, 2001; Hailey, 2001; Kothari, 2001) argue, this form of participation actually drives participants of the process to seeing and representing their world within the context of the PRA experts vision. Or perhaps, local people are simply pragmatic and are able to off-load local knowledge into predetermined structures, but with the view to realising opportunities and resources from external programmes.

The host community involved in the tourism planning process may in fact merely become actors, with participants possibly acting out roles for planners. Kothari (2001) argues that PRA represents an act with participants remaining distinct and 'contrived' roles and practitioners or facilitators acting as stage managers or directors who guide or attempt to delimit the performance of participants. Thus, planners are not gaining a balanced representative view from participants. Furthermore the participatory processes may lead a group to say what it is they think you and everyone else wants to hear, rather than what they truly believe. There also exists a further assumption that members of the community are willing and able to participate equally. Most critically some literature suggests (Taylor, 2001; Hailey, 2001; Cleaver, 2001; Mowforth & Munt, 2003) participation simultaneously veils and legitimises existing structures of power. In Taylor's (2001) view, participation is simply not working because it has been promoted by the powerful and is largely cosmetic, but most ominously because it is used as a 'hegemonic' device to secure compliance to and control by existing power structures.

Therefore, in the context of this chapter, it is understood that while participation is not a panacea and does not automatically or necessarily lead to a change in underlying structures of power, the exclusion of the host community from the involvement and decision-making process in tourism planning is today inexcusable. The actual typologies, techniques and appraisal methods of participation in tourism planning require discussion. This should act as an aid and provide possible tools to analyse the possible level and depth of host community participation in sustainable tourism planning.

Typologies of Participation

The actual concept and principle of local participation may be easy to promote and discuss in relation to sustainable development. This has been demonstrated in the LA 21 discourse on local community involvement in planning. However, the practice and actual application of host community participation is much more complex (Haywood, 1988; Mowforth & Munt,

2000; Mason, 2003; Tosun, 2004). The first issue in relation to community involvement is whether to engage in public participation at all, and if so, what degree of participation is to be pursued by the planners.

If the planners are consulting the literature, it suggests first that host community participation may be implemented in a myriad of different ways (Arnstein, 1969; Inskeep, 1987; Haywood, 1988; Green & Hunter, 1992; Gunn, 1994; Pretty, 1995; Tosun, 2000; Mowforth & Munt, 2000; Mason, 2003; Tosun, 2004), and second, these methods of facilitating host community participation have the propensity to allow varying degrees of participation. Third, host community participation may take place at different levels (local, regional or national) and various forms in numerous ways under site-specific conditions (Inskeep, 1987; Green & Hunter, 1992; Gunn, 1994).

Researchers have developed a number of models or frameworks that have been useful in this process (Arnstein, 1969; Pretty, 1995; Tosun, 2000). These typologies of community participation have emerged over the past four decades to help determine the level of participation. To ensure consistency in analysis and comparison of the typologies, they have been reviewed here in relation to tourism planning, host community involvement in the decision-making process and with respect to the distribution of power. According to Arnstein, citizen power is

> The redistribution of power that enables the have-not citizens to be deliberately included in the future. It is the means by which they can induce significant social reform, which enables them to share in the benefits of affluent society. (1969, p. 216)

Historically, Arnstein's (1971) much-cited text 'A Ladder of Citizen Participation' employed the idea of a ladder of participation to encapsulate the different meanings of community involvement. This according to Haywood (1988), Mason (2003) and Murphy and Murphy (2004) distinguished between eight different degrees of participation from manipulation, therapy, information, consultation, placation, partnership, delegated power through to full citizen control (see Table 1).

The relevance of Arnstein's model to tourism has been best illustrated by Murphy and Murphy (2004), where they highlight and provide commentary on the following levels of Arenstein's model. 'Manipulation' (nonparticipatory) at level 1 of the ladder is described as the 'decide-announce-defend' approach where the public cannot change what has been predetermined. This involves educating the public as to what will be done, often through a set presentation to local government and through supportive stories in the media. The host community involvement in the decision-making process is

Table 1. Typology of Community Participation.

1.	Manipulation	Nonparticipation
2.	Therapy	
3.	Informing	Degrees of citizen tokenism
4.	Consultation	
5.	Placation	
6.	Partnership	Degrees of citizen control
7.	Delegated power	
8.	Citizen control	

Source: Adapted from Arnstein (1971).

nonexistent at this level. There is no distribution of power from the planners to the community.

Level 2 is referred to by Arenstein as 'therapy', and appears to involve a very low level of participation. It may provide an opportunity for the public to share its frustrations and concerns, often through a 'special meeting' at the local government level. The focus may be on identifying and managing 'problem people'. In reality this may involve presenting a resort development's supposed benefits to members of the public and provide them with an opportunity to have their say on the issue without providing feedback mechanisms for modifying the proposal. The host community involvement in the decision-making process and distribution of power is tokenistic at this level.

'Informing' or level 3 involves a low level of participation and the first legitimate step to participation and distribution of power. Public concern over a pending decision can lead to minor alterations to the decision, but the scope of the changes is limited. This again may involve informing the community of a resort development concept and provide limited opportunities for them to suggest small changes, such as those relating to the appearance of a resort.

The academic commentary on Arnstein's typology (Haywood, 1988; Pretty, 1995; Tosun, 2000; Mason, 2003; Murphy & Murphy, 2004) suggests that the next level, that of 'consultation', involves minor degrees of participation, whereby special forums exist for the public to share its views through mechanisms such as surveys and workshops, designed to draw out public goals, ideas and concerns in relation to pending decisions. This level controls the extent of public discussions on tourism and uses these discussions as a means of assessing community support for the proposed resort and other pending tourism decisions. The distribution of power is still quite minimal and remains with the planners. Although some changes to the proposal will be considered in response to the public's expressed views, whether it should be built will not be questioned.

Level 5 'placation', involves a moderate level of participation. At this level the public seems to influence the decision in a broad-based manner, while certain individuals or groups have the opportunity to more closely advise the decision-making bodies. It caters for the creation of task forces, committees or other groups that are seen to represent the broader interests of the community and these groups advise the decision-making bodies. A public advisory group with members handpicked by elected representatives could be created to make recommendations for significant changes to the resort proposal. Here there is clearly some move towards placing power to make decisions with the host community. However, it must be argued at this stage that depending on the level of legitimacy that the decision-making body gives to this group, only politically palatable recommendations will be adopted while more radical recommendations are deferred for further study.

The next level referred to as 'partnerships' involves a high level of participation. The actual decision-making is shared with members of the public. Redistribution of power is through negotiation between the established decision-making bodies and members of the public through the establishment of joint committees. A joint committee made up of members from established decision-making bodies and the public reviews issues and makes recommendations that decision-making bodies adopt, as long as these recommendations are supported by all committee members.

'Delegated power' (level 7), involves a very high level of participation in terms of actual decision-making being led by members of the public. The balance of power is weighed in favour of members of the public through the establishment of joint committees. A joint committee, made up of members from established decision-making bodies and the public, where members of the public are in the majority reviews the issues and makes recommendations that the decision-making bodies will adopt as long as these recommendations are supported by a majority of the committee members.

Finally, 'citizen control', according to Arnstein and other academic commentators on the model (Haywood, 1988; Pretty, 1995; Tosun, 2000), involves top level participation. This is the highest level of public participation (level 8), in the sense that the general public holds all decision-making power, and creates cooperatives that are responsible for planning, policies and decisions that affect community members. Murphy and Murphy (2004) for instance contend that certain ecotourism groups establish cooperative tourism boards to plan and operate local tourism ventures, including resorts. The political success of such a process will be determined by the extent to which the public's representatives in this process are seen to legitimately represent their community and be in a position to make the best possible decisions for their community.

The typology provided by Arnstein and the examples and expansion provided by Murphy and Murphy (2004) of typical tourism planning application have been very useful in determining the degree of participation afforded to the host community in sustainable tourism planning in Ireland. However, current theory in this area suggests that this typology does not exist in isolation (Arnstein, 1969; Inskeep, 1987; Haywood, 1988; Green & Hunter, 1992; Gunn, 1994; Pretty, 1995; Tosun, 2000; Mowforth & Munt, 2000; Mason, 2003; Tosun, 2004). Therefore, other typologies have also to be reviewed as part of this research. Furthermore, it is also worth noting that Arnstein's model is not without its limitations and these also need to be discussed.

The rungs in the ladder need renaming and that the ladder may not be an appropriate metaphor, implying as it does a single means of ascent/descent and that the rungs are equally spaced and hence are easily attained. The ladder is also value-laden in that it implies that all communities should aspire to and ascend to the higher levels, as these are desirable in a democratic society. With these factors taken into account, it is still argued by some scholars that Arenstein's metaphor retains intuitive appeal and alerts us to degrees of participation and what is 'offered' by planning authorities or demanded by citizens (Bahaire & Elliot-White, 1999).

To ensure that the best available model for assessing participation is utilised in this chapter, it is important to examine the theory on other typologies presented in the literature that may attempt to address some of the criticisms of Arnstein's model. A significant argument put forward by Pretty (1995) was that participation can mean different things to different people. This led to the creation of a more detailed typology of participation that also included a critique of each form of participation. Furthermore, Pretty (1995) identified and described seven different types of participation ranging from 'manipulative participation', where actual power lies with groups beyond the local host community, to 'self-mobilisation', in which the power and control over all aspects of the development rest squarely with the local community (see Table 2).

In theory, the application of Pretty's typology is facilitated by a recognition of local circumstances, the unequal distribution of power between local and other interest groups, and different interpretations of the term participation (Mowforth & Munt, 2000; Mason, 2003; Tosun, 2004). Mason (2003) argues that in Pretty's typology it is only under the headings

Table 2.   Typology of Participation.

Typology	Characteristic of Each Type
Manipulative participation	Participation is simply a pretence: Peoples' representatives on official boards but they are unelected and have no power
Passive participation	People participate by being told what has been decided or has already happened: Involves announcements without listening to people's responses
Participation by consultation	People participate by being consulted or by answering questions: External agent defines problems, does not concede any share in decision-making
Participate for material incentives	People participate by contributing resources (e.g. labour) in return for food, cash, yet people have no stake in prolonging practices when incentive ends
Functional participation	Participation seen by external agencies as a means to achieve project goals, especially reduce costs: People may participate by forming groups to meet predefined project objectives
Interactive participation	People participate in joint analysis, development of action plans and strengthening of local institutions: Participation is seen as a right; the process involves interdisciplinary methodologies that seek multiple perspectives. Groups take control of local decisions and have a definite stake
Self-mobilisation	People participate by taking initiatives independently of external institutions to change systems: They develop contacts with external institutions for resources and advise; self-mobilisation can spread if governments and NGOs provide an enabling framework of support. This may or may not challenge existing distributions of wealth and power

Source: Modified from Pretty (1995).

of 'interactive participation' and self-mobilisation that local people are actively involved in decision-making. The range and type of participation presented in Pretty's model allows for different degrees of external involvement and local control (Mowforth & Munt, 2000), while also reflecting the power relationship between them. Furthermore it must be argued that for local people involved, the decision-making process is only a feature of the interactive participation and self-mobilisation level, while in the functional participation level most major decisions have been made before they are taken to the local community. The usefulness of Pretty's model to this chapter is it allows for analysis at each level for differing degrees of external involvement and local control, and attempts to reflect the power relationships between them. This should allow for clear identification of the actual level of participation afforded to host community involvement in the decision-making process in tourism planning and is also reflective of the distribution of power at all levels.

Building on Pretty's model, a final typology is presented in the literature, which it is argued is the most relevant to the chapter. This is put forward by Tosun (2004), who has purposefully developed a typology of community participation for tourism. The typology as illustrated in Table 3 classifies types of community participation under three headings: 'spontaneous community participation', 'coercive community participation' and 'induced community participation'. The appeal of the typology developed by Tosun is that it elaborates on each type of community participation with special reference to the tourism industry. It may be useful in relation to this chapter to further elaborate on this typology to gain a sound conceptual framework for the empirical component of the study.

On closer analysis the highest degree of participation in Tosun's typology, spontaneous participation corresponds to degrees of citizen power in Arnstein's typology and self-mobilisation and interactive participation in Pretty's model. It represents an ideal mode of community participation. This ideal type provides full managerial responsibility and authority to the host community (Tosun, 2004). It is typically a bottom-up or 'grass roots' style of planning. It actively encourages active participation in decision-making, and in relation to this chapter on sustainable tourism planning, represents authentic participation and is categorised by what Tosun (2004) calls self-planning.

'Induced community participation' in tourism development is comparable with degrees of citizen tokenism in Arnstein's typology, and consultation or participation for material incentives as described by Pretty (1995). Basically, in this situation the host community is to hear and be heard. In essence, they have a voice in the tourism planning process.

However, it must be argued that it is clear that they do not have the power to ensure that their views will be utilised by the remaining powerful interest groups such as multinational tourism companies, local and government bodies. As a result, it represents a certain level of tokenism in relation to host community participation within the tourism planning process. This type is the most common mode to be found in developing countries where a host community only endorses decisions regarding tourism development made for them rather than by them (Tosun, 1999). This type of participation is synonymous with traditional top-down forms of planning. On behalf of

Table 3.   Normative Typologies of Community Participation.

Pretty's (1995) Typology of Community Participation	Arnstein's (1971) Typology of Community Participation		Tosun's (1999a) Typology of Community Participation
1. Manipulative participation	1. Manipulation	Nonparticipation	*Coercive participation*: Top-down, passive; mostly indirect, formal; participation in implementation but not necessarily sharing benefits; choice between proposed limited alternatives or no choice; paternalism, nonparticipation, high degree of tokenism and manipulation.
2. Passive participation	2. Therapy		
3. Participation by consultation	3. Informing	Degrees of citizen tokenism	*Induced participation*: Top-down; passive; formal mostly indirect; degree of tokenism, manipulation; pseudo-participation; participation in implementation and sharing benefits; choice between proposed alternatives and feedback.
4. Participation for material incentives	4. Consultation		
5. Functional participation	5. Placation		
6. Interactive participation	6. Partnership	Degrees of citizen power	*Spontaneous participation*: Bottom-up; active par.; direct participation; par. in decision-making, authentic participation; self-planning
	7. Delegated power		
7. Self-mobilization	8. Citizen control		

Source: Adapted from Tosun (2005).

the community it is passive and indirect, in that they may participate in implementation and sharing the benefits of the tourism industry, but not in the decision-making process. Finally, Tosun's last degree of community involvement 'coercive participation' is manipulated and manufactured as a replacement for authentic and meaningful host community participation. In relation to Arnstein's model it represents the lowest rungs of the ladder, 'manipulation and therapy'. This coincides with the passive and manipulative participation in Pretty's typology. In fact the purpose of this level of participation is not to meaningfully engage the participants, but according to Tosun (2004, p. 494):

> It enables power holders to educate or cure host communities to turn away potential and actual threats to future tourism development. Some decisions may be taken to meet basic needs of host-communities by consulting local leaders so as to reduce socio-political risks from tourists and tourism development. Although it seems that tourism development is to take place based upon host communities' priorities, it is heavily skewed towards the fostering and development of tourism, and would primarily be concerned with meeting the needs and desires of decision makers, tourism's operators and tourists.

This level of participation accords well with the superimposed nature of tourism activity that is infrequently grafted onto an economy and society in a top-down manner (France, 1988). It is suggested by Tosun that these three typologies may be useful as a tool to identify the spectrum of community participation from passive to authentic and interactive. Therefore, the insight and debate provided by Arnstein (1971), Pretty (1995) and Tosun (2006) and the adoption of a multi-typology assessment approach allow the researcher to draw from all three typologies and utilise the discourse provided by each to assess, at a basic level, host community participation in sustainable planning for tourism. A basic means is stressed here, as these typologies are not without their limitations.

There are some limitations with these typologies. First, they do not consider the total population of citizens to be included in the tourism planning process. Also the actual time and duration of the participation is not addressed. Tosun (2004) points to the fact that there is no analysis of significant roadblocks (paternalism, racism, gender discrimination and cultural remoteness of local people to tourism). However, taking these limitations into consideration, the typologies do provide a simple way to gauge at a basic level the spectrum of participation that may be taking place during community tourism planning.

Power
The focus of power is very evident in the typology of tourism–destination community relationship scenarios: win-win, win-lose, lose-win or lose-lose, as discussed by a number of authors (Cater & Lowman, 1994; Boyd & Singh, 2003). The win-win scenario is one where both community and tourism benefit, effectively there is general power sharing. The win-lose scenario may exist where the community benefits but tourism does not necessarily, thus the community holds the majority of the power, extremely rare on a wider level. The third scenario is lose-win where the community

loses while tourism gains and the tourist industry holds the majority of power. Finally, the lose-lose scenario indicates the community and tourism both lose out. Loss of community power occurs due to short-term economic gain at the expense of long-term community and environmental loss. It is imperative to note that though the four scenarios illustrated are broad-based and generalised, their relevance in explaining the success and failures in community tourism is undeniable (Boyd & Singh, 2003, p. 30).

With these broad-based and generalised scenarios in mind, there is a need to address power in relation to host community participation in tourism planning, and this has been highlighted from the review of the typologies of participation (Arnstein, 1971; Pretty, 1995; Tosun, 2000). Power has been defined by West (1994) as the ability to 'impose one's will or advance one's own interest', while power in the decision-making process has been defined as '[t]he potential or actual ability to influence others in desired direction' (Gordon, Mondy, Sharplin, & Premeaux, 1990, p. 589). Community tourism analysts tend to assume, often implicitly according to Reed (1997), that the planning and policy process is a pluralistic one in which people have equal access to economic and political resources. Reed also argues this assumption runs through ecological models of tourism planning put forward by Murphy (1985). For example, the tourist system is frequently described as being highly fragmented. This observation, Jamal and Getz (1995, p. 193) argue, has led to the assumption that 'no single organisation or individual can exert direct control over the destination's development process'. This argument has been supported by Reed (1997) who argues that such interpretations mask the pivotal role that actions of individuals can have at the local level. At a larger scale, the design and management of, for example, Disney World in Florida have created problems in Greater Orlando that the residents perceive are exacerbated by, if not entirely created by, the Disney Corporation.

The level of participation that the public obtains is a direct reflection of the local power dynamic. Susskind and Field (1996) suggest that power is a reflection of resources, including money, intellect, experiences, negotiation and leadership skills as well as the ability to inspire. Those without substantial resources can increase their power by making strategic alliances, rallying support for their views and conducting themselves well in the collaborative decision-making process. Power is also profoundly influenced according to Murphy and Murphy (2004) by laws, institutions, cultural norms and language that largely determine the extent to which the views of various stakeholders' groups will be incorporated into tourism planning. Thus, it is worth nothing that the final steps, for example, of Arnstein's (1971), Pretty's (1995) and Tosun's (2004) models may be unachievable for political or economic reasons. Yet according to Webber (1995) there are still strong arguments for the earlier steps, such as partnerships, as a way of complementing existing systems.

Furthermore, the work by Blank (1989, p. 54) on the community tourism imperative suggests that 'community leadership is heterogeneous ... drawn from a number of power bases'. The varying power relations regarding tourism planning have been viewed as an instrument to be managed and balanced. Jamal and Getz (1995) argue that it is possible to address the issue of power and authority by including legitimate stakeholders and identifying a suitable convener at an early stage in the collaborative planning process. To these ends, they propose criteria for identifying legitimate stakeholders based on identifying the right and capacity to participate. Where power is not initially equal, they suggest that a local authority, for example local government, may be a suitable convener when the issues need to be resolved.

However, this is contested by Reed (1997), who argues that reliance on local authorities to convene power relations assumes that these authorities will be neutral arbiters in the land-development process. Yet political theorists have demonstrated that governance institutions have their own agendas in the formulation and implementation of policy (Clark, 1984; Dye, 1986; Rees, 1990), while applied researchers have illustrated how these agendas have been advanced (Reed, 1995). In specific relation to tourism development, Hollinshead (1990) argues that government agencies may act as regulators, players, or partners exercising influence and control through their regulatory and service function. This is specifically interesting in the context of Ireland, and the application of the participation models may allow the power balances to be highlighted in relation to tourism planning. It must be stressed however that this research is not intended to be a discourse on the power relation between local authorities and the host community.

Impediments to Local Participation

It is evident at this stage that some literature suggests that involving local communities in decision-making about tourism development does not necessarily ensure success (Mowforth & Munt, 1998). In fact Middleton and Hawkins (1998) suggested that there is little evidence that effective community-led tourism has been implemented; they argue that the main reason community-led planning has failed is due to the fact that a community does not really exist and hence obtaining a consensual view on tourism development is virtually impossible. Interestingly, Murphy (1985) earlier indicated that it is relatively easy for a community to unite in opposition to a tourism development. However, it is far more difficult for a community to conceptualise, agree and then achieve its own long-term tourism future (Middleton & Hawkins, 1998). The process of community engagement has been discussed by Jenkins (1993, p. 62) in detail and he suggests six impediments to local participation in tourism planning:

- The public generally has difficulty in understanding complex and technical planning issues;
- The public does not necessarily understand how the planning process operates or how decisions are made;
- The problem of attaining and maintaining representation of all views in the decision-making process;
- Apathy among some if not a majority of citizens;
- The increased cost of decision-making that takes much longer as a result of community participation;
- The overall efficiency (particularly in terms of time; money and the smooth running) of the decision-making process is adversely affected.

These impediments to local participation also highlight the difficulty in encouraging active meaningful host community participation. It will be important to discuss these in relation to the research in hand. However, taking these impediments into consideration, it is also necessary to discuss the limitations to community participation.

First it must be recognised that there is little research into this area in relation to tourism. Tosun and Timothy suggest operational, structural and cultural limits to community participation in planning (Tosun, 2000; Timothy & Tosun, 2003). However, these are in the context of developing countries. As Ireland may be considered relatively developed, this body of work is of minor relevance to this chapter, which focuses more on the various methods employed by planners to facilitate meaningful participation.

Methods of Participation

From a historical perspective the whole notion of host community partnerships and workshops to bring together industry and community emerged in the 1980s. A range of approaches or tools such as conciliation, articulation and mediation were recommended by Haywood (1988). This was followed by 'what if scenarios' to give clarity and purpose to the community (Richie, 1993). The move from cooperation to collaboration was then noted and argued for by Getz and Jamal (1994), which allowed for a process of joint decision-making within the planning process. Community involvement in tourism planning can exist in a variety of ways (Haywood, 1988; Murphy, 1988; Richie, 1993; Jamal & Getz, 1995). In deciding whether to proceed with public participation, and if so how far to move, an appraisal of the community's tourism environment may be necessary. This may ask what are the issues, who are the concerned publics and what are their reactions to these issues. The design and length of participation must be decided upon. Here Haywood (1988) argues that logistical costs and administrative convenience tend to support small groups, while the need for adequate representation can necessitate a larger one. One of the outcomes of this chapter is to determine what form, method and/or techniques of participation have been utilised in sustainable planning for tourism in Ireland. Therefore, the next section will discuss the methods and tools that are available to planners to facilitate meaningful participation from the host community when planning for sustainable tourism.

The Tools of Participation
The tourism planning literature highlights an increasing number of tools for facilitating community participation. Mowforth and Munt (1998) identify tools and techniques such as meetings, public attitude surveys, stated preference surveys, contingent valuation method, Delphi technique, and workshops. However, they also stress that

> Those techniques which allow for consultation and participation are still young in their
> development and suffer various shortcomings. (Mowforth & Munt, 1998, p. 219)

In order to assess the tools that may be utilised by local authorities to facilitate participation, they first need to be described. By far the oldest tool available is that of the public meeting, which is usually held before elected or appointed officials such as village boards or forward planners using formal rules of order and resulting in an official vote or recommendation. This is the most structured and formal method of participation used in the latter part of the planning process after most information and comments have been gathered and considered. This is a good tool for eliciting commentary and consideration by elected and appointed representatives of the community, and it gives the community's official 'stamp of approval' to the plan. This method allows participation by the public, but because it occurs late in the planning process it is not the best method for gathering the public's opinions for establishing goals and objectives of plans or choosing various alternatives. Mowforth and Munt argue:

> It is debatable whether any of the relatively sophisticated techniques that have become available recently are able to improve on the traditional and well-used technique of the meeting. Local communities the world over traditionally use both formal and informal meetings to debate the course of development and issues which may affect them. (2003, p. 221)

Meetings are not without shortfalls, for example, they are not necessarily all inclusive (Murphy, 1985; Pearce et al., 1996; Middleton & Hawkins, 1998). The use of public meetings may also be criticised for supporting low levels of participation. Arnstein (1971) viewed this as the 'decide-announce-defend' approach that involves educating the public as to what will be done, often through a set presentation to local government and through supportive stories in the media. Furthermore, the format of such meetings may differ significantly, and they may be dominated by certain individuals, which is problematic in advocating balanced inclusive community participation (Simmons, 1994; Hunter & Green, 1995; Murphy, 1985). Therefore, public meetings carried out in isolation are not seen as a particularly effective tool in facilitating host community participation.

Gunn (1972, p. 66), in one of the first texts on tourism planning, advocated for the use of forums to ensure public participation. By means of forums with community leaders and constituencies, designers can foster open discussion of the desired goals of tourism development. Forums and committees generally consist of a group of people in the community that deals with the planning of a project from conception to completion. It usually consists of volunteers or appointees who work together with officials, investing considerable time in the process. This tool can be very valuable because committee members develop a high level of investment in the project. However, it does not allow a direct method of participation for all members of the public, thus resulting in a low level of overall community participation (Tosun, 2004). Committees should be representative of residents and interest groups, where individuals may voice their views through committee members. This in reality may be difficult to ensure as members of the forum are often voluntary (Mowforth & Munt, 2003), and thus under significant pressure from other sources and the resulting time constraints. The use of focus and advisory groups made up from the community members is similar to the committee, but, unlike a committee that meets regularly during the entire length of the process, each focus group typically meets once at an early phase of the process. The focus group is a good method to promote dialogue between different groups in the community to identify issues and concerns towards establishing goals and objectives for the plan.

The charette or 'community design charette' is an innovative approach that is widely used by physical planners and designers (Murphy, 1985). This involves a workshop involving local citizens facilitated by architects, landscape architects and planners to identify opportunities and constraints on maps so that issues are spatially defined for planning purposes. The planner or facilitator then assists participants at the workshop in giving form to alternative proposals for their community through mapping and drawings. A multi-meeting intensive collaborative effort involving community members and sometimes officials helps to create a detailed design plan for a specific area (Gunn, 1994; Murphy, 1985; Bahaire & Elliot-White, 1999; Mowforth & Munt, 2003). They address and form solutions for problems in a short period, resulting in a comprehensive physical plan for a designated area of policy. Therefore, this method would not be useful for an overall general plan for a large area but might be useful for addressing a small subarea of the community. The charette is one of the fastest and well-known methods of developing consensus among various individuals and community groups; however, it is also extremely time-consuming and costly to planners.

Another method advocated by planning theory is the survey, namely, public attitude surveys and stated preference surveys, of which exist four principal types: postal, telephonic, focus group interviews and in-person (Mowforth & Munt, 2003). In-person interviews are the most expensive but reveal a great deal of in-depth qualitative data that can often be invaluable to planners, with mailed surveys proving to be the least expensive (Inskeep, 1991). However, the data are often very formal and structured and it takes a longer time to collect data, and the response rate is characteristically low. Telephone surveys are less expensive than in-person surveys and can provide statistically significant data in a relatively short time. Surveys are very useful for assessing the opinions and desires of the community to participate in tourism planning within destinations. However, they can be limited to the collection of opinions of stakeholders in order to provide fuller information for the public-sector planners. According to De Araujo and Bramwell (2000), this can be largely a one-way consultation process when there is little direct dialogue between the stakeholders and the planners. This can occur when the opinions of stakeholders are collected using self-completion questionnaires, focus group interviews, drop-in centres and telephone surveys. De Araujo and Bramwell (2000) argue that it is likely to be less complex to collect people's opinions than to involve them in direct dialogue with public-sector planners or seek negotiations and consensus-building through collaborative planning.

While these one-way processes seem less time-consuming and seem to be capable of involving a greater number of participants, they are often criticised for being one-way and advocate top-down planning (Inskeep, 1991; Bramwell & Lane, 2000; Gunn, 2002; Murphy & Murphy, 2004; Mowforth & Munt, 2004). However, it must be recognised that these practices can offer very valuable information for decision-making in collaborative working groups (Simmons, 1994; Yuksel, Bramwell, & Yuksel, 1999). It must be noted that they also allow stakeholders to be consulted at several stages in the planning process if the planners maintain a database of participants and keep them informed about the developments. Therefore, these may be useful tools if not solely used in isolation to engage meaningful host community participation. The current growth and expansion of the cyber or virtual community has witnessed increased use of electronic communications such as Web sites, e-mail, and cable television by planners and local governments to communicate with host communities. Indeed there is increased discussion on the virtual community in the literature (Shields, 1996; Castells, 2001; Delanty, 2003). Information regarding the planning process can be put on the Web site or broadcast on cable access channels with citizens posting questions and comments directly to a site or responding by e-mail. This is a convenient and relatively inexpensive tool. Citizens who may not be able to attend scheduled meetings may access the information at any time and on their own schedule.

Theory suggests that the emergence and new development of technologically mediated cyber or virtual communities are bringing about new kinds of social groups that are polymorphous, highly personalised and often expressive (Delanty, 2003). Thus, the emergence of e-planning for tourism must be recognised as a new and potentially powerful tool to facilitate host community participation and the analysis should qualify the current state of e-planning. A final technique that attempts to involve the notion of participation in the making of decisions is the Delphi technique. This is used to set threshold values or critical levels of standards for specific aspects of a development (such as maximum visitor numbers). This is a judgemental technique involving the subjective assessment of those who take part, although it is often seen as a means of collecting expert or informed opinion and of working towards consensus between experts on a given issue (Green & Hunter, 1992). The technique initially uses the actual responses from a questionnaire in relation to the planning issue, followed by a feedback second session on all responses. The third stage simply repeats the first stage but the participants have the benefit of knowing all other responses; this is simply repeated until a consensus is reached.

This model has the advantage of anonymity, or at least separation of the participants, thereby reducing peer pressure in the formation of opinions, thus permitting more honest responses. It must be argued however that a disadvantage of this technique is the method of selection of participants, which is not extensive and is made by either planners or interested parties who wish to see the proposal go ahead (Mowforth & Munt, 2003). Furthermore, in terms of Pretty's typology, though such techniques may help to improve the level of participation, they are unlikely, according to Mowforth and Munt (2003), to attain a high level unless they focus on the degree of decision-making devolved to the local community as well as its active involvement in the operation of the scheme. Therefore, it may be suggested that without adequate sustained and dedicated funding, time and trained professional application, the process is open to problems and low levels of participation.

The tourism planning literature increasingly highlights an increasing number of specific approaches, models, techniques and ladders for implementing community participation. Murphy (1988) identifies partner-ships and community workshops to bring together the industry and the community. Haywood (1988) argues participants in a community participa-tion process require a range of tools such as conciliation, mediation, articulation, and identification of superordinate goals. This has led other authors such as Richie (1993) to identify vision statements and 'what if' scenarios to give clarity and purpose to the community tourism participation process. The next section of this chapter will discuss a cross-section of approaches identified in the literature (Pine, 1984; Gray, 1985; Drake, 1991; Simmons, 1994; Jamal & Getz, 1995; Bonilla, 1997; Bramwell & Lane, 2000; Mason, 2004).

Pine's Participation Ladder

As reiterated throughout the tourism literature, community involvement in tourism can exist in a range of formats. Once a community is involved in participation however, the participation may proceed through various stages as is illustrated in Table 4. It must be highlighted that there are a number of varying processes outlined for host community participation and they all offer unique attributes depending on values within the community, the types of tourism and the resources available.

As can be seen from Table 4, Pine (1984) demonstrates a basic process of participation based on a nine-stage process. While the process is over two

Table 4.   Participation Ladder.

(1)	Information	Introduction of existing tourism policy to citizens by the authority
(2)	Animation	Stimulation of perception among citizens
(3)	Participation (stage 1)	Opening of dialogue between citizens and authority
(4)	Participation (stage 2)	Initiation of tourism planning on the basis of partnership
(5)	Participation (stage 3)	Joint research – identification of strengths and weaknesses, opportunities and threats, etc.
(6)	Participation (stage 4)	Determination of tourism objectives and strategies
(7)	Participation (stage 5)	Joint decision-making regarding resource allocation, development and management
(8)	Operationalisation	Implementation of tourism strategy by administrators
(9)	Participation (stages 6–1)	Review of tourism policy and achievements

Source: Adapted from Pine (1984).

decades old, it still holds some important features relevant to the process of participation today. What is interesting about this process is it was based on three case studies in Finland, England and Ireland. This represents the first mention in the literature in relation to host community participation, and while it is not specifically relevant to tourism it does address community development and voluntary associations. However, Pine's ladder of participation is problematic in its assumptions and simplicity. It, for example, offers no time line for the process or numbers of participants that can be facilitated, nor does it address what resources are needed to move through the ladder to the next stage.

Drake's Model of Local Participation in Tourism Development
In contrast to Pine's ladder and within the context of nature-based tourism, Drake (1991) suggested a model of local participation in tourism development. Drake argued that local participation referred to the ability of local communities to influence the outcomes of development projects that had an impact upon them. He created a nine-phase model that is presented in Table 5.

Drake's model, it must be argued, tends to lend itself more to real application within the field of tourism planning than Pine's ladder and therefore may facilitate more integrated community involvement in

Table 5. Drake's Nine-Phase Model of Local Participation in Nature-Based Tourism.

Phase 1: Determine the role of local participation in the project. This includes an assessment of how local people can help

Phase 2: Choose research team. The team should include a broad selection

Phase 3: Conduct preliminary studies. The political, economic and social conditions of the community should be studied, via documents and surveys. The following should be identified: needs, local leaders, community commitment to the project, media involvement/interest, traditional use of land, role of women, land ownership and cultural values

Phase 4: Determine the level of local involvement. This will be somewhere along a continuum from low to high intensity

Phase 5: Determine an appropriate participation mechanism. This is linked to the intensity of involvement, the nature of existing institutions and characteristics of local people. It is likely to involve consultation and sharing

Phase 6: Initiate dialogue and educational efforts. The use of the press is important in this phase as a means by which to build consensus through public awareness. Key community representatives can be used in this process. Workshops or public meetings could be organised to identify strengths and weaknesses of the project

Phase 7: Collective decision-making. This is a critical stage that synthesizes all research and information from the local population. The project team presents the findings of their research to the community, together with an action plan. Community members are asked to react to the plan, with the possible end result being a forum through which the team and local people negotiate to reach a final consensus based on the impact of the project

Phase 8: Development of an action plan and implementation scheme

Phase 9: Monitoring and evaluation. Although often neglected, this should occur frequently and over the long term. The key evaluation is to discover whether goals and objectives set out early in the project's life cycle have been accomplished or not

Source: Modified from Mason (2004, p. 119).

sustainable tourism planning. Research objective 3 '[t]o critically examine the process in place to facilitate host community participation in tourism planning' within this chapter will examine if any particular process as identified by Drake and Pine is being utilised by local authority planners in Ireland.

Participatory Ecotourism Planning Model
Another model that seems to be growing in use is the participatory ecotourism planning model that has been utilised with some success according to Bonilla (1997). It is not possible to go into a detailed account of each participation method discussed in this literature review, however, for the purpose of illustration a short summary is provided (see Table 6). The process evolved between 1996 and 1997 when Conservation International

Table 6.   Participatory Ecotourism Planning Model.

Phase I: Preliminary assessment
  Phase I permits the assessment of three critical issues necessary to the success of the process.
  These are
      (a) Relevant aspects of the industry, including data on the current offer, demand and
          trends
      (b) Existing legal and administrative framework
      (c) Stakeholders involved in the local and regional tourism scene
Phase II: Strategic participatory planning workshops
  Phase II involves stakeholders in a three-stage planning process:
      (a) Participatory analysis of the actual tourism situation, identifying barriers and
          bottlenecks for the activity in the region
      (b) Classification of barriers and bottlenecks according to two relevant factors: Aspects of
          the activity, including business, socioeconomic, environmental and legal-
          administrative; and geographic distribution, establishing priorities and the main
          barriers for each area that supports or has potential for tourism activity
      (c) Definition of strategic plan, defining general principles of policy, priorities, strategies,
          actions, who is responsible for the action and indicators of progress
Phase III: Validation and conformation of steering committee
  Once a strategic plan is created, it is critical that proper follow-up puts into action the
  strategies proposed. The next step is then the establishing of a steering committee that
  includes all sectors involved, maintains the communication flow and implements the action
  plan

Source: Modified from Bonilla (1997, p. 23).

conducted two participatory ecotourism planning processes in major regions of the Peten, Guatemala and Inca Region, Perú. Despite obvious differences, both countries and regions share problems created by a rapid development of the tourism industry and a poor or nonexisting planning framework. As a result of processes occurring simultaneously, both were enriched by the exchange of experiences and the original plan of each one was subsequently improved by the new ideas and methods developed by the other. Bonilla (1997) put forward this overview of the methodology used.

The first workshop in Peten took place over 3 days with more than 40 essential problems and barriers identified, and more than 60 corrective or preventive actions proposed. Even though during the first day of work old conflicts between stakeholders were revived, the methodology employed permitted all of the discussion to concentrate on the proposal, which allowed concrete principles and actions to be generated that had the approval of all sectors involved. The second workshop in Peten also took place over 3 days and generated the base for the tourism policy, presenting principles, guidelines and actions, considering all aspects of the situation such as environment, legal, socioeconomic and business. The single most important issue in the success of the methodology according to Bonilla (1997) is the participation of all those involved in the activity. The actors and builders of the policy are all those who will be affected or must take responsibility for its implementation. Of course, it is impossible to have everybody involved in tourism in the region attend a workshop, so the identification of suitable representatives of all sectors is critical.

Typically, there are four major sectors involved in tourism in a given region: government sector, private sector, community sector and non-government sector. The core of the methodology is composed by the planning workshops (see Table 6). These 3-day-long workshops follow an interactive methodology loosely based in ZOPP (ziel-orientated project planning or objective-orientated project planning), a participatory planning strategy developed by the German cooperation agency GTZ in the 1980s. The main virtue of ZOPP is that it provides a graphic interface to understand how barriers and problems relate to each other, from cause to consequence. Because it is based on the writing of concise sentences in 4×6-in. cards, it prevents long verbal discussions and makes it easier to admit or attack an idea or concept without involving the person who proposed it. The objectives of the workshops are:

- To generate participatory analysis of the actual tourism situation, identifying barriers and bottlenecks for the activity in the region;
- To classify barriers and bottlenecks according to two relevant factors: (i) Aspects of the activity, including business, socioeconomic, environmental and legal-administrative. (ii) Geographic distribution, establishing priorities and the main barriers for each area that supports or has potential for tourism activity;
- To create a strategic plan, defining general principles of policy, priorities, strategies, actions, who is responsible for the action and indicators of progress.

The process outlined is centred on community participation and this may lead one to ask how many planning workshops are necessary. The information gathered during Phase I might decide the number of workshops. If the region for which the strategy is being planned is divided into subregions that have very different degrees of tourism development, or very marked differences, then probably it is a good idea to have at least one workshop for each region.

The resources, expertise, time and detail needed to engage a community in sustainable tourism planning has become increasingly more obvious from the literature and examples explained. The process just discussed should offer enough detail to determine if similar models, time and resources are being employed in tourism planning. The works of Bonilla (1997) and Mowforth and Munt (2003) have also highlighted a trend for participatory approaches to enquiry and research. Participatory Action Research (PAR), Participatory Research Methodology (PRM), PRA and Rapid Ethnographic Assessment (REA) and a bewildering array of other acronyms and initials have entered into use (Mowforth & Munt, 2003). Although they are often formally stated to involve many steps in the process, essentially they follow the three-step procedure of participatory enquiry, collective analysis and action in the locality.

More sophisticated survey techniques, public attitude surveys, stated preference technique and contingent valuation methods all suffer the disadvantage of being conducted, administered, promoted and published by persons outside the local community affected by tourism development (Mowforth & Munt, 2003). However, the degree of attention within the current literature in relation to the collaborative and partnership approach offers the public a collaborative or partnership role with the planning process.

Collaboration and Partnership
The collaboration process for tourism planning has been advocated by many tourism scholars (Haywood, 1988; Gray, 1989; Inskeep, 1991; Jamal & Getz, 1995; Gunn, 2002; Reid, Mair, & George, 2004; Murphy, 2005). There are a number of interpretations and models put forward by the relevant tourism commentators that are similar in essence. However, the collaborative process can vary according to many dimensions, and for analytical purposes it is helpful to conceptualise each dimension as a continuum, along which specific examples can be located. In this context, some authors place the ideas of collaboration between stakeholders within a broader conceptual framework of the network of stakeholders relevant to an issue and of the diverse relations between these parties (Amin & Thrift, 1995; Healey, 1998; Thompson, Mitchell, Levacic, & Francis, 1991; Bramwell & Lane, 2000). Collaborative planning in tourist destinations is usually considered to involve direct dialogue among the participating stakeholders including the public-sectors planners, and thus has the potential to lead to negotiation, shared decision-making and consensus-building about planning goals and actions (Bramwell & Sharman, 1999).

For the purpose of developing this argument, the author will concentrate on the definition and model put forward by Jamal and Getz (1995) in their seminal paper 'Collaboration Theory and Community Tourism Planning'.

The definition put forward was adapted from Gray's (1989) work on collaboration theory and is as follows: 'Collaboration for community-based tourism planning is a process of joint decision-making among autonomous, key stakeholders of an inter-organisational, community tourism domain to resolve planning problems of the domain and/or manage issues related to the planning and development of the domain' (Jamal & Getz, 1995, p. 188). With this definition in mind for participation in tourism planning it is worth considering the five key characteristics of collaboration that have been outlined by Gray (1985, p. 236):

1. The stakeholders are independent;
2. Solutions emerge by dealing constructively with differences;
3. Joint ownership of decisions is involved;
4. The stakeholders assume collective responsibility for ongoing direction of the domain;
5. Collaboration is an emergent process, where collaborative initiatives can be understood as emergent organisational arrangements through which organisations collectively cope with the growing complexities of their environment.

Gray suggested a three-stage model through which collaboration develops (see Table 7). The first stage consists of an initial problem setting that helps identify key stakeholders and issues. This is then followed by the second stage in the process that is concerned with direction setting. This helps identify and create a shared vision of future collaborative interpretations, allowing a sense of common purpose to emerge.

The final stage of the process is implementation, where a shared vision, plan or strategy is implemented with a focus on selecting a suitable structure for institutionalising the process. Here tasks and goals may be assigned along with monitoring of ongoing processes to ensure compliance to collaboration decisions. The literature suggests numerous potential benefits for collaboration when the rich diversity of stakeholders affected by tourism attempts to collaborate and generate tourism plans. Some of these are quite obvious, like decreasing conflict from stakeholders who realise they need to work together towards a common shared goal. Overall the stakeholders may benefit from fewer adverse tourism impacts, increased competitiveness and enhanced equality (Gray, 1985; Bramwell & Lane, 2000). A comprehensive list of potential benefits of collaboration and partnerships in tourism planning has been generated by Bramwell and Lane (2000) and can be seen in Table 8. There are also limitations and obvious potential problems with collaboration in tourism planning. The most obvious is the need, if it arises,

Table 7. A Collaborative Process for Community-Based
Tourism Planning.

Stages and Propositions	Facilitating Conditions	Actions/Steps
Stage 1: Problem-setting Propositions applicable: P1, P2, P3, P4, P5	Recognition of interdependence; identification of a required number of stakeholders; legitimate/skilled convener; positive beliefs about outcomes; shared access power; mandate (external or internal); adequate resources for process	Define purpose and domain; identify convener; convene stakeholders; define issues to resolve; identify and legitimise stakeholders; build commitment to collaborate by raising awareness of interdependence; balance power differences; address stakeholders concerns; ensure adequate resources available to allow collaboration
Stage 2: Direction-setting Propositions applicable: P1, P2, P3, P5	Coincidence of values; distribution of power among stakeholders	Collect and share information; appreciate shared values; enhance perceived interdependence; ensure rules and agenda for direction-setting; organize subgroups if required; list alternatives; discuss various options; select appropriate solutions; arrive at shared vision or plan
Stage 3: Implementation Propositions applicable: P1, P2, P5	High degree of ongoing interdependence; external mandates; redistribution of power; influencing the contextual environment	Discuss means of implantation and monitoring solutions, shared vision and plan or strategy; select suitable structure for institutionalising process; assign goals and tasks; monitor ongoing progress and ensure compliance to collaboration decisions

Source: Modified from Gray (1985) and Jamel and Getz (1995).

to overcome the whole issue of mistrust that may have already set into the tourist destination.

This may be connected to environmental impacts that in itself raise complicated issues on guardianship and long-term management of resources. Another significant potential problem relates to the issue of power, the process may challenge the vested interests and power of otherwise dominant

Table 8. Benefits of Collaboration and Partnership in Tourism Planning.

There may be involvement by a range of stakeholders, all of whom are affected by the multiple issues of tourism development and may be well placed to introduce change and improvement

Decision-making power and control may diffuse to the multiple stakeholders that are affected by the issue, which is favourable for democracy

The involvement of several stakeholders may increase the social acceptance of policies, so that implementation and enforcement may be easier to affect

More constructive and less adversarial attitudes might result as a consequence of working together

The parties who are directly affected by the issues may bring their knowledge, attitudes and other capacities to the policy-making process

A creative synergy may result from working together, perhaps leading to greater innovation and effectiveness

Partnership can promote learning about the work, skills and potential of the other partners, and also develop the group interaction and negotiating skills that help to make partnerships successful

Parties involved in policy-making may have a greater commitment to putting the resulting policies into practice

There may be improved coordination of policies and related actions of the multiple stakeholders

There may be greater consideration of the diverse economic, environmental and social issues that affect the sustainable development of resources

When multiple stakeholders are engaged in decision-making, the resulting policies may be more flexible and also more sensitive to local communities and to changing conditions

Nontourism activities may be encouraged, leading to a broadening of the economic, employment and societal base of a given community or region

Source: Adapted from Bramwell and Lane (2000).

organisations (Gray, 1985; Bramwell & Lane, 2000). The collaboration or partnership may be set up as a tokenistic gesture to avoid tackling the bigger issues directly with all citizens involved.

Again Bramwell and Lane (2000) have provided a list of potential problems that are shown in Table 9. There are numerous examples in the literature of specific case studies demonstrating the success of collaborative community tourism planning (Murphy, 1988; Jamal & Getz, 1995; Bahaire & Elliot-White, 1999; Bramwell & Lane, 2000; Hall, 2000; Mason, 2003; Burns, 2004; Tosun, 2005). These case studies have been useful in providing in-depth insight into the process. They allow the researcher to identify the resources needed, time and the number of people involved within the process. Murphy (1988) for example provides an insight into such a collaborative planning exercise in Greater Victoria, British Columbia, Canada. Here 53 agencies and groups collaborated to solve the logistical and marketing difficulties

Table 9.   Problems of Collaboration and Partnerships in
Tourism Planning.

In some places and for some issues, there may be only a limited tradition of stakeholders
participating in policy-making
A partnership may be set up simply as 'window dressing' to avoid tackling real problems head-
on with all interests
Healthy conflict may be stifled
Collaborative efforts may be under-resourced in relation to requirements for additional staff
time, leadership and administrative resources
Actors may not be disposed to reduce their own power or to work together with unfamiliar
partners or previous adversaries
Those stakeholders with less power may be excluded from the process of collaborative working
or may have less influence on the process
Power within collaborative arrangements could pass to groups or individuals with more
effective political skills
Some key parties may be uninterested or inactive in working with others, sometimes because
they decide to rely on others to produce the benefits resulting from partnership
Some partners might coerce others by threatening to leave the partnership in order to press their
own case
The involvement of democratically elected government in collaborative working and consensus-
building may compromise its ability to protect the 'public interest'
Accountability to various constituencies may become blurred as the greater institutional
complexity of collaboration can obscure who is accountable to whom and for what
Collaboration may increase uncertainty about the future as the policies developed by multiple
stakeholders are more difficult to predict than those developed by an authority
The vested interests and established practices of the multiple stakeholders involved in
collaborative working may block innovation
Some collaborative arrangements may outline their usefulness, with their bureaucracies seeking
to extend their lives unreasonably

Source: Adapted from Bramwell and Lane (2000).

being faced by this fragmented domain. The process involved a 2-day
workshop attended by 150 people; with the result being shared common
marketing vision and objectives. From the work put forward by the
aforementioned authors, it is evident that the collaborative process for
community-based tourism planning may offer a very applicable process that
could be utilised in local-based tourism planning.

The collaboration process for community-based tourism planning
provides a dynamic process-orientated strategy that Jamal and Getz
(1995) suggest may be suitable to manage turbulent planning domains at
the local level. It aids public–private sector interactions and should therefore
provide an effective mechanism for community involvement in tourism

planning in Ireland, through the selection of key stakeholders to represent the public interests. It is also worth pointing out that Jamal and Getz (1995) argue that with the pace of change associated with tourism and intensifying competition resulting from the globalisation, sustainable tourism development at the local and global level will therefore require much greater cooperation than practised to date. What is even more significant is they suggest that in the future in emerging tourism domains, it may be necessary to specifically implement a collaborative community-based planning process and form relevant organisations to manage the tourism development affairs of the community and the region. This raises the question as to what form of method of participation, if any, was being deployed at the local authority level in Ireland. Furthermore, despite wide-scale recognition of the value of the various tools available to facilitate participation (Delbecq & Van de Ven, 1971; Glass, 1979; Murphy, 1985; Simmons, 1994; Middleton & Hawkins, 1998; Pearce et al., 1996; Pretty, 1995; Richards & Hall, 2000; Tosun, 2004; Murphy & Murphy, 2004), on closer analysis of the theory on community participation in tourism planning, it is evident that little in-depth critical appraisal has been carried out of the various tools available for facilitating participation. Research by Simmons (1994) only provides a subjective rather than empirical appraisal of methods (see Table 10). This clearly establishes a knowledge gap that if filled may facilitate tourism planners to utilise the best tools available to encourage meaningful and appropriate host community participation in sustainable tourism planning.

Table 10. Education of Citizen Participation Methods in Tourism.

Method	Type of Communication	Number of Participants	Representativeness of Participants	Efficiency, Cost and Time	Perceived Personal Usefulness for Public and for Planners
Interviews with key stakeholders	Two way	Low	High	High-medium	Medium-low
Community survey	One way	High	High	High-high	Low-medium
Focus groups (including a nominal group technique session)	Two way	Low	Medium	Medium-medium	High-high

Source: Modified from Simmons (1994).

Towards a Framework of Assessing Host Community Participation

Sustainable development must be built by, through and with the commitment of local communities. Stewart and Hams (1991) argue that the requirements of sustainable development cannot merely be imposed; active participation by local communities is needed. The absence of an existing framework that could be used to assess levels of host community participation in sustainable planning for tourism in Ireland resulted in the development of a specific framework being generated for the purpose of this chapter.

In order to probe planners and analyse the actual level of host community participation in the sustainable planning process, it was necessary to construct a framework capable of incorporating the majority of themes that have emerged from the literature review. This includes the host community problematic, methods of facilitating participation through to typologies of participation such as Tosun's (1999) normative typologies of community participation. Additionally, the framework needed to incorporate the legal or statutory obligation to consult, as well as the process for designing new Local Development Plans. In light of the discussion around this literature, this chapter requires a framework for assessing community participation in local authority tourism planning. It is however important to put this framework into the context of the Local Authority County Development Planning process involving communication and interrelationships (Table 11) in order to appreciate the complexities and stages of the planning process within which participation takes place.

The first theme is concerned with the need to define host community in order to facilitate meaningful participation. It assesses if the local authorities and any state tourism–related bodies have defined or identified community, host community, destination community or stakeholders. It also analyses local authorities' legal obligation and legal processes outlined for public consultation. In particular, it assesses the legal process of consultation followed in terms of communication, notification of public meetings, oral submissions and manager's reports on submissions.

Theme 2 assesses if specific participation models were applied to facilitate host community involvement. It identifies if an external facilitator was used and if the local authority had a particular mechanism in place for community consultation. It then breaks the process up into the following subcategories to ensure that all the components were assessed: number of public consultation meetings held, time of public meetings, presentations and exhibitions given, question and answer sessions facilitated, participatory workshops facilitated at public meetings, written submissions taken at

Table 11. An Outline of the Framework for Assessing Community Participation in Local Authority Tourism Planning in Ireland.

1. Host community
   The need to plan for tourism communities addressed
   Legal obligation to consult addressed and fulfilled
   Communication of the initiation of the consultation process
2. Process of consultation
   Specific participation model used
   External facilitator used
   Mechanism in place for consultation
   Method of participation (tools used)
3. Host community and stakeholders submissions on planning concerns
4. Draft plan
   Inspection copy of draft plan made available to host community and sent to various
     stakeholders and authorities
   Alterations and impacts to draft plan from host community and various agencies submitted
5. Information host community of changes to draft plan and final plan, e-planning
6. Training and support for planners to facilitate consultation
7. Community participation at higher levels (regional, national and EU)

meetings and individual clinic facilitation. Theme 3 is concerned with the assessment of submissions. In order to identify the level of participation it is necessary to assess the number of submissions made at the various stages of the planning process and identify through content analysis how many of these submissions directly relate to tourism. The framework allows these results to be compared and contrasted on a national level between counties in terms of tourist arrivals to the region.

Theme 4 examines some aspects of the draft plan preparation and its exposure to the host community and prescribed bodies. In particular it determines the nature of alterations to the draft plan, focusing on the local authority's impact on the alteration of the plan and the second manager's report on relevant submissions from community, stakeholder or prescribed bodies. Theme 5 of the framework examines communication within the planning process and the emergent area of e-planning and assesses the level of e-planning engaged in by local authorities. It is also concerned with determining the detail and depth of the e-planning portals being employed by the forward planners.

Theme 6 within the framework incorporates the assessment of levels of training and support available to planners who were responsible for facilitating this process. In particular, it notes external and in-house training for planners on public consultation. It assesses the level of support offered by literature and guides on the consultation process available to planners and finally assesses if the available resources provided by the local authority for running the consultation process is a limitation. Theme 7 addresses levels of community participation at a regional, national and European level. This allows the researcher to provide a bottom-up assessment of participation, assessing levels of community involvement from the local plan level to the wider European level.

CONCLUSION

The need for community participation in sustainable tourism planning has been clearly identified from world summit level to the implementation of LA 21. However, this reality is yet to be fully realised. Some concern has been raised in relation to the problematic of community in that the term 'host community' has been used widely by planners, academics and policy writers with assumptions made in relation to the definition, homogeneity and willingness to participate in sustainable tourism planning processes. Although there is an abundance of international literature and case studies on the need for and application of community involvement in tourism planning, there still exists the fundamental debate as to whether communities exist in a functional sense, and if they do, are they prepared and willing to be involved in determining their own futures.

There exists the need for more specific and in-depth assessment in order to help define the host community and assess the validity of engaging in and uses of particular methods employed to facilitate long-term meaningful host community participation in sustainable tourism planning. There is also a need to identify the actual relative impediments and limitations encountered by local authorities planners when facilitating this process. Furthermore, community involvement or public participation in tourism planning remains an ambiguous concept and relatively little research exists on the topic to date. This research should attempt to address this gap and help clarify some of the issues for local authority planners, Fáilte Ireland, and host communities. In order to assess the extent of host community participation in sustainable tourism planning, the most relevant themes from the literature were taken and incorporated into a framework. The level of host community participation, however, needs to be assessed in context of the process, depth and application of planning for sustainable tourism.

REFERENCES

Amin, A., & Thrift, N. (1995). Globalisation, institutional 'thickness' and the local economy. In: P. Healy, S. Davoudi, S. Graham & A. Madani-Pour (Eds), *Managing cities: The new urban context* (pp. 91–108). Chichester: Wiley.

Anderson, B. (1983). *Imagined communities: Reflections on the origin and spread of nationalism.* London: Verso.

Arnstein, R. S. (1969). A ladder of citizen participation. *Journal of the American Institute of Planners, 35,* 216–224.

Arnstein, S. R. (1971). A ladder of citizen participation. *Journal of the Royal Town Planning Institute,* April.

Bahaire, T., & Elliot-White, M. (1999). The application of geographic information systems (GIS) in sustainable tourism planning: A review. *Journal of Sustainable Tourism, 7*(2), 159–177.

Bell, C., & Newby, H. (1976). Community, communion, class and community action: The social sources of the new urban politics. In: D. T. Herbert & R. J. Johnston (Eds), *Social areas in cities* (Vol. 2). London: Wiley.

Blank, U. (1989). *The community tourism imperative: The necessity, the opportunities, its potential.* State College, TX: Venture Publishing.

Bochner, S. (1982). *Cultures in contact: Studies in cross cultural interaction.* Oxford, NY: Pergamon Press.

Boissevain, J. (1979). Impact of tourism on a dependent Island: Gozo, Malta. *Annals of Tourism Research, 6,* 76–90.

Bonilla, J. C. (1997). *Participatory ecotourism planning.* London: Conservation International.

Bosselman, F. P. (1979). *In the wake of the tourist: Managing special places in eight countries.* Washington, DC: The Conservation Foundation.

Boyd, S. W., & Singh, S. (2003). Destination communities: Structures, resources and types. In: S. Singh, D. J. Timothy & R. K. Dowling (Eds), *Tourism in destination communities* (pp. 32–41). Bristol, UK: CAB International.

Bramwell, B., & Lane, B. (1999). *Tourism collaboration and partnerships, aspects of tourism.* Bristol, UK: Channel View publications.

Bramwell, B., & Lane, B. (2000). *Tourism, collaboration and partnerships (aspects of tourism).* Bristol, UK: Channel View Publications.

Bramwell, B., & Sharman, A. (1999). Collaboration in local tourism policy making. *Annals of Tourism Research, 26*(2), 392–415.

Brandon, K. (1993). Basic steps toward encouraging local participation in nature tourism projects. In: K. Lindberg & D. E. Hawkins (Eds), *Ecotourism: A guide for planners and managers* (pp. 134–151). North Bennington: The Ecotourism Society.

Bryson, J. M., & Crosby, B. C. (1992). *Leadership for the common good: Tackling public problems in a shared-power world.* San Francisco: Jossey-Bass.

Burns, P. (2004). Tourism planning: A third way? *Annals of Tourism Research, 31*(1), 24–43. ISSN 0160-7383.

Castells, M. (2001). *The internet galaxy: Reflections on the internet, business and society.* Oxford: Oxford University Press.

Cater, E., & Lowman, G. (1994). *Ecotourism: A sustainable option?* New York: Wiley.

Choy, D. J. L. (1984). Tourism and development: The case of American Samoa. *Annals of Tourism Research, 11,* 573–590.

Clark, G. (1984). A theory of local autonomy. *Annals of the Association of American Geographers, 74,* 195–208.

Cleaver, F. (2001). Institutions, agency and the limitations of participatory approaches to development. In: B. Cooke & U. Kothari (Eds), *Participation: The new tyranny.* London: Zed Books.

Cohen, A. (1985). *The symbolic construction of community.* London: Tavistock.

Cohen, E. (1971). Arab boys and tourist girls in a mixed Jewish/Arab community. *International Journal of Comparative Sociology, 12,* 217–233.

Cohen, E. (1988). Authenticity and commoditization in tourism. *Annals of Tourism Research, 15,* 371–386.

Cooke, B. (2000). Rules of thumb for participatory change agents. In: S. Hickey & G. Mohan (Eds), *Participation from tyranny to transformation?* (pp. 42–56). London: Zed Books.

Cooke, B., & Kothari, U. (Eds). (2001). *Participation: The new tyranny.* London: Zed Books.

Cooke, K. (1982). Guidelines for socially appropriate tourism development in British Columbia. *Journal of Tourism Research, 21*(1), 22–28.

Dalton, S., & Dalton, R. (1975). *Community and its relevance to Australian society.* Canberra: Department of Tourism and Recreation.

D'Amore, L. (1983). Guidelines to planning harmony with host community. In: P. Murphy (Ed.), *Tourism in Canada: Selected issues and options* (pp. 135–159). Victoria, BC: University of Victoria, Western Geographic Series 21.

Dann, G. (1978). Tourist satisfaction; a highly complex variable. *Annals of Tourism Research, 5*(4), 440–443.

De Araujo, M., & Bramwell, B. (2000). Stakeholder assessment and collaborative tourism planning. In: B. Bramwell & B. Lane (Eds), *Tourism collaboration and partnerships, aspects of tourism.* Bristol, UK: Channel View publications.

de Kadt, E. (Ed.) (1979). *Tourism: Passport to development.* Oxford: Oxford University Press.

Delanty, G. (2003). *Community.* London: Routledge.

Delbecq, A. L., & Van de Ven, A. H. (1971). A group process model for problem identification and program planning. *Journal of Applied Behaviour Science, 7,* 466–492.

Doxey, G. (1975). When enough's enough: The natives are restless in old Niagara. *Heritage Canada, 2,* 26–27.

Drake, S. (1991). Local participation in ecotourism projects. In: T. Whelan (Ed.), *Nature tourism.* Washington: Island Press.

Dye, T. R. (1986). Community power and public policy. In: R. J. Waste (Ed.), *Community power: Directions for future research* (pp. 29–51). Beverly Hills, CA: Sage.

European Commission Enterprise and Industry. (2007). *Actions for more sustainable European tourism.* Report of the Tourism Sustainability Group, European Commission.

Foucault, M. (1980). *Power and knowledge.* Hemel Hempstead: Harvester Wheatsheaf.

Getz, D., & Jamal, T. B. (1994). The environment-community symbiosis: A case for collaborative tourism planning. *Journal of Sustainable Tourism, 2*(3), 152–173.

Glass, J. J. (1979). Citizen participation: The relationship between objectives and techniques. *Journal of American Planning Association, 45,* 180–189.

Gordon, J. R., Mondy, R. W., Sharplin, A., & Premeaux, S. R. (1990). *Management and organisational behaviour.* Boston: Allyn & Bacon.

Gray, B. (1985). Conditions facilitating interorganisational collaboration. *Human Relations, 38*(10), 911–936.

Gray, B. (1989). *Collaboration finding common ground for multi-party problems.* San Francisco: Jossey-Bass.

Green, H., & Hunter, C. (1992). The environmental impact assessment of tourism development. In: P. Johnson & B. Thomas (Eds), *Perspectives on tourism policy.* London: Mansell.

Gunn, C. (1972). *Vacationscape.* New York: Van Nostrand Reinhold.

Gunn, C. (1988). Participatory planning a view of tourism in Indonesia. *Annals of Tourism Research, 26*(2), 371–391.

Gunn, C. (1994). *Tourism planning, basic concepts cases* (3rd ed). New York: Taylor and Francis.

Gunn, C. (2002). *Tourism planning, basic concepts cases* (3rd ed.). New York: Taylor and Francis.

Gunn, C. A. (2002). *Tourism planning: Basics, concepts, cases* (4th ed.). New York: Routledge.

Hall, C. M. (2000). *Tourism planning: Policies, processes and relationships.* Essex: Prentice Hall.

Hall, M. (1984). *Tourism and politics.* Chichester: Wiley.

Haywood, K. M. (1988). Responsible and responsive tourism planning in the community. *Tourism Management, 9,* 105–118.

Healey, P. (1998). Collaborative planning in a stakeholder society. *Town Planning Review, 69*(1), 1–21.

Henkel, H., & Stirrat, R. (2001). Participation as spiritual duty; empowerment as secular subjection. In: B. Cooke & U. Kothari (Eds), *Participation: The new tyranny.* London: Zed Books.

Hillery, G. A. (1955). Definitions of community: Areas of agreement. *Rural Sociology, 20*(2), 111–123.

Hollinshead, K. (1990). The powers behind play: The political environments for recreation and tourism. *Australia Journal of Park and Recreation Administration, 8,* 35–50.

Hunter, C., & Green, H. (1995). *Tourism and the environment: A sustainable relationship?* London and New York: Routledge.

Inskeep, E. (1987). Environmental planning for tourism. *Annals of Tourism Research, 14*(1), 118–135.

Inskeep, E. (1991). *Tourism planning: An integrated and sustainable development approach.* New York: Van Nostrand Reinhold.

Jackson, G., & Morpeth, N. (1999). Local Agenda 21 and community participation in tourism policy and planning: Future or fallacy. *Current Issues in Tourism, 2*(1), 39–46.

Jamal, T., & Getz, D. (1995). Collaboration theory and community tourism planning. *Annals of Tourism Research, 22*(2), 186–204.

Jenkins, C. L. (1993). Tourism in developing countries: The privatisation issue. In: A. V. Seaton (Ed.), *Tourism: The state of the art* (pp. 3–9). Chichester, England: Wiley.

Joppe, M. (1996). Sustainable community tourism development revisited. *Tourism Management, 17*(7), 475–479.

Keogh, B. (1990). Public participation in community tourism planning. *Annals of Tourism Research, 17,* 449–465.

Knopp, T. B. (1980). Tourism, the local interests and the function of public lands. In: D. Hawkins & E. Shafer (Eds), *Tourism planning and development issues.* London: Sage.

Kothari, U. (2001). Power knowledge and social control in participatory development. In: B. Cooke & U. Kothari (Eds), *Participation: The new tyranny.* London: Zed Books.

Krippendorf, J. (1982). Towards new tourism policies. *Tourism management, 3,* 135–148.

Lankford, V. (1994). Attitudes and perceptions toward tourism and rural regional development. *Journal of Travel Research, 32*(2), 35–43.

Li, W., & Yu, L. (1974). Interpersonal contact and racial prejudice: A comparative study of American and Chinese students. *The Sociological Quarterly, 15*, 559–566.

Long, P. T., & Richardson S. L. (1989). Integrating recreation and tourism development in small winter cities. *Leisure Today, 60*(8), 26–29.

Mason, D. (2004). Guest perceptions and uncertainty: A study of the hotel booking process. *International Journal of Hospitality and Tourism Administration, 5*(3).

Mason, P. (2003). *Tourism impacts, planning and management.* London: Heinemann.

Mathieson, A., & Wall, G. (1982). *Tourism: Economic, physical and social impacts.* London: Longman.

Mayo, M. (2000). *Cultures, communities, identities.* London: Palgrave.

McIntosh, R. W., & Goeldner, C. R. (1990). *Tourism; principles, practices, philosophies* (6th ed.). New York: Wiley.

Medlick, S. (2003). *Dictionary of travel, tourism and hospitality.* London: Heinemann.

Middleton, V. T. C., & Hawkins, R. (1998). *Sustainable tourism: A marketing perspective.* Oxford: Heinemann.

Mowforth, M., & Munt, I. (1998). *Tourism and sustainability: Development and new tourism in the third world.* London: Routledge.

Mowforth, M., & Munt, I. (2000). *Tourism and sustainability: Development and new tourism in the third world* (2nd ed.). London: Routledge.

Mowforth, M., & Munt, I. (2003). *Tourism and sustainability: New tourism in the third world* (2nd ed., 338p.). London: Routledge.

Mowforth, M., & Munt, I. (2004). *Tourism and sustainability: Development and new tourism in the third world* (3rd ed.). London: Routledge.

Murphy, L. (2005). High tech versus high touch: Visitor responses to the use of technology in tourist attractions. *Tourism Recreation Research Special Issue on Cybertourism, 30*(3), 37–47.

Murphy, P. (1984). Perceptions and attitudes of decision-making groups in tourism centers. *Journal of Travel Research, 21*(3), 8–12.

Murphy, P. (1985). *Tourism: A community approach.* New York: Methuen.

Murphy, P. (1988). *Tourism Management, 9*(2), 96–104.

Murphy, P. (1999). Tourism and sustainable development. In: W. Theobald (Ed.), *Global tourism* (2nd ed., pp. 173–190). Oxford: Heinemann.

Murphy, P., & Murphy, A. (2004). *Strategic management for tourism communities (aspects of tourism, 16).* Bristol, UK: Channel View Publications.

O'Carroll. J. P. (1985). Community and society. *Social Studies, 8*, 17–42. Irish Press.

Oppermann, M., & Weaver, D. (2000). *Tourism management.* Brisban, Australia: Wiley.

Page, S. J., & Dowling, R. K. (2002). *Ecotourism.* Harlow: Prentice Hall.

Pearce, D., Moscardo, G., & Ross, G. F. (1996). *Tourism community relationships.* Oxford: Elsevier Science Ltd.

Peck, J. G., & Lepie, A. S. (1977). Tourism and development in three North Carolina coastal towns. In: V. Smith (Ed.), *Hosts and guests: An anthropology of tourism* (pp. 159–172). Philadelphia: University of Pennsylvania Press.

Pine, R. (1984). Public participation and natural resource decision-making. *Journal of Natural Resources, 27*(1), 123–155.

Porteous, J. F. (1989). *Planned to death.* Toronto: University of Toronto.

Pretty, J. (1995). The many interpretations of participation. *Focus, 16*, 4–5.

Rahnema, M. (1992). Participation. In: W. Sachs (Ed.), *The development dictionary: A guide to knowledge as power.* London: Zed Books.

Reed, M. (1995). Co-operative management of environmental resources: A case study from Northern Ontario, Canada. Economic Geography, *71*, 132–149.

Reed, M. G. (1997). Power relations and community-based tourism planning. *Annals of Tourism Research, 24*(3), 566–591.

Rees, J. (1990). *Natural resources: Allocation, economics and policy* (2nd ed.). London: Routledge.

Reid, D. G., Mair, H., & George, E. W. (2004). Community tourism planning: A self-assessment instrument. *Annals of Tourism Research, 31*(3), 623–639.

Reisinger, Y., & Turner, L. W. (2003). *Cross-cultural behaviour in tourism.* London: Elsevier.

Richards, G., & Hall, D. (Eds). (2000). Tourism and sustainable community development. USA: Sage.

Richie, J. R. (1993). Crafting a destination vision: Putting the concept of resident-responsive tourism into practice. *Tourism Management, 15*(5), 379–389.

Ritchie, J. R. B. (1988). Crafting a destination vision. In: J. R. B. Ritchie & C. R. Goeldner (Eds), *Travel tourism and hospitality research* (2nd ed., pp. 29–38). New York: Wiley.

Shields, R. (Ed.) (1996). *Cultures of the internet.* London: Sage.

Simmons, D. G. (1994). Community participation in tourism planning. *Tourism Management, 15*, 98–108.

Sproule, K., & Suhandi, S. (1998). Guidelines for community-based ecotourism programs. *The Ecotourism Society, 5*, 215–235.

Stewart, J., & Hams, T. (1991). *Local Government for Sustainability.* Luton: Local Government Management Board.

Susskind, L., & Field, P. (1996). *Dealing with an angry public: The mutual gains approach to resolving disputes.* New York: The Free Press.

Swarbrooke, J. (1999). *Sustainable tourism management.* Wallingford: CABI Publications.

Syme, G., MacPherson, D., & Seiligman, C. (1991). Factors motivating community participation in regional water allocation planning – A test of an expectancy value model. *Environment and Planning A, 23*, 1779–1795.

Taylor, H. (2001). Insights into participation from critical management and labour process perspective. In: B. Cooke & U. Kothari (Eds), *Participation: The new tyranny.* London: Zed Books.

Thompson, G., Mitchell, J., Levacic, R., & Francis, J. (1991). *Markets, hierarchies and networks: The coordination of social life.* London: Sage.

Timothy, D. J. (1998). Cooperative tourism planning in a developing destination. *Journal of Sustainable Tourism, 6*(1), 52–68.

Timothy, D. J., & Tosun, C. (2003). Appropriate planning for tourism in destination communities: Participation, incremental growth and collaboration. In: S. Singh, D. J. Timothy & R. K. Dowling (Eds), *Tourism in destination communities* (pp. 181–204). Wallingford: CAB International.

Tosun, C. (1998). Roots of unsustainable tourism development at the local level: The case of Urgup in Turkey. *Tourism Management, 19*, 595–610.

Tosun, C. (1999). Towards a typology of community participation in the tourism development process. *International Journal of Tourism and Hospitality, 10*, 113–134.

Tosun, C. (2000). Limits to community participation in the tourism development process in developing countries. *Tourism Management, 21*(6), 613–633.

Tosun, C. (2004). Expected nature of community participation in tourism development. *Tourism management, 27*(3), 493–504.

Tosun, C. (2005). Sustainable tourism development in the developing world: The case of Turkey. *Tourism Management, 22*, 289–303.

Tosun, C. (2006). Perceptions of tourism impacts: A comparative study. *Annals of Tourism Research, 28*, 231–253.

Tovey, H. (1984). Local community, a defence of a much-criticized concept. *Social Studies, 8*, 17–29. Irish Press.

UNESCO. (1976). The effects of tourism on socio-cultural values. *Annals of Tourism Research, 4*(2), 74–103.

United Nations Food and Agriculture Organisation (UNFAO). (1990). *The community's tool box*. Rome: FAO.

UNWTO. (2005). Making tourism more sustainable, a guide for policy makers UNWTO/UNEP. Madrid: WTO.

Warren, R. (1977). *Social change and human purpose*. Chicago: Rand McNally.

Webber, T. (1995). Right discourse in citizen participation: An evaluative yardstick. In: O. Renn, T. Webler & P. Wiedemann (Eds), *Fairness and competence in citizen participation: Evaluating models for environmental discourse* (pp. 35–86). The Netherlands: Kluwer Academic press.

West, P. (1994). Natural resources and the persistence of rural poverty in America: A Weberian Perspective on the role of power, domination, and natural resources bureaucracy. *Society and Natural Resources, 7*, 415–427.

Williams, A. M. (1996). Mass tourism and international tour companies. In: M. Barke, J. Towner & M. T. Newton (Eds), *Tourism in Spain: Critical issues*. Wallingford: CAB International.

Young, G. (1973). *Tourism: Blessing or blight?* London: Penguin Books.

Yuksel, F., Bramwell, B., & Yuksel, A. (1999). Stakeholder interviews and tourism planning at Pamukkale, Turkey. *Tourism Management, 20*, 351–360.

CHAPTER 10

THE POLITICS OF WASTE, CONSUMPTION AND SUSTAINABILITY IN THE REPUBLIC OF IRELAND

G. Honor Fagan

INTRODUCTION: THE POLITICS OF GROWTH AND WASTE

Grotesque wasting has been, and is, generated in a series of spatial levels or scales and in association with accelerated growth rates. A key political challenge for environmental sustainability in the approaching post–consumerist phase of globalisation is to innovate, plan and implement a fresh waste future as part of the wider evolving green revolution. This challenge of addressing the structures and practices of wasting can only be pursued through a multiplex response in production, governance, consumption patterns, scientific advances, national mindset and personal attitudes.

Growth in the production and consumption has generated volatile levels of wasting, to the extent that sustainable development is not viable without a total review of the logic of wasting. Sustainable development as a concept contains two competing elements. The word development can primarily

Global Ecological Politics
Advances in Ecopolitics, Volume 5, 221–240
Copyright © 2010 by Emerald Group Publishing Limited
All rights of reproduction in any form reserved
ISSN: 2041-806X/doi:10.1108/S2041-806X(2010)0000005014

refer to economic growth, increased production and increased profitability in production. On the contrary, sustainability refers to a way of meeting our needs without compromising the capacity of the children of this generation to in turn meet its needs by depleting earth's resources or not taking into account its limitations. The sustainability argument is premised on the necessity of reconstructing our theoretical conceptions of productivity, profit and consumerism in ways that 'build in' the waste component. Social and economic theorists, producers, consumers and politicians alike have traditionally relegated this constituent element of production – wasting-to obscurity. However, more recently a major shift in approach is evident with the 'zero waste' environmental campaigns and the clean production agenda that creates possibilities of new waste futures.

This chapter describes the politics of growth and waste management in the Republic of Ireland during the 'Celtic Tiger' decade of rapid economic growth between 1996 and 2006. It advances a multi-scalar analysis of the various actors involved in waste governance as they sought seek to deal with what has become known as the 'waste crisis' and identifies shifts and continuities within the counter-posed sustainability and competitiveness paradigms in those Celtic Tiger years. It moves on to discuss how in 'after the extreme partying' mode of the post-boom conjuncture the notion of sustainability may find a fresh resonance with people. This chapter argues for prioritising, communicating and symbolising a 'green' component to Irish identity and developing a new reflective politics of clean production and consumption. Given that the excesses of ungoverned accelerated growth are now very visible and extreme wasting has been witnessed it is, perhaps, more likely that an appetite for sustainable development will emerge.

MEASURING SMART GROWTH

Although sustainability is a nebulous concept and has been critiqued for being so broad as to appear to be the conceptualisation of 'environmental politics gone astray' (Fisher & Hayer, 1999), there is evidence that to some extent indicators of sustainability will be quite concretely built into all future development. How does one evaluate a period of national economic growth in the twenty-first century? Economists typically measure it in terms of Gross Domestic Product (GDP). Sociologists typically measure it on the basis of increased household earnings, and other sociologists of a more radical persuasion measure it on the basis of increased equality in incomes, whether in terms of earnings between classes, spatially diverse locations, genders or races. Increasingly at the micro-level citizens choose to understand, conceptualise and measure it on the basis of growth in their individual or family income, their increased spending and purchasing power, and their greater access to social facilities such as education, health and their access and control over decision making in government policies that impact their lives and life chances. Hence, there is a variation and indeed a politics to measuring development. Structures of economic development traditionally operate to increase production. Economic development is likewise dependent on growth in consumption, where the ability of consumers to buy the outputs from production is linked directly to the calculations on profit. Although that equation works out quite well in the short term, it does not take into account the real material factor of the environment in which this structural activity is organised. In other words, it does not cost in the exploitation of the environment nor factor in the material reality of the earth as a limited resource, usually reduced by economists to mere 'externalities'. From a structural perspective it can be argued then that the prioritisation of economic growth has led to a total array of structural conditions that support production for profit regardless of the lack of sustainability of such patterns of production and consumption.

However, more recently, an interesting shift is occurring at the macro level of economic governance in the global era where measuring the success of growth through GDP indicators is being subtly but irreversibly altered. Now the argument is being developed, due to environmental pressures, for a shift from GDP indicators to 'smart GDP' measurements where good things count positively and bad things count negatively (McGlade, 2007). Measurements of GDP are inaccurate and misleading given that a GDP can soar after a natural disaster for example, because of the inevitable increase in production to rebuild after the loss of human life and infrastructure. Given the current pressures on the environment, global sustainability necessitates the redesign of production and consumption patterns. So-called smart GDP (McGlade, 2007) indicators will drive this, regulating production in ways that provide opportunities for systemic changes in diets and lifestyles. The redesign is currently under development in the context of the action plans of the European Commission such as the dual and interlinked development of the Action Plan on Sustainable Consumption and Production and the Action Plan on Sustainable Industrial Policy.

Was the 'Celtic Tiger' boom based on a 'smart economy' or 'Smart' GDP indicators? If we look at the waste scenario, we can argue that it fell very short of being smart. In fact the prioritisation of economic growth that characterised the boom years led to a total array of structural conditions that supported production for profit regardless of the lack of sustainability of such patterns of production and consumption. In the context of the debate on 'Smart' GDPs we can ask have principles around Ireland's sustainability been addressed in relation to production, consumption and waste policy in its Celtic Tiger years? How have various forces shaped the waste policy, and to what degree has sustainability or competitiveness entered calculations?

THE 'CELTIC TIGER' AND THE POLITICAL ECONOMY OF WASTE

Internationally, the pattern of waste flows in the 1980s and 1990s was marked by wholesale increases in the production of waste, with particularly fast increases in the richer nations. US waste generation grew from 2.7 pounds per person in 1960 to 3.3 pounds per person in 1980 and up to 4.4 pounds per person in 1993.[1] Over 1.8 billion tonnes of waste was generated each year in Europe equivalent to 3.5 tonnes per person. This was mainly made up of waste coming from households, commercial activities (e.g. shops, restaurants and hospitals), industry (e.g. pharmaceutical companies and clothes manufacturers), agriculture (e.g. slurry), construction and demolition projects, mining and quarrying activities and from the generation of energy. In all European Union (EU) countries, the quantity of waste is continuously increasing, however, in the Republic of Ireland, there was an above average growth rate in its production due to the economic boom of the 'Celtic Tiger'. Between 1995 and 1998, waste flows in Ireland increased by a phenomenal 89 per cent. Clearly one principal child of the economic boom was unsightly and unsustainable waste production, and clearly the debris of globalised Ireland's production and consumption boom left a visible malign geographic footprint. The position on its management in 2000 was, according to an Environmental Protection Agency staff member interviewed then, that:

We have done very little in the waste area through the 1970s and 1980s, and it wasn't until the 1990s that any kind of focus started on waste. And because we didn't start when we should have, we are twenty-five years behind others. (Fagan, O'Hearn, Mc Cann, & Murray, 2001, p. 13)

In other words, before the Republic of Ireland was networked into a European system of waste management, they were simply not governing waste; they were 'disposing' of it in landfill sites. Agricultural waste, at 70 per cent of the total, constitutes the largest proportion, although it is decreasing from previous years. Construction and demolition waste constitutes the next biggest proportion at 12 per cent of the total. The bulk of the 15 per cent increase in total generation of waste between 2001 and 2004 is attributed to the trebling of the waste produced in this category. Municipal waste, which got a disproportionate amount of attention in the 'waste crisis' debate, constitutes only 4 per cent of the waste produced. However, it too is fast increasing.

Municipal waste increased by 1 per cent from 2001 to 2002, but from 2002 to 2003 it increased by 10 per cent, where for the first time municipal waste exceeded three million tonnes (EPA, 2003, p. 6).[2] Although municipal waste did increase in 2004 by 4 per cent, a new statistical calculation on the part of the EPA leaves the overall figure to be still at just over 3 million tonnes (EPA, 2004, p. vii) (Table 1).

Table 1. The Irish Total Waste Generation in 2004.

Waste Category	2004	
	Tonnes	%
Construction and demolition waste	11,167,599	13.1
Manufacturing waste	5,044,243	5.9
Mining and quarrying waste	4,044,511	4.7
Municipal waste	3,034,566	3.6
End-of-life vehicles and scrap metal	491,960	0.6
Hazardous waste	366,291	0.4
Contaminated soil	307,340	0.4
Energy, gas and water supply waste	284,647	0.3
Dredge spoils	238,565	0.3
Drinking water sludges	59,741	0.1
Urban wastewater sludges	42,298	0.0
Sub-total non-agricultural waste	25,081,660	29.4
Agricultural waste	60,175,025	70.6
Total	85,256,685	–

Source: EPA (2004).

At the level of individual consumption, each person in the Republic of Ireland in the year 2000 'produced' practically double the European average of 1 kg of municipal waste per day. The Irish Environmental Protection Agency (EPA, 2002) estimated that in 2000 every citizen of the Republic produced an average of 600 kg of waste a year. The average generation of household waste per person was calculated at 398 kg per capita in 2003, still increasing from 2002, but with just a 2 per cent rate of increase (EPA, 2003, p. 8). The methodologies for calculation have been changed, and there have been improvements in the collection of data from local authorities since 2003 (EPA, 2004, p. 8). However, although there is variation between national calculation methods, and data to some extent may not be comparable, still Ireland ranks as the largest per capita generator of municipal waste in the EU [European Environmental Agency (EEA), 2005].

Applying the concept of environmental sustainability to recent economic development trends in Ireland highlights the boom's disastrous eco-social consequences. Are there any real achievements in terms of waste reduction given increased pressure from the EU to regulate waste? Table 2 shows the major waste indicators for 2001, 2002 and 2003. It provides figures for the latest waste produced, recovered and disposed of in landfill for these years during which there has in fact been an implementation of waste management policy.

Although the figures highlight huge efforts to manage waste, particularly at the three lower levels of the waste hierarchy, as in the rest of Europe, these efforts are not effectively counteracting the increases. National and EU regulations are not enough in themselves to stem flows in waste. In addition to this policy failure, there has been in Ireland considerable illegal waste activity recorded since the introduction of the Waste Management Act in 1996. Large-scale dumping occurred in Wicklow from 1997 to 2002, and in 2005 there were still 25 unauthorised landfills and fifteen unauthorised waste handling facilities (EPA, 2005, p. 1). There has also been considerable cross-border illegal movement of waste. Statistics for 2003 show that one in five households were either not served or not availing of a waste collection service, which in itself could involve almost 300,000 tonnes of waste unaccounted for annually (EPA, 2005, p. 2). The 2005 EPA report on *The Nature and Extent of Unauthorised Activity in Ireland* indicates that first the nature of illegal activity is changing in that large-scale illegal dumping no longer takes place, that illegal cross-border movement of waste has reduced significantly, but that there has been increased unauthorised waste collection, fly-tipping (sporadic, small-scale dumping) and uncontrolled burning of waste. It is estimated that 17 of the 25 unauthorised

Table 2. Waste Indicators, 2001–2003.

Indicator	2001	2002	2003
Municipal waste			
Municipal waste collected/person	0.59 tonnes	0.61 tonnes	0.65 tonnes
Municipal waste arising/person	0.69 tonnes	0.69 tonnes	0.77 tonnes
Disposal rate for household and commercial waste collected	86.7%	79.3%	71.6%
Recovery rate for household and commercial waste collected	13.3%	20.7%	28.4%
Number of landfills accepting municipal waste	48	39	35
Number of bring banks	1,436	1,636	1,692
Household waste			
Household waste collected/person	0.34 tonnes	0.36 tonnes	0.36 tonnes
Household waste arising/person	0.37 tonnes	0.39 tonnes	0.41 tonnes
Disposal rate for household waste	94.4%	90.7%	86.9%
Recovery rate for household waste	5.6%	9.3%	13.1%
Commercial waste			
Commercial waste collected/person	0.25 tonnes	0.25 tonnes	0.29 tonnes
Disposal rate for commercial waste collected	76.2%	62.5%	52.7%
Recovery rate for commercial waste collected	23.8%	37.5%	47.4%
Packaging waste			
Best estimate of total quantity arising	872,917 tonnes	899,125 tonnes	1,006,287 tonnes
Packaging waste arising/person	0.223 tonnes	0.229 tonnes	0.257 tonnes
Best estimate of packaging waste recovered	221,266 tonnes	296,389 tonnes	419,600 tonnes
Packaging waste recovered/person	0.056 tonnes	0.076 tonnes	0.107 tonnes
National recovery rate	25.3%	33%	41.7%
Hazardous waste			
Quantity of hazardous waste exported	275,309 tonnes 226,904 recovery 47,979 disposal 475 unspecified	249,439 tonnes 203,156 recovery 42,419 disposal 3,364 unspecified	389,199 tonnes 224,749 recovery 162,821 disposal 1,629 unspecified

Source: EPA (2004, p. 28).

landfills contained commercial and industrial waste, with construction and demolition waste accounting for the greatest level of illegal activity.

Over 80 per cent of the waste found in unauthorised landfills was construction and demolition waste and local authorities had received more complaints about this type of waste than about all the other streams put together. Given these figures on illegal activity, the EPA strongly advocates enforcement as key to progress on waste management (EPA, 2002, p. 2). However, although enforcement in these cases is indeed a priority, it is clearly the mark of the failure of Irish policy in general. Focusing on enforcement is indeed a distraction, but perhaps a necessary one for the EPA, given that the seismic shifts necessary to address the problem of waste and to engineer a sustainable future for Ireland, is not evident. Regardless of the policies on how to deal with waste, such as whether to divert it from landfill, recycle it, or incinerate it, we can clearly conclude that the Celtic Tiger has excreted all over the Irish landscape and environment. The 'green Ireland' of myth and folklore has been noticeably marked by its economic boom, and the overall trend of increased waste generation remains an unresolved issue and a key matter of concern that requires revolutionary redress over the years to come.

TECHNOCRACY, PROBLEM SOLVING AND PLANNING?

Having looked at the material reality of waste production and disposal in the Celtic Tiger years, the chapter now turns to the emerging opportunities and obstacles in the policy arena. Ireland at the height of its economic boom moved into the grip of what has been commonly referred to as a 'waste management crisis' (Fagan et al., 2001) in the late 1990s and the early 2000s. There were two aspects to this crisis. First, there was the material and environmental problem of the increase in the quantity and types of waste and, second, the interlocked problem of its management. With the EU able to enforce sanctions on the nation-state and the national Government needing to radically change the direction and composition of waste flows, the drawing up and implementation of strategy quickly became an issue of governance at a national level. Stoker (1998, p. 21) argues that 'governance recognises the blurring of boundaries and responsibilities for tackling social and economic issues'. Government by central decree on the waste management issue was not an option since the Irish Government had moved to a governance model patterned on consensual politics and multi-agency partnerships. From this perspective, self-governing networks in relation to waste management were very much favoured by the Irish State. The capacity to 'get things done' did not simply rest on the power of Government to command, and commands would only be invoked in a last instance scenario. This reflects the European context where the communicative turn had begun to take effect in policy development. Consultation on policy was a legal requirement of the EU, although the extent or parameters of that consultation were not legislated for. In the European governance scenario, planning, the main tool to change society was to shift towards a collaborative or communicative form. Good governance was about bringing citizens and stakeholders together to *participate* and take responsibility in a well-functioning planning *process*, where the ideal of 'communicative planning' was the external referent. Communicative planning according to Sager (1994) is characterised by a view of planning as a long-term process in which the focus lies on the process and on communications within that process, as much as on calculations and the planning object.

In terms of the levels of power of different actors in the waste governance scenario, the EU is a key player in that it regulates waste and sets the scene for its regulation at national level. The cornerstones of European policy on waste were established as hierarchically organised objectives:

Prevent waste in the first place,
Recycle waste,
Turn waste into a 'greenhouse neutral' energy source,
Optimise the final disposal of waste, including its transport.

Although the European agenda informed by sustainable environment concerns can be clearly seen with its hierarchisation of objectives, equally the market-driven notions of development are being played out when it comes to its implementation, with its fourth objective at that point often being prioritised. Waste legislation clearly takes cognisance of networked green politics, but at the implementation stage, the contradiction between the concepts of development (market-driven in its capitalist form) and sustainability (the earth as limited resource) is in constant contention with each other. European policy in the 1990s pointed towards degrees of sustainability in its waste hierarchy, but the EU also put legislation in place that set targets for its constituent countries to reduce all waste streams, and set very specific timeframes for national governments to meet these reductions.

For example, for the Republic of Ireland's municipal waste stream, there is a national target to be achieved of 35 per cent (currently at 34 per cent) recycling by 2013 and a household waste diversion from landfill target of 50 per cent (currently at 19 per cent) by 2013. In the Republic of Ireland in 2001, there was a need for an estimated investment of one billion euros, over a three- to five-year period to implement the waste development plan (Forfás, 2001, p. vi), and the National Development Plan envisaged this coming mainly from the private sector. Clearly, given its history of reliance on landfill, Ireland faced a gruelling task to organise a strategy to divert waste away from landfill, to reach targets set at a five-fold increase in recycling and to find the finance for the infrastructure especially if the objective was for the private sector to answer this call as envisaged in the Irish state's National Development Plan. Private capital was thus seen as a key stakeholder, as a necessary 'node' in the governance of waste management (Fagan, 2004). In particular the government's gaze focused on the private sector and on the waste industry's multi-national giants, and sustainability concerns became secondary to costs and to citizens' and communities' concerns. To reach the targets it was considered necessary by the government of the day to bring key players such as 'private enterprise' into some form of partnership, in other words a prioritisation of the 'stakeholder' over the citizen was clearly part of the solution to the waste problem. Waste governance, from this perspective, could not be resolved at its most radical level – that of sustainability. As it emerged the plans relied heavily on the treatment of waste through regional 'thermal treatment plants' and on recycling to be funded primarily through private enterprise.

The plans were brought to a standstill as opposition focused around the local planning authorities at regional level where the incineration plants were to be sited. Those environmentalists and environmental scientists who contested waste management plans were worried about the growing influence of commercial interests, specifically waste companies coming into the Irish globalised waste market. The key concern from the environmentalist's point of view was the role of 'big business', that is incineration companies, in the implementation of the plan. They argued that there had been aggressive attempts by incinerator companies to lobby the government (Fagan et al., 2001, p. 17) and to lead strategy. This concurs with O'Brien's interpretation at a global level where he comments on waste industrialists:

> This is a market whose rational economic actors are begging, cajoling, threatening and coercing the states of Europe to intervene politically into the circulation of wastes precisely because the 'spontaneous' emergence of markets does not generate the values they want out of the rubbish heap. (O'Brien, 1999, p. 292)

Environmentalists have argued that the new government response of building incinerators simply mirrored the previous landfilling strategy – 'Okay so we can't dump everything anymore, so let's just burn it' seemed to be the strategy. They believed that in both cases the government was 'being wooed by, or was wooing', large international companies and taking little responsibility for negative impacts on localised communities (Fagan et al., 2001, pp. 16–17). Those in opposition to the plans felt that they failed to contextualise waste in anything other than a framework for industrial 'competitiveness' and profitability as opposed to sustainability. Although governance necessitated a consultation process and the introduction of key players into the process, the unequal balance of power in the consultations and the fact that some partners were 'more equal than others' resulted in outright contestation of the plans, thus the situation spiralled into a political crisis. On what discursive basis did communities and activists contest the Irish government's preferred waste management strategy? The environmentalists and local communities feeling threatened by incineration plans were deeply critical of what they perceived as the 'façade' of consultation that had been put in place (Fagan et al., 2001, p. 18). There was a widespread perception at community level that government 'consultations' (often dictated by EU regulations) on the development of incinerators were simply empty rhetorical exercises for communities to 'let off steam' but were not designed to change decisions already taken on technical grounds (Fagan et al., 2001, p. 19).

The opposition to the location of incineration plants began, fuelled by anger about the nature of the consultation process that had produced the plans, and drove the waste management strategy into political crisis in 2000–2001 as local communities blocked the sub-regional plans. The state, however, reacted and the Minister at the time, Noel Dempsey, removed local councillors from the decision making process (who had been subject to public will) and replaced them with the county manager, a government employee. So here, in response to challenge from 'below', a central decree (government as opposed to governance) was used to achieve the localising or embedding of waste management. This is not to say that the state moved entirely back to traditional government or rejected the principal of consensus politics and failed to involve itself in multi-agency partnership, but, rather, that they removed the locality from involvement in the decision-making process. The Environment Minister, Martin Cullen, stated quite openly that the planning process on waste management was 'over-democratised' and that he did not believe it was 'adding anything to it by having so many layers involved' (Mc Donald, *Irish Times*, 12 August 2002).

The so-called 'fast-tracking' for waste management plans had to be implemented, and An Board Pleánala (The Planning Board) became a 'one-stop shop' for assessing all plans for new waste management facilities. The Minister, rather contradictorily, insisted that he was not removing any groups or individual rights to express their views – 'That is sacrosanct, but I don't see a need for these views to be expressed at so many different levels.' (Mc Donald, *Irish Times*, 12 August 2002). In other words, a repeat of oppositional views at multiple levels in a multi-layered process of governance was a source of irritation for government.[3]

POWER, COMMUNICATION AND CONFLICT

The issue of power of the various actors became central in the multi-faceted and shifting dynamic of the governance process and to the communicative planning scenario. Some actors had more power than others. Some gained more power than others because of their alignment with technocratic short-term profitable solutions given the urgency and materiality of the waste crisis. Others lost considerable power in the complex political process that unfolded, local authorities and communities being big 'losers' in the almost final settlement. That local communities were important players in the dynamic is without question, but there were ebbs and flows in their political power. Theoretically expanding governance through such mechanisms as consultation processes, increased participation and communicative planning could deliver better democracy, quicker consensus, and stronger legitimacy. Communicative planning has been derived from Habermas' (1994) theory of communicative action that argues for a new universal model for discursive rationality (de Sousa Santos, 1995). Communicative planning relies on the potential of communicative rationality as a system of critical assessment of alternatives towards reaching consensus. However, conflict, unequal power bases, short-term solutions and decreased legitimacy mark the implementation of environmental planning in the Celtic Tiger years, even within that expanded governance scenario. Consultation processes and more specifically communicative planning are designed to give different actors access to decision-making processes. Indeed it often holds out the promise of equalising their influence on the planning process. However, it failed to deliver in the development of Irish waste management policy, where the 'façade' of the consultation processes described by citizens and communities was central to triggering their anger with the process, and central to their articulation of grievance. Second, the political crisis erupted in reaction to what was seen as the false assumption (from the point of view of the government) or false promise (from the point of view of the communities and environmentalists) of a communicative process, that of the equalisation of different actors' influence on the planning process. The environmentalists saw the 'wooing' of the government by big incineration businesses as central to the outcome, and they saw that the technocrats dictated the outcome, given that the government employed one engineering company to 'manage' the consultation process with communities and citizens.

In terms of analysing obstacles and opportunities for implementing sustainable planning locally through communicative planning, Mannenberg and Wilbourg (2008) argue that communicative planning (now the norm) is a planning ideal that, in applied contexts, carries certain risks for delivering sustainable development and indeed for democracy more generally. First there is the risk of the communicative process becoming the focus rather than the plan itself; second, the traditional model of representative democracy is challenged; third, legitimacy is challenged; and fourth, it relies on achieving consensus that risks hiding political conflict (Mannenberg & Wilbourg, 2008, p. 36). In terms of various outcomes possible for different actors they argue that where communicative processes are strong, the citizens and stakeholders can gain influence, where the professional planner and local politician who have to be accountable can be weakened. They further argue that 'communicative planning is a friend of all strong actors and a foe to those in less favourable positions' (Mannenberg & Wilbourg, 2008, p. 42). In the case of the planning process in Ireland, the citizens and communities definitely found communicative planning, or what they would consider the illusion of communicative planning, a foe. Second, those stakeholders with finance and with profitability as their goal were advantaged by the communicative planning process – as stakeholders their position was strengthened. Finally, in the short term, the government's advantage was that it could change the rules of the communicative game at will, removing weaker players from the planning process.

This is not to infer that the governance processes described earlier adhered to the ideal of communicative planning, but rather that in practice the discourse of communicative planning and the illusion of communicative planning marked the development of Ireland's waste management policies. That the policies in the Republic of Ireland were derived from the basis of a weak communicative process, and the government responded to the contestation of these plans with a further weakening of the communicative process is without doubt. Given the symbiotic relationship between the social and the environmental, a major challenge for governance is to identify the means by which to implement sustainable development practically and concretely. A major challenge for governance at this particular moment, when powerful corporate actors who produce and 'dispose' of waste are strengthening their role, is to ensure that the discourses of all the players are heard, that all the nodes in the networks are uncovered, and that all are contextualised within a broader framework than economic profitability. What the repercussions of the above debacle in the exercise of governance are is as yet unknown. However, what is interesting is that with a communicative process, or the illusion of a communicative process in place, conflict and contestation was still the fate of the waste management plans. This outcome makes clear the limitations of communicative rationality as a universal model insofar as it downplays power struggles and political contradictions. As a useful and progressive way to progress change, communicative planning cannot be left out of the equation when it comes to reorientating policy on wasting. However, we must be at the same time cognisant of the vested interests and conflicts that emerge, and how this may strengthen or weaken any deepening of democratic processes in bringing about social and material change toward sustainable development.

PRODUCTIVITY AND SUSTAINABILITY – BINARY OPPOSITES?

To focus on waste alone, rather than on regulating production and consumption when engineering sustainability is simply not logical, and the fact is that the early waste management plans did just this. It would be the equivalent of legislating for how to bin the shaving that came off the platform of a nuclear reactor's base, rather than legislating around the production and use of the nuclear reactor itself. Without production being governed by criteria of sustainability, there is no point in managing waste. In essence the waste situation is deteriorating and waste disposal policies are not improving the waste situation as quickly as the problem warrants internationally. This is certainly the case for Europe and for Ireland. Waste policies were officially seen to be clearly failing as early as by the end of 1999 in Europe. The environment action programmes were unable to stem the generation of waste and thus were failing to meet their foremost objective – the prevention of waste in the first place. Despite the hierarchisation of objectives and targets set by the EU, the Environmental Agency by the year 1999 presented a chaotic scenario unfolding: 'The expected waste trends during the outlook period [up to 2005] suggest that existing policies, although providing some degree of success, will not be sufficient to stabilise waste arising, meet policy objectives, or progress towards sustainability' (EEA, 1999, p. 215). The sheer material quantity of waste in circulation during this period was extraordinary.

The EEA statistics on the EU for 1999 showed that 2000 million tonnes of waste were being generated per year and that the amount had increased by 10 per cent per annum over the previous six years. It was estimated that *all* waste streams would continue to increase steadily (EEA, 1999, p. 215). Essentially waste generation was spiralling out of control. To begin with, a wide range of different waste streams were increasing in volume, from consumers generating too much household waste to more wastewater treatment plants producing larger amounts of sewage sludge. Waste disposal methods were not coping with the increased loads, with several countries increasing the amount of biodegradable waste sent to landfill. Gradually and most importantly what was known in lay terms began to be officially recognised – that *waste generation was strongly linked to economic activity*, meaning that, as Europe's economy would grow, so too would the waste problem. The data generated under the Directives of the EU revealed a particularly close link between economic growth and waste from the construction industry (EEA, 2000). The Republic of Ireland statistics directly reflected this trend of increased economic growth, and the out of control spiral of waste emerging from the construction industry.

In the light of the failure of previous policies a further phase of policy making began in the early years of 2000. Although the waste hierarchy was not removed as a solution, further emphasis was placed on the first point, the prevention of waste, and the link between economic activity and waste production became the focus of further policy. The EU sixth environment action programme called for 'absolute decoupling', that is an overall reduction in the volumes of waste generated. Decoupling occurs if the growth rate of waste amounts is less than the growth rate of a given economic driving force over a certain period of time. Relative decoupling occurs when waste amounts continue to grow, although at a slower rate than the underlying economic driver. Absolute decoupling is when environmental pressure is decreasing during a period of economic growth (EEA, 2005, p. 27). Projections drawn up for the years 2000 to 2020 on the basis of current policy in place, indicates that in the EU, most waste streams are expected to decouple relatively, but not significantly, from GDP by 2020 (EEA, 2005). None are expected to decouple absolutely. So the further waste target of absolute decoupling will not to be met in the foreseeable future.

The construction, demolition and industrial waste streams are expected to produce about 650 million tonnes per year by 2020, and municipal waste is expected to produce 250 million per year by that year (EEA, 2005, p. 32). Policy, therefore, at European level is destined to fail to achieve its principle objectives (EEA, 2005).

Hence, it can be argued that current trends in waste management are unsustainable and that increases are not being counteracted effectively. Options to treat and dispose of waste are seen to be diminishing as quantities increase and concerns about their potential impacts grow (EEA, 2004, p. 6). There is growing evidence of the harm caused by the toxic emissions of incinerators and they are increasingly being perceived as at core 'dirty technologies' (Murray, 2004, p. 7). Landfill options are often limited by space and fears of soil and groundwater contamination and their impacts on human health.

The EEA (2004, p. 6) state that 'The current policy tools for dealing with waste are inadequate and need to be complemented by approaches that promote smarter resource use by changing production and consumption patters and through innovation'. Hence, clean and cleaner production is now recognised to be essential in sustainable development. Cleaner production is the continuous application of an integrated preventive environmental strategy to processes, products and services to increase overall efficiency and reduce risks to humans and the environment. Cleaner production can be applied to the processes used in any industry, to products themselves and to various services provided in society. As Lakhani (2006, p. 1391) puts it, 'Begin with a sustainable product, that uses a sustainable process, based on sustainable materials and sustainable energy and water use, or else we will never reach genuinely sustainable development'. However, achieving clean production is largely an aspiration at the moment. The radical changes towards sustainable products and clean and safe production have yet to be developed and implemented in all sectors of industry. Arguably, Ireland is at a turning point in relation to waste management. Efforts to manage waste, with or without enforcement, are no longer seen as sufficient unless integrated with processes of production and consumption. Discussing waste amounts and striving for the waste management hierarchy of more recycling and less disposal is still a necessity. However, there is also need for a more integrated approach that would examine where and from what mechanisms the waste comes, what types of waste should not be produced, what resources go into the waste stream, and what resources can successfully be lifted out of the stream altogether. Understanding waste flows and paving the way for better waste regulation thus would become integrated into the debate on production and consumption patterns and resource management. If the global of waste remains unresolved, society can choose either to continue attempting to incrementally reduce wastes and lessen impacts, or to consider a more ambitious approach. Greyson (2006, p. 1382) argues that paradoxically this approach may be easier to implement and suggests how an approach designed to prevent waste and other global impacts could be based on the established practices of precycling, circular economic policy and recycling insurance.

The structures and consumption patters of contemporary society encourage wasteful consumption and unsustainable patterns of production that lead to waste. Sustainable production and consumption are the only viable long-term options for society, but there is a long way to go to get there. Factoring in the production of waste to economic growth and providing a waste costing system where the allocation of waste costs to producers and consumers would be conducted fairly would provide part of a structural solution only. Scientific innovation is also a necessary component of the switch to sustainability. Building on resource productivity is one of the key ways the scientific community can transform structural conditions. Very interesting in this regard is the new 'materials revolution' being proposed by environmental engineers and scientists and some are making the argument that materials productivity as opposed to labour productivity will form the basis of the post-industrial era (Weizsaker, Lovins, & Lovins, 1998). It is only in the shift towards this 'materials revolution' and social patterns of sustainable consumption that production and sustainability can be complementary as opposed to oppositional.

TOWARDS A GREEN IRELAND?

Although natural scientists and politicians already have a clear role to play in regard to environmental sustainability, the role of the social sciences and humanities are also vital to develop a holistic and sustainable approach. Changing the social practices around consumerism should be part of developing sustainable consumerism. A social practice approach looks at how patterns of social behaviour create, support and recreate structures, suggesting that there are no structures without supporting behaviours. If this approach to wasting is followed, a waste future where lifestyles in relation to wasting are addressed could emerge. The environmental pressures of consumption are generally lower than those of production, but grew significantly in boom years. Consumption patterns around eating, housing, travel and tourism are, as in the recent past, growing significantly and this marks a shift in the environmental burden away from production to consumption. Given this shift, it can be argued that it is necessary to develop innovative governance strategies for dealing with sharply rising patterns of consumption. The development of these governance strategies would be designed by citizens and governments together inspired by the critical need to organise sustainable patterns of consumption. Shifts in lifestyles and societal preferences can make a huge difference in a world organised around consumerism (Spaargaren, Moll, & Buttel, 2000). A drop in consumption such as the one currently being experienced in the Republic of Ireland does result in a decrease in waste production, but more is needed. Restructuring various consumption patterns can be crucial in the future, and this is possible if the focus is on the intersection of the structure of production with the lifestyle of the citizen/ consumer, and not on the individual or the structures alone. Consumption is based on a premise of disposability, but in reality nothing is disposable – it is either abandoned to contaminate or it can be assimilated into some part of the ecological cycle. This understanding is critical to the change required. In a post-boom period, with consumption patterns and spending ability decreasing, and extravagance going out of fashion, there is a slight possibility that this challenge to the logic of wasting may in fact complement the economic climate rather than running contrary to it as in the boom period.

Without a lead being given in the matter of innovation in production and consumption, the reality is that the imagined 'Green' Ireland is fast disappearing in the sense that its air and water quality is being progressively compromised. It's continued 'greenness' is only possible through an ecological transformation whereby production and consumption patterns and their resultant waste streams are reorganised to protect the health of the environment and its dependents. Ireland's future in this bleak economic period need not be all doom if we put renewed energy into smart planning for sustainability and if it develops the ability of its politicians, citizens, scientists and business leaders to plan a more progressive Irish role in the wider evolving green revolution that it is hoped will mark the post–consumerist phase of globalisation. An analysis is needed that engages and imagines towards the politics of contingency[4] where the socio-economic politics of limiting wasting and greening production come into vogue as something more structured than a cosmopolitan lifestyle choice. Here 'good waste' (Murray, 2004) (i.e. recyclable) would be instantly recognisable and promoted, and likewise unclean production, un-recyclable waste and wasting consumption patterns would be immediately recognisable as bad things in a 'new' Irish model of sustainability. Given the link between accelerated growth rates and wasting, Ireland in a deflated or 'bust' economy will never be in a better position than it is now to make the necessary changes.

NOTES

1. Figures sourced at www.epagov/grtlakes/seahome/housewaste/src/intro.htm.
2. The EPA cannot account for this 10 per cent increase other than to say that local authorities believe that the dramatic increase from 2002–2003 is likely to be because of increased quality of data as well as increased resource use and waste generation on the part of consumers and business (EPA, 2003, p. 7). In 2004 they calculate that the municipal waste is at just over 3 million tonnes although there has been a 4 per cent increase, because they have produced the figures based on a new methodology.
3. For discussion on how the multi-level governance approach of waste management has impacted at the local level, see Murray (2003).
4. Laclau and Mouffe (1989) assert that nothing is predetermined and that points of contingency hold potential for transformative change.

REFERENCES

de Sousa Santos, B. (1995). *Toward a new common sense*. New York: Routledge.
EPA. (2002). *Environment in focus, 2002: Key environmental indicators for Ireland*. Dublin: Environmental Protection Agency.
EPA. (2003). *National waste database 2003, interim report*. Wexford: Environmental Protection Agency.
EPA. (2005). The nature and extent of unauthorised activity in Ireland. Press release, Thursday, 15 September 2005. Available at www.epa.ie/NewsCentre/Press Release/Main Body,7789,en.html
EPA. (2004). *National Waste Report 2004*. Dublin: Environmental Protection Agency.
European Environment Agency (EEA). (1999). *Environment in the European union at the turn of the century*. Luxemburg: EC Publications.
European Environment Agency. (2000). *Environmental signals*. Luxemburg: EC Publications.
European Environment Agency. (2004). *EEA signals 2004 – A European environment agency update on selected issues*. Luxemburg: EC Publications.
European Environment Agency. (2005). *European environment outlook report no. 4*. Luxemburg: EC Publications.
Fagan, G. H. (2004). Waste management and its contestation in the republic of Ireland. *Capitalism, Nature, Socialism*, *15*(1), 83–102.
Fagan, G. H., O' Hearn, D., Mc Cann, G., & Murray, M. (2001). *Waste management strategy: A cross border perspective*. Maynooth: National Institute for Regional and Spatial Analysis.
Fisher, F., & Hayer, M. A. (1999). Beyond global discourse: The rediscovery of culture. In: F. Fisher & M. A. Hayer (Eds), *Environmental politics. Living with nature*. Oxford: Oxford University Press.

Forfás. (2001). Key waste management issues in Ireland. Dublin: Forfás.

Greyson, J. (2006). An economic instrument for zero waste, economic growth and sustainability. *Journal of Cleaner Production, 15*(13–14), 1382–1390.

Habermas, J. (1994). *The theory of communicative action.* Cambridge: Polity.

Laclau, E., & Mouffe, C. (1989). *Hegemony and socialist strategy: Towards a radical democratic politics.* London: Verso.

Lakhani, M. (2006). The need for clean production and product re-design. *Journal of Cleaner Production, 15*(13–14), 1391–1394.

Mannenberg, M., & Wilbourg, E. (2008). Communicative planning – friend or foe? Obstacles and opportunities for implementing sustainable development locally. *Sustainable Development, 16*, 35–43.

Mc Donald, F. (2002). Minister wants to fast-track planning on waste. *Irish Times*, August 12.

McGlade, J. (2007). Finding pathways towards sustainable consumption and production in Europe, at the EEA time for action: Towards sustainable consumption and production in Europe conference, Ljubljana. Slovenia, 27–29 September 2007. Available at www.eea.europa.eu/pressroom/peeches/finding-the-pathways-.

Murray, M. (2003). *Waste management in Ireland: A case study on the impact of transnationalisation on governance.* Ph.D. Thesis, NUI Maynooth.

Murray, R. (1999). *Creating wealth from waste.* London: Demos.

Murray, R. (2004). *Zero waste.* London: Greenpeace Environmental Trust.

O'Brien, M. (1999). Rubbish values: Reflections on the political economy of waste. *Science as Culture, 8*(3), 269–295.

Sager, T. (1994). *Communicative planning theory.* Avesbury: Aldershot.

Spaargaren, G., Moll, G., & Buttel, F. (Eds). (2000). *Consuming cultures: Power and resistance.* London: Macmillan.

Stoker, G. (1998). Governance as theory: Five propositions. *Journal of International Social Science, 155*, 119–131.

Weizsaker, E., Lovins, A., & Lovins, L. (1998). *Factor four, doubling resources, halving resource use.* London: Earthscan.